Migration and Transnationalism Between Switzerland and Bulgaria

Marina Richter • Paolo Ruspini
Dotcho Mihailov • Vesselin Mintchev
Michael Nollert

Editors

Migration and Transnationalism Between Switzerland and Bulgaria

 Springer

Editors
Marina Richter
Social Policies and Social Work
University of Fribourg
Fribourg, Switzerland

Paolo Ruspini
Faculty of Communication Sciences
University of Lugano (USI)
Lugano, Switzerland

Dotcho Mihailov
Agency for Socioeconomic Analyses
Sofia, Bulgaria

Vesselin Mintchev
Economic Research Institute
Bulgarian Academy of Sciences
Sofia, Bulgaria

Michael Nollert
Social Policies and Social Work
University of Fribourg
Fribourg, Switzerland

ISBN 978-3-319-31944-5   ISBN 978-3-319-31946-9   (eBook)
DOI 10.1007/978-3-319-31946-9

Library of Congress Control Number: 2016936980

Printed on acid-free paper

This Springer imprint is published by Springer Nature
The registered company is Springer International Publishing AG Switzerland

Foreword

In the European context, East–West migration has been a fertile ground for research for almost two decades as a consequence of the EU enlargement processes and the geographical and political reshaping of the European continent. EU enlargement raised a lot of expectations regarding the end of the East–West divide and the reunification of Europe as a single polity. The current political situation in different EU national contexts proves, however, to be a different reality. The concept of East as a category of alterity constructed by the Western narratives is far from being totally dismantled. Growing Euroscepticism and populist movements show that Vaclav Havel's "wall in our heads", namely, the mutual ignorance and prejudices built up during the decades of the Cold War division of Europe, still remains a difficult state of mind to eradicate. This persistent psychological mindset has an impact on general public attitude. Its leverage on migrant inclusion in different local contexts should not be underestimated either. The exchange of scientifically sound knowledge and fair learning practices is thus more essential than ever at this historical juncture.

In the East–West mobility framework, we have now acquired a good amount of knowledge on short-term and long-term migrant configurations, circular, transnational or return patterns of migration framed by the EU policymaking processes. A lot of empirical and comparative research has been conducted, ranging from single-case studies to the collection of large quantitative and qualitative datasets. Lessons learnt include the importance of avoiding a single explanatory framework for understanding migration flows characterised by mutable direction and varied intensity. Notwithstanding the current level of knowledge, there are however geographical areas still left out of the mainstream East–West research which mainly covers the EU region.

The Bulgarian–Swiss endeavour, which has been investigated by my colleagues in this book, pertains to one of the above neglected research contexts. This country-specific case represents a small but interesting pattern of East–West (and West–East, as we are talking about transnational and return) migration. Therefore knowledge about it is of the utmost importance for migration scholars, practitioners and policymakers at different levels of governance. It includes the perspective of both a sending and a receiving country, linking one recent EU member state to a non-EU member, in this case Switzerland. Both these countries have been permeated by EU regional integration processes, which have impacted to various degrees on their migration and asylum policy framework.

Two particular aspects which pertain to the adopted theoretical and empirical approaches make this book innovative in comparative terms. The theoretical framework includes an attempt to link transnational migration to the investigation of social inequalities, regional disparities and the current national and European policy dimension. Researching social inequalities and regional disparities with a sending- and receiving-country perspective helps to better elucidate the different migration drivers and determinants which underpin the Bulgarian–Swiss case study. This research standpoint also represents a substantial contribution to the understanding of the different rural–urban (and vice versa) mobility patterns, in what has been until recently an under-researched domain in international migration. The focus on inequality provides instead the opportunity for a distinction per ethnic lines of different categories of more and less successful Bulgarian migrants and their experience of inclusion and exclusion in the host country as well as remigration in the home country. Finally, the emphasis on migration policy aims at capturing the changing political framework in Switzerland and Bulgaria. This helps, on the one hand, to understand the impact of a restrictive admission policy which makes Switzerland a better option for highly skilled Bulgarian labour migrants compared to lower skilled ones who mainly head towards other European destinations. The selective character of the Bulgarian return migration framework coupled with the negative demographic outlook and persistent unemployment explains, on the other hand, the relative degree of attractiveness of remigration options.

The empirical approach builds on the transnational method adopted. Large datasets derived from quantitative and qualitative analysis both in Switzerland and Bulgaria have been gathered. Although not new, this mixed-method approach with a two-country perspective is important for capturing the extent and size of multiple migration flows as well as the aspirations and capabilities of potential and actual migrants, and the "floating population", across several locations. On this basis, socio-demographic profiles of different categories of Bulgarian migrants have been drawn up and then compared. As a result, this book has provided a valuable contribution to further knowledge on migration and mobility processes in Europe.

Marek Okólski

Acknowledgements

The various chapters of this book are the result of a research collaboration between Bulgarian and Swiss researchers. This collaboration was possible thanks to the Bulgarian–Swiss Research Programme, which runs from 2011 to 2016 as part of the framework agreement between the government of Bulgaria and the Swiss Federal Council. The Swiss National Science Foundation and the Ministry of Education and Science were commissioned with the Bulgarian–Swiss Research Programme by the Swiss Agency for Development and Cooperation (SDC) of the Federal Department of Foreign Affairs. Fieldwork and the preparation of this book were also generously supported by funds of the University of Fribourg (Switzerland).

We would like to thank all the interviewers and results processors who were involved in the data collection and data entry throughout our surveys. This book would not have been possible without the interviews conducted in Switzerland as well as in Bulgaria and the data collected in both countries.

We are also grateful to Bill Brodie who unified our differing levels of English and Daniela Krupala who was a great help in preparing the manuscript and formatting it. Nevena Antova and Anina Geninasca were involved in the collection of data and the preparation of qualitative data reports in Switzerland and in Bulgaria. Further, we are thankful for the support we received from the former Bulgarian ambassador in Switzerland, Meglena Plugtschieva, and the director of "Bulgarian Communities and Information Services" at the Directorate in the State Agency for Bulgarians Abroad, Koyanka Dimitrova, as well as the honorary consul in Lugano, Fabrizio Mion, and the honorary consul in Zurich, Felix Fischer.

Finally, we are very much indebted to the people who gave of their precious time and told us about their experiences in our surveys and qualitative research.

Marina Richter, Fribourg, Switzerland
Paolo Ruspini, Lugano, Switzerland
Dotcho Mihailov, Sofia, Bulgaria
Vesselin Mintchev, Sofia, Bulgaria
Michael Nollert, Fribourg, Switzerland

Contents

Abbreviations

BG	Bulgaria
BGN	Bulgarian National Currency (Leva)
CEC	Commission of the European Communities
CEE	Central and Eastern Europe
CH	Switzerland
CHF	Swiss National Currency (Francs)
EC	European Commission
EEA	European Economic Area
EFTA	European Free Trade Association
EP	European Parliament
EU	European Union
FOM	Federal Office for Migration (since 1.1.2015 SEM), Switzerland
GDP	Gross Domestic Product
GVA	Gross Value Added
IOM	International Organization for Migration
MIPEX	Migration Integration Policy Index
NSI	National Statistical Institute, Bulgaria
NUTS	Nomenclature d'Unités Territoriales Statistiques (Statistical Territorial Entities, EU Geocode Standard)
OECD	Organisation for Economic Co-operation and Development
PPS	Purchasing Power Standard
SEM	State Secretariat for Migration, Switzerland
SFSO	Swiss Federal Statistical Office, Switzerland
UN	United Nations

Contributors

Venelin Boshnakov University of National and World Economy, Sofia, Bulgaria

Iordan Kaltchev "Neofit Rilski" South-West University, Blagoevgrad, Bulgaria

Dotcho Mihailov Agency for Socioeconomic Analyses, Sofia, Bulgaria

Vesselin Mintchev Economic Research Institute at the Bulgarian Academy of Sciences, Sofia, Bulgaria

Michael Nollert Social Policies and Social Work, University of Fribourg, Fribourg, Switzerland

Marina Richter Social Policies and Social Work, University of Fribourg, Fribourg, Switzerland

Paolo Ruspini Faculty of Communication Sciences, University of Lugano (USI), Lugano, Switzerland

Georgi Shopov Economic Research Institute at the Bulgarian Academy of Sciences, Sofia, Bulgaria

Irena Zareva Economic Research Institute at the Bulgarian Academy of Sciences, Sofia, Bulgaria

About the Editors

Marina Richter is a sociologist and geographer who is presently working at a department for sociology, social policy and social work and has since her graduate school in gender studies worked in various projects with people from different disciplines. She is an expert in migration to Switzerland and has mostly published on Spanish migration to Switzerland. She has conducted research on transnational aspects of migration such as networks and has in this realm also published on methodological aspects. Her research perspective on migration also includes aspects such as emotional attachment to place, gender differences as an example of social inequalities and in particular questions of deskilling. Her major publications include: Richter, Marina and Michael Nollert. 2014. Transnational networks and transcultural belonging: a study of the Spanish second generation in Switzerland. Global Networks. 2014(04), 458-176; Richter, Marina. 2012. Researching transnational social spaces: A qualitative study of the Spanish second generation in Switzerland [40 paragraphs]. Forum Qualitative Sozialforschung/Forum: Qualitative Social Research, 13(3), Art. 8; Richter, Marina. 2011. "A country full of snow". Spanish migrants in Switzerland and their ways of engaging with places, memories, and personal migration history. Emotion, Space and Society. 4. 221-228; Richter, Marina. 2006. Integration, Identität, Differenz. Der Integrationsprozess aus der Sicht spanischer Migrantinnen und Migranten. Bern: Peter Lang.

Paolo Ruspini is a senior researcher at the Faculty of Communication Sciences of the University of Lugano (USI) since February 2008 and honorary research fellow at the Department of Social Sciences, University of Roehampton, London. A political scientist, he has been researching issues of international and European migration and integration since 1997 with a comparative approach and by drawing on qualitative and policy analyses. The geographical focus of his research spans from Western to Central and Southeastern Europe and covers also the post-Soviet migration space with emphasis on the dynamics and multimodal character of migration flows in a changing policy context. He has been working in many collaborative projects at national and European level, and he is active in research networks regarding international migration and social cohesion as well as being an advisor for national and international organisations. From October 2013 until May 2014, he was visiting professor at the Scuola Superiore Sant'Anna, Institute of Law, Politics and Development (DIRPOLIS) in Pisa. He has also been an associate fellow at the Centre for Research in Ethnic Relations (CRER) of the University of Warwick for 10 years until the CRER closed in September 2011. In the year 2001, Paolo Ruspini received a Marie Curie postdoctoral fellowship for his project "Living on the Edge: Irregular Migrants in Europe" (2001–2002), and he also received a German Marshall Fund and other smaller grants for holding the position of principal investigator at CRER for the research project in collaboration with the Centre of Migration Research of Warsaw University, "In Search for a New Europe: Contrasting Migratory Experiences" (2001–2005). He was a visiting scholar at the Mershon Center for Education, Ohio State University (1998), and worked for the United Nations Industrial Development Organization (1995–1996). He combines research activities with routine lectures in a number of universities and international institutions. Besides a significant number of papers on migration and contributions to international conferences, he is the author of *Migration in the New Europe: East-West Revisited* (2004, Palgrave-Macmillan, co-editor), *Prostitution and Human Trafficking: Focus on Clients* (2009, Springer, co-editor), South-Eastern Europe and the European Migration System: East-West Mobility in Flux (2010, *The Romanian Journal of European Studies*, Special Issue, No.7-8/2009, guest editor) and A Decade of EU Enlargement: A Changing Framework and Patterns of Migration (2014, *Central and Eastern European Migration Review*, Special Issue, Vol. 3, No. 2, December 2014, co-editor).

Dotcho Mihailov is a survey researcher and a manager of the research agency "Agency for Socioeconomic Analyses" (ASA), which is partnering with the ERI on the Bulgarian side of the project "Migration and Transnationalism Between Switzerland and Bulgaria". Holding a Ph.D. in social psychology, Dr. Mihailov has coordinated and has contributed as a lead author to a number of policy reports for Bulgaria, addressing the issues of regional disparities and social inequality. Among them are the 2003 UNDP National Human Development Report "Rural Regions: Overcoming Development Disparities", the UNDP 2002 National Human Development Index: "Municipalities in the Context of Districts" and the UN National Millennium Development Goals reports for Bulgaria for 2003 and 2008. During the last 15 years, Dotcho Mihailov has been providing consultancies mainly in the fields of rural development and social inclusion for a number of development agencies such as the Swiss Agency for Development and Cooperation, the UNDP, the World Bank and others. As an associate of Blackstone Corporation Resource Management Consultants, Canada, he has carried out project evaluations and development consultancy missions in Eastern Europe, Africa, India and China. In terms of survey experience, Dotcho Mihailov has coordinated more than 100 national and topical surveys, including two on migration in cooperation with Mintchev, Kalchev, Boshnakov and Zareva.

Vesselin Mintchev is an economist. His research background is in the field of corporate governance and international economics. He analysed, among others, the attitudes of potential migrants, effects of return migration and remittances in Southeast Europe (Mintchev, V. (2009), "International migration and remittances in the Balkans: the case of Bulgaria", in E. Novotny, P. Mooslechner and D. Ritzberger-Grunwald (eds.), The Integration of European Labour Markets, Cheltenham: Edward Elgar, 177–204). He was interested by the interaction among family models and migration patterns (Mihailov, D., V. Mintchev, V. Bosnakov, and K. Nikolova (2007), Family models and migration, National Representative Survey, Sofia: Agency for Social and Economic Analysis and Center for Comparative Studies). He analysed migration as factor of income inequality in Bulgaria (Mintchev V., V. Boshnakov and A. Naydenov (2010), "Source of Income Inequality: Empirical Evidence from Bulgaria", Economic Studies, 4, 39–65) as well. More recently, he concentrated on the study of the Bulgarian diaspora in Spain, identifying the models of adaptation, the contacts with the home country, etc. He coordinated and participated in a number of research projects in the field mentioned above commissioned by different institutions such as the UNFPA, Global Development Network and National Science Fund of Bulgaria.

Michael Nollert is a sociologist and has worked extensively on social inequalities and social exclusion and the impact of policies on social stratification. He analysed economic inequalities in the world system, in Latin America, in intergenerational reproduction of social status (social mobility regimes) and in the reproduction of economic elites. He also studied the influence of European umbrella associations in the decision-making process of the EU, the transnational ties of big European companies and their impact on the Single European Act in the 1980s and the class formation of transnational elites. One of his recent research projects analysed the regional varieties of gender inequalities in the Swiss labour market and the impact of policies on these inequalities (M. Nollert and S. Schief, Cantonal patterns of gender-specific time-inequalities in paid and unpaid work: Empirical results and political-institutional conclusions, in: B. Liebig et al. 2016, Gender Inequality in Context: Policies and Practices in Switzerland. Opladen: Barbara Budrich). His recent contributions to migration research stem from a broader project, where also Marina Richter was collaborating (Richter and Nollert 2014), and a current research project which focuses on the identities and attitudes of migrants which engage in Muslim organisations in Switzerland (M. Nollert and A. Sheikhzadegan 2016, Gesellschaften zwischen Multi- und Transkulturalität. Zürich: Seismo). His geographical focus is on Europe, Latin America, the Netherlands, Germany and Switzerland. Most of his studies are based on a comparative perspective.

Chapter 1
An Introduction to Migration and Transnationalism Between Switzerland and Bulgaria

Marina Richter and Paolo Ruspini

Migration from Eastern and South Eastern European countries to destinations in the Western part of the continent has been acquiring the growing interest of migration stakeholders and has become a focus of academic research since the end of the Cold War. East–West migration from rural to urban, less developed to more developed areas of the European continent is a longstanding phenomenon dating back centuries, but the scale, intensity and magnitude of these processes gained its momentum in the last decades. The fall of the Iron Curtain provoked changes in the political order of borders: opening some borders, creating new ones or hardening others. This has, on the one hand, fuelled the number of people on the move between different regions of Europe and, on the other hand, has created new research ground for migration scholars.

The different types of large East–West migration flows sparked by historical developments of the post-Second World War era in the European continent can be summarized as follows: (1) waves of asylum-seeking and irregular migration from the East to the West of Europe as a consequence of the Fall of the Berlin Wall (1989) and the demise of the Soviet Union (1991); (2) mixed regional migration flows composed of refugees, displaced persons and labour migrants directed towards specific Western European destination countries resulting from the political upheavals and conflicts that caused the break-up of the former Yugoslavia during the early 1990s; (3) income-seeking post-2004 and 2007 European Union (EU) enlargement migration with different features and destinations, which occurred because of the opening of borders between European regions at diverse paths of development; and lastly (4) West–East return and different patterns of migration initiated by the

M. Richter (✉)
Social Policies and Social Work, University of Fribourg, Fribourg, Switzerland
e-mail: marina.richter@unifr.ch

P. Ruspini
Faculty of Communication Sciences, University of Lugano (USI), Lugano, Switzerland
e-mail: paolo.ruspini@usi.ch

© Springer International Publishing Switzerland 2017
M. Richter et al. (eds.), *Migration and Transnationalism Between Switzerland and Bulgaria*, DOI 10.1007/978-3-319-31946-9_1

economic crisis which has been sweeping the European continent from the first decade of the twenty-first century.

During the Cold War, the Central and Eastern European (CEE) region has been considered as a "buffer zone" for migration in between East and West. The role of the region was functional to Western Europe: thanks to the Schengen border the West aimed at being protected by uncontrolled inflows of illegal labour-seeking migrants or *mala fide* asylum seekers from the East (Stola 2001). As a consequence, the CEE region became the second best destination for migrants travelling from the bordering countries on their Eastern flank or even through the extremities of the Eurasian continent in search for a landing place in the West. The 1990s were characterized by "circular or incomplete migration" in CEE, e.g. back and forth movements thanks to border opening and the wage differentials between bordering regions whose economic development is moving at a different pace (Okólski 2001).

The main features of the CEE circular migration patterns have been described as income-seeking, opportunistic or overly exploitative (e.g. Morawska 2008). Related migrant networks, which developed throughout the region, are functional to this work-related dimension. Circular migration and its transnational dimension are therefore intrinsic to the geographical and economic characteristics of the CEE region from the early 1990s. The European migration regime contributed substantially to this migration framework by dictating the pace of "openings" and "closures" in terms of borders and access to opportunities in the local labour markets (e.g. Jileva 2002). The open borders facilitated temporary, circular and transnational mobility governed rather by the ebb and flow of economic demand than by long-term permanent immigration and asylum-seeking (Favell 2008).

Apart from the relevant historical background and regional focus on new migratory movements, there are also specific characteristics that make these movements worth looking at and include some rather novel aspects that can be of help to further our understandings of migration processes as such. Among these characteristics are (1) the movements originate from post-socialist countries (Eade and Valkanova 2009; Kaneff and Pine 2011); (2) the political structure is a complicated one: some borders are relatively open (within the Schengen area) while others are heavily guarded (at the fringes of the Schengen area) reflecting the political developments between countries of the overall Eastern region; (3) the space in which these movements occur is relatively limited, which results in relatively short distances, in particular if combined with modern means of transportation; (4) the movements are finally characterized by a high degree of mobility usually for short periods of time.

Changes in migration regimes and the concurrent role of different economic factors have varying impact on the directions and extent of these migration patterns, making the European space an interesting area for comparative research on the changing nature of international migration. The majority of the CEE countries still remain net labour exporters. This potential generated serious discussions and evaluations of the East–West migration before the eastward enlargement of the EU (e.g. Kahanec and Zimmermann 2010; Boeri and Bruecker 2001; Bauer and Zimmermann 1999) and urged some EU member states to call for transitional arrangements for the free movement of labour in 2004 and 2007. These transitional arrangements coupled with the economic crisis had a significant impact in re-addressing flows across Europe or on the characteristics and types of migration flows from the new EU Eastern European members.

The case we are presenting here is situated in the context described earlier. For the purpose of verifying the nature and scope of changing migration in the European continent, we deliberately picked two countries which are characterized by different degrees of economic and regional developments—one in the South East and the other in the West European region—to gain a deep understanding of the migratory movements that occur between these two countries, their casual factors and different historical stages. The case of Switzerland, as a country of destination, also brings in additional specificities since the country is part of Schengen but it is not a member of the European Union (EU). Instead the relationship with other EU countries and in particular the question of the permeability of borders is dealt with in bilateral agreements. The effective impact of these agreements and related transitional arrangements in restricting Bulgarians from entering Switzerland and accessing the Swiss labour market has been one important focus of this research.

Our perspective on migration between Bulgaria and Switzerland is therefore framed by the changing European migration regime as well as by the specific case Switzerland presents. Diverse macro, meso and micro level of analysis including structural policy and economic factors, social networks, households and migrant agency have been considered. In this way, we try to understand the reasons why people migrate, the impact of migration control and regulations on actual flows, what the patterns are that evolve from diverse migration determinants and how migration impacts on the social structure in the countries that are affected by these flows. In particular, we look at the social inequalities that structure migration processes in many ways: they provide the reason to leave a country in search for better earnings or a better place to live, and they also provide the resources on which migrants count when they decide to migrate. At the same time the impact of migration on social inequalities—an aspect that is usually discussed under the label of the migration–development nexus has been also explored. As we are looking more closely at two countries in particular, we are also able to analyse regional disparities within the countries in order to understand how migration and social inequalities are not only interlinked but also regionally patterned. Entry strategies have been analysed in close conjunction with inclusion and exclusion patterns and perspective in Switzerland, but also in relation to migrants' relatives, non-migrants' and return migrants' strategies in Bulgaria. We aim at effectively linking perspectives from traditional sending and destination countries as well as understanding possible secondary movements or migrant ties with other destinations in Europe. In a certain way, we are thus matching a comparative perspective with a strategy that looks in an opposite direction to the one usually aimed at countering the critique of methodological nationalism (Wimmer and Glick Schiller 2002). Instead of diversifying only across ethnical and national boundaries, we also diversify within: on the one hand, in ethnical terms, as there are various ethnic groups in the Bulgarian population, on the other hand, in terms of varying the notion of migration across regions and social status.

In what follows, some background information to frame the presented research is provided. In the first section, we will discuss the conceptual terms that guide our analysis. We will start the section with a discussion of the terminology concerning migration, as we face a variety of migration patterns which demand a broad understanding of the shape and forms of migration. In the continuation, we discuss how social inequalities interact with migration and how they need to be linked to questions of geographical distribution and patterns. The way relevant policy changes at different levels of governance impact on migration as well as the consequences of migration on the national policy framework is also discussed both in the destination and source country. Second, we will address the regional context in which our research is situated and will give background information regarding the two countries and the respective migration history that contextualizes the case. This leads us, third, to a brief presentation of the study conducted, its design and its methods. Last, we present an overview of the book and the following chapters.

1.1 Concepts

1.1.1 Migrant Transnationalism

The various forms of migration we can currently observe in East and South East Europe have little in common with the prototype of a migrant who emigrates from one country in order to settle down for good in another and forget about his or her origin and the people related to it. Rather there is a variety of forms termed, for instance shuttle, pendular or circular migration. These migration patterns can be voluntary or promoted by governments and policymakers for several political reasons, especially in the broad case of circular migration. They are usually the result of changes in policy, but they are also made possible by the revolution in means of communication and transportation initiated by the processes of globalization. Nevertheless, this mutable migration landscape does not exclude forms of permanent migration of people who leave their country in order to settle down or who after contrary intentions end up staying for good in the country they migrated to.

For the people involved in these types of movements, they are all migrants in one way or another. This is among others, a reason, why we did not decide to concentrate on one sole form of migration, but wanted to analyse the full picture. Framing the current complex and changing migration dynamics allows us to overcome the binary immigrant–emigrant opposition and thus understand the total and all-embracing nature of this process for the actors involved. This means that we use the term migration in a very broad sense that follows the transnationalist approach.

There are two debates in the field of transnational migration studies that have been developing and need to be considered herein. One regards transnationalism as a new phenomenon characterized by continuous, ongoing and lasting activities over international borders (Portes et al. 1999) that create new social formations and social spaces which have a transnational span (Faist 2004). In this context, the notion of transnationalism has been generally used to refer to ongoing ties of migrants with source countries. Portes et al. (1999: 217) argue that "while back-and-forth movements by immigrants have always existed, they have not acquired until recently the critical mass and complexity necessary to speak of an emergent social field. This field is composed of a growing number of persons who live dual lives: speaking two languages, having homes in two countries, and making a living through continuous regular contact across national borders." Defining the concept as "the processes and activities that transcend international borders", Bauböck (2008) provides also an attentive distinction from similar social phenomena as well as a categorization of the social actors involved. Countries of origin, countries of destination and the individual migrant create a triangular framework that is often expanded through the presence of other agents, including migrant associations and non-state political entities, such as hometown municipalities (Bauböck 2008). Transnational relationships and activities include, according to Boccagni (2012), forms of economic, political as well as social and cultural transnationalism. Economic transnationalism includes the sending and receiving of remittances, investment in land, housing and business in the country of origin, as well as trading and consumption of goods from the home country or from a country abroad. Political transnationalism encompasses activities that are related to patriotism, long-distance nationalism or homeland-related political activism. Finally, social and cultural transnationalism is related to nostalgia and identification with the culture and folk-lore of the homeland; the 'myth of return'; visits to kin and friends left behind; various forms of non-corporeal communication; participation in or support for a variety of civic, recreational, religious or cultural initiatives and events (see also King et al. 2013). Different types of transnationalism encompassing the reactive, resource-based and border transnationalism are also studied according to certain cultural and legal assumptions which imply different identity, economic and cultural effects and implications for the sending communities in terms of remittances, development and strategy to overcome poverty and marginalization (Castaneda et al. 2014).

The other perspective has more to do with the development of theory in migration research and with the ontological definition of how we define the subject of our research. Transnationalism then stands for a shift in the paradigms of migration research and opens up the definition of what can be counted—and therefore studied—as migration (King et al. 2013). People increasingly move for short periods of time of only several months, but do this repeatedly. The traditional United Nations (1998) definition of migration defines an international migrant as a person staying for at least 12 months in a country where he/she was not born. This definition is not free from statistical and conceptual weaknesses: (1) in view of the well-known lack of availability, accuracy and comparability of statistics on international migration (e.g. Fassmann and Musil 2013; Fassmann et al. 2009); but also because (2) it fails to capture longstanding short-term, seasonal and circular movements such as those in East and South East Europe. Similar migratory flows cannot be grasped by such a normative stance alone.

On the one hand, we understand migration in the broad term inspired by the second debate on transnationalism. On the other hand, we also look at concrete transnational activities that correspond to the definitions advanced in the first instance. This means that for the purpose of our research the transnationalist approach proposes a good working framework for studying different kinds of migration between two countries and for analysing the different kinds of linkages these migration flows create. Migrants are seen as capable of negotiating their place in society and are able to form a double identity instead of conflicting identities. The regular contacts migrants maintain with the country of origin as well as the back and forth movement illustrate the transnational mobility (Portes et al. 1999). As noted by Chapman and Prothero (1983) thanks to the transnationalist approach it is possible to question the binary structuralist vision of cross border movements, taking into account the circularity of migration movements which facilitates migrants' mobility.

1.1.2   Migrant Transnationalism and Social Inequality

Social inequality refers to the unequal distribution of access to resources in a society. Resources can be material ones such as money, goods or land, but also immaterial resources such as knowledge, education or—particularly important in the context of migration—social networks (Amelina 2013). The unequal distribution results in the social status of individuals. The link between migrant transnationalism and social inequality falls into various subfields. First, social inequality is a driver for migration but also a factor that structures the migratory process as such. Low social status is a strong driver for migration. At the same time, the poorest strata of a country are lacking the necessary resources in terms of human and social capital to migrate. The social status of an individual and his or her family has an enabling function when it provides access to necessary resources such as networks, money or knowledge.

Migration literature has recently recognized the importance of the meso level of analysis. Migration scholars have therefore widely acknowledged and debated the role of social networks moving from the seminal work of Granovetter (1973) to more recent conceptualizations. In particular literature on migration networks takes into account that there are different types and functions of networks which include a heterogeneity of actors based on gender, ethnicity, race and generation (Boyd and Nowak 2013).

Second, there is the migration–development nexus that has been looked at from various perspectives. In general, migration is seen as a means for development in countries of origin (Faist 2008). Nevertheless, other innovative approaches on the migration–development nexus emerged recently, connecting, for instance, local migrant incorporation to migrants' transnational development practices (Østergaard-Nielsen 2011), or making the development link in both ways by reverse remittances (Mazzucato 2011). There is no clear answer whether migration has an effect at all on development and whether this effect is positive or negative. The various answers depend mostly on the theoretical standpoint of the researchers involved. While functional perspectives in general tend to emphasize the positive effects of migration on development, structuralist perspectives (such as Neo-Marxist or Dependencia theory) tend to stress the negative impacts of migration (de Haas 2007; 2010a). Currently, there has been a renewal in the debate (Faist 2008) and the pendulum is presently swinging back to a functional perspective. Another point of discussion is the term *development* itself. Many authors argue that economic indicators alone cannot account for development as it also includes aspects linked to well-being such as health or education, as they are described in the Human Development Index (de Haas 2010a; Babić 2013).

To understand the drivers of international migration processes and analyse different forms of migrations between Bulgaria and Switzerland within the transnational perspective adopted by our research, it is also worth including structure and agency according to the Sen's capabilities-based development concept and as such describing migration as a function of (1) capabilities, (2) aspirations and, on a macro level (3) opportunity rather than income differentials alone (de Haas 2010b).

Third, social inequality is often analysed with reference to processes of inclusion and exclusion. Barriers to social, economic and political participation in society are often built on categories of social inequality (Girard and Bauder 2007; Mountz 2011). Social inequality is therefore also an important issue for research in the society where migrants are living.

Social inequalities as a condition that structures migration have been addressed for Switzerland, for instance, in studies that discuss labour market integration of highly skilled migrants (Pecoraro 2005; Riaño and Baghdadi 2007). Most of these studies discuss the barriers migrants encounter when entering the labour market, often intersecting the social category of migrant or foreigner with gender (Wanner et al. 2005; Baghdadi and Riaño 2011; Riaño 2011), thereby showing, how migrant women are confronted with stereotype roles that attach them rather to home work and child-bearing than to the workplace (Baghdadi and Riaño 2014). Deskilling of migrants on the labour market is often discussed in relation to women, but affects men as well (Richter 2011) and is highly influenced by the country of origin. For instance, migrants from the United States and from EU countries are three times less likely to experience deskilling than migrants from Africa, Latin America and other countries (Haug 2006). At the same time, some sectors of the economy such as the care and health sector are in need of skilled personnel and have to recruit them abroad (Jaccard Ruedin and Weaver 2009).

Social differences such as country of origin, gender or religion often translate into social inequalities, resulting in restricted access to resources. This then results in reduced possibilities for social mobility and economically and socially powerful positions. It is, in particular, the political debate around integration, which is very much shaped in a discourse of (cultural) difference (Wessendorf 2008). A fact that is mirrored in the politics of naturalization: Swiss nationality is still sanctioned by the local community and can therefore be subject to discriminatory practices based on the nationality or religion of the applicants (D'Amato 2001; D'Amato and Fibbi 2007).

Fourth, social inequality also needs to be looked at from a transnational perspective, which means not to disentangle the contexts of origin and destination but to think of them as interlocking elements of a social reality. The way migrants deal with transnational lives and how they bridge often difficult gaps between their transnational status in two or more countries has been conceptualized in the notion of a transnational habitus (Guarnizo 1997; Kelly and Lusis 2006). Although there are interesting perspectives on the topic, there is a need for a deeper understanding of how social inequality is experienced internationally. In particular, it is important to explore and link the often differing statuses of migrants in different places and ground them in the local context. This reminds us of the importance of analysing migration as an integral part of wider developmental and transformation processes.

1.1.3   Regional Disparities and Migration

The discussions on regional aspects of migration dynamics had an important momentum in the 1980s when it was mostly debated around questions of internal migration (Polese 1981). The regional question dealt with migration that did not cross international borders and the special focus therefore was on disparities within the countries. This recalls the laws of migration by Ravenstein (1885, 1889) which also made statements about distance and about the characteristics of rural–urban migration within Great Britain in the late nineteenth century.

At present, the debate on regional disparities within migration studies focuses mostly on the case of China. Migration in China is mostly characterized as internal, as the country includes social inequalities as well as disparities in local economic and employment structure on a level comparable to other migration systems that include various countries (e.g. Gransow 2012). Also the sheer size of the country reduces the need for international migration.

In general, there is relatively scarce research on regional aspects of migration. In addition, most research that focuses on local contexts tends to choose urban contexts as the site of their research (e.g. Body-Gendrot and Martiniello 2000; Martiniello and Rath 2010; Krase 2012). The relative interest in the regional and rural contexts of migration (contexts of origin or of destination) might be coupled in the sense that cities are seen as the beehives of a society. Global cities became hotspots for analysis of social transformation processes and immigrant incorporation making the cosmopolitan and trans-local interesting dimensions for theoretical and empirical investigation, which are also relevant for small-scale geographical contexts (e.g. Ang 2004; Yeoh 2013). The trans-local dimension brings us back to the description of different forms of migration and the current multidimensional character of East–West migration in Europe.

A recent renewal of interest in research for rural–urban or urban–rural migration is, in fact, related to the EU enlargement processes and the resurgence of new forms of migration as circular or return migration resulting from freedom of movement, economic development, ethnic networks and more recently the economic crisis

(Sandu 2005; Anghel 2008; Napierała and Trevena 2010; Mintchev and Boshnakov 2010; Klein-Hitpaß 2013; Farrell et al. 2014). Similar discussions are also of great importance for a still predominantly emigration country as Bulgaria where we can ask how regional disparities are interlinked with different forms of internal, international or potential migration.

Regional disparities appear to be in the focus of many Bulgarian authors (Yankova et al. 2003; Totev 2004, 2006). Very often the focus is on the development and application of quantitative methods, such as the taxonomic method (Yankova 2007), cluster analysis (Rangelova 1995, 2008), factorial analysis (Shopov et al. 2011) or sample method of measuring admissible differences between the regions (Totev 2011). Although, the relation between migration and regional disparities in Bulgaria is still a research "gap", Totev and Kaltchev (2000) propose a region-specific profile of potential migration. They use three main regional types—peripheral region, region with declining industries and competitive regions.

For Switzerland, the regional aspect seems inherent to Swiss federal organization and to the language divide between the German speaking and the French and Italian speaking parts of the country. Research on these issues is still lacking. More controversial evidences are available regarding the differences between urban and rural contexts in Switzerland and their impact on the process of integration of migrants (Tangram 2011; Manatschal 2010).

The incorporation of the trans-local dimension allows us to fill a gap in research and to cast a bridge between regions at different phases of development. It aims at considering the processes of urban and rural transformation as well as inclusion and exclusion of different migrant cohorts across time and space in Switzerland or Bulgaria.

1.1.4 Changing Policies

Migration is nowadays very much connected to processes of interdependence between countries and regions. Changing migration regimes at different levels of governance do have, on the one hand, an impact on migration flows according to the degree of policy transfer and country-specific immigration history. Migration flows do have, on the other hand, an impact on migration regimes, causing resistance, adaptation and/or change in legislation and policymaking (e.g. Zincone et al. 2011). Policy provisions such as transitional arrangements to access the labour market, readmission agreements with countries of origin or mass regularizations have proved to lead to initiating or redirecting migration to countries and regions in Europe. Migration also causes changes in the very same law regulations originating from competing interests and divergent political systems: for instance, sudden mixed flows driven by conflicts or regime changes in the European neighbourhood result in policy answers either in terms of control, humanitarian measures or often a combination of these two approaches.

In comparison to the widely studied North-American migration model, which has been extensively describing migration dynamics between the United States and Mexico, the supranational dimension pertaining to the European Union provides some uniqueness in the theory of European integration (Geddes 2003). Policy implementation at the EU level had historically a substantial leverage on changes in different forms of migration in the whole continent (Górny and Ruspini 2004; Ruspini 2008b). The influence and specificity of this supranational actor in sparking transnational migration in Europe has been also recognized as a distinctive feature of East–West mobility (Ruspini 2011; 2010). Although not all migrants are transnational, different migrant cohorts in Europe are becoming so, putting traditional classifications of emigrant–immigrant under discussion and pushing for changes in the traditional models of immigrant integration.

In this mutable migration landscape, the role and specificity of single countries such as the non-EU member state, Switzerland, and the new EU member state, Bulgaria, have added new challenges for research while providing fertile ground to compare and contrast case studies in migration relations between European countries. As a matter of fact, we aim at comparing a longstanding country of immigration featuring a "guest worker" regime in the past and a current selective model of incorporation as Switzerland to a substantially emigration country as Bulgaria, which only recently has started to receive occasional labour and circular migrants and more recently consistent flows of asylum seekers transiting through Turkey.

Different historical stages pertaining to both these countries have been considered including for Bulgaria: the fall of the Berlin wall (1989), the removal of the country from the visa blacklist (2001) and the accession to the European Union (2007); whereas for Switzerland: the signature of the EU bilateral agreements (2002), the adoption of transitional arrangements for CEE migrants to access the Swiss labour market (2009) as well as newest policy developments, such as the popular referendum on "mass immigration" (2014). The latter initiative has, in fact, put into discussion the overall Swiss–EU bilateral framework providing for future restrictions to admission of the whole EU citizenry to the national labour market.

These events have been considered in close relation to changes in the extent and characteristics of migration from Bulgaria to Switzerland stemming from the quantitative and qualitative analyses carried out in both countries. The final scope of this specific research aims at detecting possible convergences and differences in the composition of migration flows and comparing them with other empirical studies of migration and transnational formations between European countries.

1.2 Context of the Study

1.2.1 The Case of Bulgaria

A transnational migration system can be identified among South and South-Eastern European countries as well: between Romania and Italy/Spain, between Albania and Bulgaria and Greece/Italy, between Bulgaria and Turkey/Spain, etc. For instance, over 40 % of potential Bulgarian migrants choose South European destinations (Mintchev et al. 2004). Respectively, an important share of return/circular migration is from these main countries. Even more—there are net gender difference in preferred destinations of potential migrants. Greece, for instance, is preferred by female migrants, and Spain by men. Concerning Bulgaria itself, the population of the country has decreased by 17.7 % between 1985 and 2011. This is mainly due to the exodus of the Bulgarian Turks (before 1989) (Gächter 2002), the negative natural growth as well as the economic migration since the beginning of the transition (National Statistical Institute, 2011, see also Mansoor and Quillin 2007).

According to the NSI of Bulgaria about 22,000 people have emigrated annually between 1992 and 2001 (NSI 2002a, b). Between the last two censuses (2001–2011), emigration for good decreased, however, by half compared with the previous period. The Agency for Bulgarians Abroad (2015) reports that the Bulgarian Diaspora currently amounts to roughly 2.5–3 million people (taking into account both old and new permanent migration), while those living in the country are estimated to be 7.3 million.

The National Statistical Institute (NSI) conducted the first national study on external migration after the political changes of 1989. Its main goals were to evaluate the scope and intensity of potential migration. It presents the first socio-demographic composition of potential migrants and establishes the causes that generate and define external migration. Similar studies were carried out in the country in 1992 and 1996 with the methodological and financial support of the International Organization for Migration (IOM 1999). The NSI carries out observations on the emigration process also through its census surveys. The 2001 census comprises a survey on the territorial mobility in the country and on the external migration. It includes estimations of the scope and intensity of external migration, including migration destinations by country, socio-demographic structures and reasons for emigration (NSI 2002a, b). A similar survey is included in the 2011 census. These surveys provide data suitable for our analysis. During the period of 1991–1996, NSI conducted specialized sample surveys on selected border points. Similar surveys are carried out on a monthly basis. The surveys involve samples of all Bulgarian and foreign citizens entering and leaving the country. These surveys produce estimations about the national, demographic and socio-economic status of the passengers as well as reasons for travel.

Evidences on Bulgarian transnational migration are well documented (Mancheva and Troeva 2009; Gómez-Mestres and Molina 2010; Deneva 2012). Preliminary attempts to gather the extent of 'inward' and 'outward' circular migration in

Bulgaria refer to Krasteva et al. (2011). Transnational patterns of Bulgarian migration and identity are also explored in studies on Bulgarian return migration (Maleev 2010).

The influence of European migration policy on Bulgarian patterns of migration is significant. In 1993, the country was placed on the EU's visa 'blacklist'. This restrictive visa regime implied a significant change in its migration flows towards the EU countries. Official emigration to Western Europe decreased significantly, while the extent of migration to Greece and Italy became largely undocumented. Once Bulgaria was removed from the Schengen 'blacklist' in 2001, temporary and seasonal migration augmented as a result of the 3 month travel possibilities provided to Bulgarian citizens. Seasonal and circular migration pushed by the high unemployment rate in selected Bulgarian regions became ethnically and regionally specific (Guentcheva et al. 2004; Markova 2010).

1.2.2 Switzerland: A Receiving Country

Switzerland has long been a country with high immigration. Several research projects and publications have analysed this fact (D'Amato 2001; Wicker et al. 2003; Dahinden 2005; Mahnig 2005). Today, the majority of migrants living in Switzerland have a European passport (84.89 %). The three most important countries of origin are Italy (15.3 %), Germany (14.9 %) and Portugal (13.01 %) (Swiss Federal Statistical Office, 2014), thereby reflecting the old guest-worker regime and the long migratory tradition from Germany, serving partly as a basis for new migration flows occurring under the present bilateral agreements on the Free Movement of Persons between the EU and Switzerland. The EU-2 (Romania and Bulgaria) only make 0.8 % (Federal Office of Migration, 2014) of the whole migrant population in Switzerland (5826 Bulgarians according to 31.12.2014 SFSO data).[1] These numbers only represent the migrants who have an official permit to stay in the country and are therefore registered as living in the country. The group of people we have researched is therefore a very small but growing group that has until now not received major attention by the scientific community.

Regarding the question of migration policy, Bulgarian migration to Switzerland is structured by the fact that the European integration process indirectly shapes Swiss migration policies (Ruspini 2008a). Since the 1st of June 2009, the bilateral agreement[2] has been extended to Bulgaria and Romania. There is a 7-year clause

---

[1] There are two datasets available for the migrant population in Switzerland: one is by the Swiss Federal Statistical Office (SFSO) and the other one by the State Secretariat for Migration (SEM), until the 1.1.2015 known as Federal Office for Migration (FOM). While the SFSO data is published yearly for the 31st of December, the data of the SEM is updated more frequently. This results in slight differences. Throughout the book we have attempted to use mostly the SFSO data as it is usually done in Swiss research.

[2] Personenfreizügigkeit, document number 0.142.112.618.

that allows the Swiss state to exert regulations over the incoming migration from these countries. In the popular vote of the 8th of February 2009, the Swiss people voted in favour of prolonging the bilateral agreement between the EU and Switzerland and also accepted the inclusion of the new EU member states (Bulgaria and Romania) into the agreement. The Second Protocol[3] to the bilateral agreement defines a period of a maximum of 7 years (until 31.5.2016) during which the Swiss state can manage the migration flows from these countries in transitional arrangements. Three years after this period, and at the latest up to 10 years after the enforcement of the protocol (31.5.2019), Switzerland can still impose restrictions if immigration increases from 1 year to another by at least 10 %.

At present, Bulgarian migrants wanting to live and work in Switzerland are confronted with the following restrictions: (1) preference for Swiss citizens (and EU-25 and EFTA citizens) on the labour market, (2) control of salary and working conditions and (3) control of the numbers of migrants entering the country. The policy is not only controlling the numbers of Bulgarians entering the country, but it is also favouring migrants with short-term projects, thereby enhancing forms of mobility that are adapted to such a time pattern. As a result of the initiative against "mass immigration" which was accepted on the 9th of February 2014 with 50.3 % of votes, the legislative framework might evolve again and become more restrictive by February 2017. The consequences of this popular vote include that: (1) instead of bilateral agreements with the EU (free movement of persons) a system of quotas is to be implemented; (2) on the labour market there will be preference for Swiss workers; (3) for Bulgaria, the transitional arrangements will not be changed into freedom of movement, resulting in a worsening of access to the country and to the labour market.

A group that has, for instance, often been studied because of its circular and temporal character—but also because of its precarious situation (Chimienti 2009)—are the so-called cabaret dancers. Bulgarian women are, as research shows, also employed in this sector (Dahinden and Stants 2006). These women are allowed into Switzerland by a specific work permit that allows them to work as cabaret dancers for some months.

Very often people who do not have access to legal entry to the country might choose irregular ways of migrating. Various studies on irregular migrants have shown the importance of irregular migration for Switzerland (D'Amato et al. 2005; gfs.bern 2005), and how irregular migrants cope with working conditions, health issues and other aspects of daily life in a highly regularized society (Achermann and Chimienti 2006; Schweizerisches Rotes Kreuz 2006).

---

[3] Personenfreizügigkeit Bulgarien-Rumänien, document number 0.142.112.618.1.

1.3   Research Design and Methodology

1.3.1   Research Objectives and Instruments

The four concepts of our study put forward the following three main research objectives: (1) to link migration between Switzerland and Bulgaria to questions of social inequalities and regional disparities we have analysed who migrates, why, and what are the interrelations of migration, social inequality and regional disparities; (2) to draw a picture of the various patterns of migration in Switzerland and Bulgaria we have researched which types of migration (return, transnational, circular, permanent, etc.) connect Bulgaria, Switzerland as well as other destination countries for Bulgarian migrants in Europe and the way these different types of migration are linked to social inequalities/processes of exclusion and regional disparities; (3) to analyse Bulgarian–Swiss migration within the framework of EU enlargement we have looked at the changing migration policy and legal framework in both countries in the context of EU and national migration policies and legislation.

The study analyses migration in a manner that combines multiple scales (from the individual person to national and European legislation), different types of perspectives (economic, political, social) as well as different sites (in Bulgaria and in Switzerland). To achieve its research objectives a mixed-method approach covering both countries was adopted since it was considered the most useful to study complex phenomena that include numbers of people (migration flows); socio-economic data (statistics); policy frameworks (national and European level); as well as individual intentions, strategies and motivations (qualitative and individual perspective).

This methodology aims at bringing together quantitative and qualitative instruments, including (1) a representative survey in Bulgaria on the regional level and a mail-based survey of the Bulgarian migrants in Switzerland to collect information not available from official statistical sources; (2) an in-depth qualitative study on Bulgarian migrants in Switzerland and on migrants, returnees or potential migrants in Bulgaria, with a view to drawing up migrant profiles which cover past and current migration experiences and migration intentions; and finally (3) a comprehensive desk research on institutional data and policy documents to assess the framework within which migration flows between Bulgaria and Switzerland take place.

Table 1.1 Overview of data gathered

Empirical approach	Quantitative/qualitative	Country	Number
1. National surveys	Quantitative	Bulgaria	3907
		Switzerland	1137 (26%)
2. Semi-structured interviews	Qualitative	Bulgaria	25
		Switzerland	23
3. Desk research	Qualitative/quantitative	Bulgaria, Switzerland, EU	

1.3.2   Data Gathered

Table 1.1 gives an overview of the data gathered based on the four empirical approaches, their quantitative or qualitative perspective, the country they focus on and the number of records/interviews they produced. The data gathered, the sample size and model are then explained in detail afterwards.

National Quantitative Surveys. Quantitative data covers results collected through the main surveys of our research. A total of 3907 face-to-face interviews were carried out in Bulgaria. A total of 4962 mail-back surveys were posted in Switzerland. Taking into account the wrong addresses and other neutral returns, the total sample includes 4307 cases. Additional data was gathered through the online version of the Swiss questionnaire published in December 2013 on the website of the project. At the end of March 2014, the response rate of the Swiss survey was 26%, i.e. 907 paper and 230 online questionnaires for a total of 1137 surveys filled in. Data in Bulgaria was collected through face-to-face interviews applying a standardized questionnaire. It was collected by local teams situated in the 28 districts of the country of the Agency for Socioeconomic Analyses (ASA) one of the Bulgarian partners.

The sample design of the Bulgarian survey comprised the following steps and main features: (a) *sample size*, i.e. 3907 completed interviews, representative for Bulgarian population (aged 15–65) with completed sample of cases by region as follows: Northwest—428, North central—457, Northeast—520, Southwest—1157 (including Sofia), South central—787, Southeast—558; (b) *sample model*, i.e. two-stage probability cluster sample stratified by place of residence (Sofia/regional centre/other towns/rural); (c) *selecting the respondent within the household's address*, normally when the number of eligible persons in a household is greater than 1, the Kish's (1965) approach, based on the nearest birthday date for determining the eligible person, was applied.

The collected data was subjected to on-field local control, post-field 10% telephone reliability checks and post-field logical control. The data was entered through an entry mask, limiting operators' errors and processed by SPSS. The generated data reproduces the structure of the general population in Bulgaria by district, sex and age with a very high level of reliability. The maximal margin of error at the NUTS II level (on average 650 respondents) is 3.84% for the 95% confidence interval at a 50% relative frequency. The same error on the national level (3900 respondents) is 1.57%.

Two main subsamples were addressed by the survey instrument: (a) return migrants, defined as people who have stayed more than 1 month abroad for the last 5 years—606 respondents or 15.5% of the sample are identified; and (b) potential migrants, defined by particular indicators measuring the strength of the migration attitude and the proximity of the migration horizon—in total 24.9% potential migrants (including short-term, long-term and potential resettling migrants as well as students and return migrants).

These two sub-samples were analysed separately, though the questionnaire comprised some "mirror" questions, e.g. addressing migration from the perspective of a return migrant and a potential migrant or non-migrant. There is however a caveat concerning these data. They rest on the assumption that the social structure of the persons who return back to the sending country mirrors or represents the structure of the current migrants abroad. Long-term migrants, permanent residents abroad or students who rarely return to the home country may be underestimated and short-term or circular migrants possibly overestimated.

In Switzerland, a survey that applies a "self-completion and mail back" data collection method was conducted. The questionnaire addressed issues regarding people over 18, having migrated themselves to Switzerland, i.e. first generation. As we could not control whether somebody is a first- or second-generation migrant before sending the questionnaires, we explained the sample in the accompanying letter. The questionnaire was written both in Bulgarian and in the locally spoken language (German or French). Face-to-face interviews like those carried out in Bulgaria were not possible because of the high costs of travelling and personnel in Switzerland.

The survey provides data such as socio-demographic profile, earnings, remittances and future migration plans and it comprised the following steps: (a) acquiring the available post mail addresses of all migrants of Bulgarian origin who live officially in Switzerland with support from the State Secretariat for Migration for a total number of 4962, resulting in 4302 valid addresses; (b) weighting the data with official statistics which resulted in an exhaustive sample of Bulgarians living in Switzerland and a response rate of 26 %, i.e. 907 paper and 230 online questionnaires for a total of 1137 surveys filled in; (c) statistically processing the data in a similar way to the Bulgarian survey.

Semi-structured Interviews In Switzerland, the qualitative work comprised 23 semi-structured interviews which were conducted in the German, French and Italian-speaking regions in late 2013 and early 2014. The contacts for the interviews were obtained partly thanks to the e-mails the Bulgarian addressees provided when filling out the national quantitative questionnaire or through personal contacts and snowball techniques as explained further. Most of the interviews took place in Bulgarian, a few in English, while the interviews in the Canton of Ticino were conducted in Italian. They were all recorded, transcribed, and where necessary translated or summarized in English afterwards.

The Canton of Ticino represents a special case study in our fieldwork due to the geographical and labour market's features of this region in between North and South, the German speaking part of Switzerland and Northern Italy. Eight semi-structured interviews were collected at different times in two locations, both in Lugano or Mendrisio, a small town closer to the Swiss–Italian border. The persons interviewed were selected with some help from the Bulgarian Honorary Consul in Lugano, NGOs working in the field of migration and integration and snowball methods. Available SEM statistics show the presence of 101 men out of a total of 320 official Bulgarian residents in the Canton of Ticino at the end of August 2015 with a resulting gender ratio of about 70 % women against 30 % men. In spite of this minor number of men, during the fieldwork we were frequently reminded about the self-perceived presence in this region of only Bulgarian women because of the long-standing migration regime and labour market's demand which would allow female migration. As a result, the interviewed sample includes only women, mainly highly skilled and one student in the 23–60 age range.

In Bulgaria, 25 return migrants were interviewed about their migration experience, the reasons why they left, their economic and work conditions abroad as well as presently in Bulgaria. The interviewed persons came back, either because they did not succeed abroad or because their intention never was to stay abroad. The interviews were conducted by a native speaker, recorded and later translated in a summarized form in English. The sample is derived primarily from the regional contacts of the ASA network, but some persons were approached through snowball methods as well. Sometimes the interviews took place in a rather formal setting, i.e. house or a public place, other times a group conversation resulted from the simultaneous interviews of various persons in a bar or the office of a mayor of the local town. In similar contexts, the grid of questions guided us in collecting the same information from every person. The conversational character helped to recall particular aspects and elaborate them further than in an interview sensu stricto.

Desk Research Desk research includes statistics, articles, publications, grey literature related to theoretical and empirical research on migration, particularly transnational migration, and migration linked to development, social inequality and regional disparities. The collected research data covers, in particular, Bulgarian and Swiss migration and legislation as well as comparative perspectives encompassing other Central and South-Eastern European countries and the EU policy and legislation.

Regional disparities between Bulgaria and Switzerland and between selected Bulgarian regions were then addressed by in-depth desk research. This specific research endeavour included, first, a general picture of macroeconomic disparities in Bulgaria and Switzerland after 2007 on the basis of major socio-economic indicators like territorial structure at NUTS 3 level, GDP/per capita (PPS), rates of fertility and mortality, unemployment and employment, real adjusted gross disposable income of households per capita (PPS), at-risk-of-poverty population, share in GDP of the public expenditures for education and health and expenditures on social protection/per inhabitant (PPS).

Second, special emphasis went on the evaluation of the socio-economic disparities between the six Bulgarian NUTS 2 regions after 2007 with a two-level analysis encompassing various specific indicators describing the demographic and ethnical structure of the population, situation on the local labour market, development of the local economy, status of the transportation infrastructure, household incomes, education (e.g. student share of the population), health (e.g. number of medicines/10,000 inhabitants). By means of the taxonomic method, the selected indicators generated a summary evaluation.

1.4 Organization of the Book

After this introduction, in the second chapter "Determinants of Migration and Types of Migration and Mobility Between Switzerland and Bulgaria" by Vesselin Mintchev, Venelin Boshnakov, Marina Richter and Paolo Ruspini, the different forms of Bulgarian migration and mobility between Switzerland and Bulgaria are explored moving from the concepts of individual aspirations and capabilities of potential and actual migrants. The transnational approach allows capturing the characteristics and linkages of different migratory trajectories and intentions between the two countries, such as permanent, return or circular migration. Particular attention is given to the theoretical and methodological definitions and to the specific determinants of various migration types as well as the respective implications resulting from them. Socio-economic and demographic profiles of these migration patterns are also drawn by relying on descriptive statistics, qualitative hints and a multivariate logistic regression analysis.

The third chapter, "Social Inequality and Migration" by Dotcho Mihailov and Michael Nollert, addresses the links between social inequality and migration. Social status in terms of profession, occupational position and income is studied as a driver and as an outcome of migration. A particular focus is put on the shifts in social status resulting from migration. Detailed socio-demographic patterns are provided for the various shifts in the social status of migrants. These observations are being made on data derived from return migrants identified in Bulgaria and Bulgarian migrants identified in Switzerland. Hypotheses of increasing and decreasing social status are tested among migrants once they are located in the receiving country and once they are back home in the sending country.

The fourth chapter "Regional Disparities in Bulgaria and Switzerland" by Venelin Boshnakov, Vesselin Mintchev, Georgi Shopov and Iordan Kaltchev considers regional differences in Bulgaria as well as interregional disparities in Switzerland as possible elements for primary or secondary migratory movements between Bulgaria and Switzerland, between Bulgarian regions at different stages of their development or between rural and urban areas and vice versa in both countries. This contribution advances some evidences as to the search of Bulgarians in Switzerland for migrant niches in relatively less developed cantons and the avoidance of higher concentration of migrants of other origin. It also suggests that educational differences as well as diversity in professional occupations amongst Bulgarian residents in Switzerland are related to the regional divergence in the respective Swiss cantons.

In the fifth chapter, "Migration Policies in Bulgaria and Switzerland" by Irena Zareva the role and impact of policy and legislation in the migration relations between the two countries are explored in the period of time before and after the Bulgarian accession to the EU in 2007 and the extension in 2009 of Swiss–EU bilateral agreements to Bulgaria. Transitional arrangements, which allow Switzerland to exert regulations over incoming labour migration from Bulgaria, hampered however the acquired freedom of movement by Bulgarian citizens. More recently, the

Swiss popular referendum on "mass immigration" held in February 2014 may have a restrictive impact on the Swiss–EU policy framework as well as on the size and structure of migration inflows to Switzerland. Migration policies are then considered as the framework that affects all Bulgarian migrants, but in different ways over time and according to certain categories such as education, labour market skills and factors as current employers' needs.

The sixth chapter, "Social Networks and Transnational Migration Practices" by Dotcho Mihailov, Marina Richter and Paolo Ruspini, examines the process of social networking and transnational interactions throughout the entire migration experience starting from the analysis of the Bulgarian–Swiss case. Therefore, social networking and transnationalism are addressed either as determinants or outcomes of particular migration patterns and models of adaptation between the receiving and sending society. A particular section deals with the shifts in cultural values and social identity driven by the migrants' experience. Thereafter, socio-economic and demographic profiles of the studied indicators are provided in terms of regional, income, gender, educational, ethnic and other basic determinants. Various forms of transnational practices, including travel and non-travel communications and contacts are also considered in light of the different forms of migrant settlement. The basic hypothesis is that migration experience fosters higher levels of multiculturalism and transnational values, resulting in shifts in interactions, professions, socio-economic status, but also bringing about major changes in social identity and cultural values.

In the "Conclusions", by Paolo Ruspini, Dotcho Mihailov and Marina Richter, the transnational practices between Switzerland and Bulgaria are considered in a final discussion covering the four researched concepts (i.e. transnationalism, social inequality, regional disparity and migration policies) and the geographical scope of the Bulgarian communities and diaspora abroad. Consideration of similar case studies is useful for moving beyond the Bulgarian–Swiss framework and analysing convergences and divergences affecting the process of migration and inclusion of Bulgarians in Europe. Finally, the conclusions also critically evaluate the adopted theoretical and empirical approach and discuss the challenges that lie ahead for future research.

References

Achermann, C., & Chimienti, M. (2006). *Migration, Prekarität und Gesundheit*. Ressourcen und Risiken von vorläufig Aufgenommenen und Sans-Papiers in Genf und Zürich. Neuchâtel: Swiss Forum for Migration and Population Studies.

Agency for Bulgarians Abroad. (2015). Retrieved November 27, 2015, from http://www.aba.government.bg/?show=english.

Amelina, A. (2013). Hierarchies and categorical power in cross-border science: Analyzing Scientists' transnational mobility between Ukraine and Germany. *Southeast European and Black Sea Studies, 13*(2), 141–155.

Ang, I. (2004). Beyond transnational nationalism: Questioning the borders of the Chinese diaspora in the global city. In B. S. A. Yeoh & K. Willis (Eds.), *State/nation/transnation: Perspectives of transnationalism in the Asia-Pacific* (pp. 179–198). London: Routledge.

Anghel, R. G. (2008). Changing statutes: Freedom of movement, locality and transnationality of irregular Romanian migrants in Italy. *Journal of Ethnic and Migration Studies, 34*(5), 787–802.

Babić, B. (2013). The migration–development nexus in Bosnia and Herzegovina: Center for Local Development and Diaspora seen 'from below'. *Southeast European and Black Sea Studies, 13*(2), 211–225.

Baghdadi, N., & Riaño, Y. (2014). Familie und Beruf vereinbaren? Vorstellungen und Strategien hochqualifizierter Migrant/innen. In Passagen (Ed.), *Migration und Geschlecht in der Schweiz* (pp. 36–57). Zürich: Seismo.

Baghdadi, N., & Riaño, Y. (2011). Negotiating spaces of participation. Experiences and strategies of skilled immigrant women to achieve professional integration. In E. H. Oleksy, J. Hearn, & D. Golanska (Eds.), *The limits of gendered citizenship. Contexts and complexities* (pp. 176–196). New York: Routledge.

Bauböck, R. (2008). *Ties across borders: The growing salience of transnationalism and Diaspora politics* (IMISCOE Policy Brief 13, October 2008).

Bauer, T., & Zimmermjann, K. (1999). *Assessment of possible migration pressure and its labor market impact following EU enlargement to Central and Eastern Europe* (IZA Research Report, No. 3).

Boccagni, P. (2012). Even a transnational social field must have its boundaries: Methodological options, potentials and dilemmas for researching transnationalism. In C. Vargas-Silva (Ed.), *Handbook of research methods in migration* (pp. 295–318). Cheltenham: Edward Elgar.

Body-Gendrot, S., & Martiniello, M. (Eds.). (2000). *Minorities in European cities. The dynamics of social integration and social exclusion at the neighbourhood level.* Basingstoke: Macmillan/St. Martin's Press.

Boeri, T., & Bruecker, H. (2001). *Eastern enlargement and EU-labour-markets: Perceptions, challenges and opportunities* (IZA Discussion Paper, No. 256).

Boyd, M., & Nowak, J. (2013). Social networks and international migration. In M. Martiniello & J. Rath (Eds.), *An introduction to international migration studies: European perspectives* (pp. 79–105). Amsterdam: Amsterdam University Press. IMISCOE Textbooks.

Castaneda, E., Morales, M. C., & Ochoa, O. (2014). Transnational behavior in comparative perspective: The relationship between immigrant integration and transnationalism in New York, El Paso, and Paris. *Comparative Migration Studies, 2*(3), 325.

Chapman, M., & Prothero, R. M. (1983). Themes on circulation in the third world. *International Migration Review, 17*(4), 597–632.

Chimienti, M. (2009). *Prostitution et migration. La dynamique de l'agir faible.* Zürich: Seismo.

D'Amato, G. (2001). *Vom Ausländer zum Bürger. Der Streit um die politische Integration von Einwanderern in Deutschland, Frankreich und der Schweiz.* Münster: LIT.

D'Amato, G., & Fibbi, R. (2007). Bürgerschaftspolitik statt Neopatriotismus. *Zur Debatte über Integration. Widerspruch, 51,* 75–83.

D'Amato, G., Gerber, B., & Kamm, M. (2005). *Menschenschmuggel und irreguläre Migration in der Schweiz.* Neuchâtel: Swiss Forum for Migration and Population Studies.

Dahinden, J. (2005). *Prishtina—Schlieren. Albanische Migrationsnetzwerke im transnationalen Raum.* Zürich: Seismo.

Dahinden, J., & Stants, F. (2006). *Arbeits- und Lebensbedingungen von Cabaret-Tänzerinnen in der Schweiz.* Neuchâtel: Studien SFM 48.

De Haas, H. (2007). *Remittances, migration and social development. A conceptual review of the literature.* United Nations Research Institute for Social Development, Social Policy and Development Programme, 34, pp. 1–35.

De Haas, H. (2010a). Migration and development: A theoretical perspective. *International Migration Review, 44*(1), 227–264.

De Haas, H. (2010b). *Migration transitions: A theoretical and empirical inquiry into the develop-mental drivers of international migration* (IMI/DEMIG Working Paper No. 24). Oxford: International Migration Institute, University of Oxford.

Deneva, N. (2012). Transnational aging carers: On transformation of kinship and citizenship in the context of migration among Bulgarian Muslims in Spain. *Social Politics, 19*(1), 105–128.

Eade, J., & Valkanova, Y. (Eds.). (2009). *Accession and migration. Changing policy, society, and culture in an enlarged Europe*. Farnham: Ashgate.

Faist, T. (2004). The border-crossing expansion of social space. Concepts, questions and topics. In T. Faist & E. Özveren (Eds.), *Transnational social spaces. Agents, networks and institutions* (pp. 1–34). Hants: Ashgate.

Faist, T. (2008). Migrants as transnational development agents. An inquiry into the newest round of the migration-development nexus. *Population, Space and Place, 14*(1), 21–42.

Farrell, M., Kairytė, E., Nienaber, B., McDonagh, J., & Mahon, M. (2014). Rural return migration: Comparative analysis between Ireland and Lithuania. *Central and Eastern European Migration Review, 3*(2), 127–149.

Fassmann, H., & Musil, E. (2013). *Conceptual framework for modelling longer term migratory, labour market and human capital processes* (SEEMIG Working Paper, No. 1). Vienna: Universität Wien.

Fassmann, H., Reeger, U., & Sievers, W. (Eds.) (2009). *Statistics and reality. Concepts and mea-surements of migration in Europe* (IMISCOE Reports). Amsterdam: Amsterdam University Press.

Favell, A. (2008). The new face of east-west migration in Europe. *Journal of Ethnic and Migration Studies, 34*(5), 701–716.

Federal Office for Migration, FOM. (2014). http://www.bfs.admin.ch/bfs/portal/de/index/the-men/01/07/blank/key/01/01.html. Retrieved August 31, 2014.

Gächter, A. (2002). *The ambiguities of emigration: Bulgaria since 1988* (International Migration Papers No. 39). Geneva: ILO.

Geddes, A. (2003). The politics of migration in an integrating Europe. In A. Geddes (Ed.), *The politics of migration and immigration in Europe* (pp. 126–148). London: Sage.

gfs.bern. (2005). *Sans Papiers in der Schweiz: Arbeitsmarkt, nicht Asylpolitik ist entscheidend*. Bern: Bundesamt für Migration.

Girard, E., & Bauder, H. (2007). Assimilation and exclusion of foreign trained engineers in Canada. Inside a professional regulatory organization. *Antipode, 39*(1), 35–53.

Gómez-Mestres, S., & Molina, J. L. (2010). Les nouvelles migrations dans l'Europe: chaînes migratoires, établissement et réseaux sociaux des Bulgares en Espagne et en Catalogne. *Balkanologie, XII*(2), 64 par.

Górny, A., & Ruspini, P. (Eds.). (2004). *Migration in the new Europe: East-west revisited*. Basingstoke: Palgrave-Macmillan.

Gransow, B. (2012, December). *Internal migration in China: Opportunity or trap. Focus migra-tion* (Policy Brief No. 19).

Granovetter, M. S. (1973). The strength of weak ties. *American Journal of Sociology, 78*(6), 1360–1380.

Guarnizo, L. E. (1997). The emergence of a transnational social formation and the mirage of return migration among Dominican transmigrants. *Identities, 4*(2), 281–322.

Guentcheva, R., Kabakchieva, P., & Kolarski, P. (2004). Bulgaria: The social impact of seasonal migration. In *Migration trends in selected applicant countries* (Vol. 1). Geneva: International Organization for Migration.

Haug, W. (2006). *Migranten und ihre Nachkommen auf dem Arbeitsmarkt: Ein Überblick*. Demos Informationen aus der Demographie. Neuchâtel: Bundesamt für Statistik.

Klein-Hitpaß, K. (2013). Regional selectivity of return migration. The locational choice of high-skilled return migrants in Poland. In B. Glorius, I. Grabowska-Lusinska, & A. Kuvik (Eds.), *Mobility in transition. Migration patterns after EU enlargement* (pp. 237–257). Amsterdam: Amsterdam University Press. IMISCOE Research.

IOM. (1999). *Migration potential in central and eastern Europe.* Geneva: IOM.

Jaccard Ruedin, H., & Weaver, F. (2009). *Ageing workforce in an ageing society. Wieviel Health Professionals braucht das Schweizer Gesundheitssystem bis 2030?* (Careum Working Papers).

Jileva, E. (2002). Visa and free movement of labour: The uneven imposition of the EU acquis on the accession states. *Journal of Ethnic and Migration Studies, 28*(4), 683–700.

Kahanec, M., & Zimmermann, K. (Eds.). (2010). *EU labor markets after post-enlargement migration.* Berlin: Springer.

Kaneff, D., & Pine, F. (2011). *Global connections and emerging inequalities in Europe. Perspectives on poverty and transnational migration.* London: Anthem Press.

Kelly, P., & Lusis, T. (2006). Migration and the transnational habitus: Evidence from Canada and the Philippines. *Environment and Planning A, 38*(5), 831–847.

King, R., Povrzanović Frykman, M., & Vullnetari, J. (2013). Migration, transnationalism and development on the southeastern flank of Europe. *Southeast European and Black Sea Studies, 13*(2), 125–140.

Kish, L. (1965). *Survey sampling.* New York: Wiley.

Krase, J. (2012). *Seeing cities change. Local culture and class.* Farnham: Ashgate.

Krasteva, A., Otova, I., & Staykova, E. (2011). *Temporary and Circular Migration in Bulgaria: Empirical evidences, current policy practice and future option 2004–2009* (Research report for the European Migration Network). Sofia: Centre for European Refugees, Migration and Ethnic Studies.

Mahnig, H. (Ed.). (2005). *Histoire de la politique de migration, d'asile et d'intégration en Suisse depuis 1948.* Zürich: Seismo.

Maleev, A. (2010). Bulgarian return migration. In A. Krasteva, A. Kasabova, & D. Karabinova (Eds.), *Migrations from and to Southeastern Europe* (pp. 267–276). Ravenna: Longo Editore.

Manatschal, A. (2010). *integration policies in federal settings: Assessing the impact of exclusionary citizenship conceptions on cantonal integration policies* (Center for Comparative and International Studies (CIS) Working Paper, 55/2010). Zurich: ETH and University of Zurich.

Mancheva, M., & Troeva, E. (2009). *Bulgaria—Context analysis and methodology.* Review Report (WP2) for the Gender, Migration and Intercultural Interaction in South-East Europe (Ge.M.IC.) project.

Mansoor, A., & Quillin, B. (Eds.). (2007). *Migration and remittances: Eastern Europe and the former Soviet Union.* New York: World Bank.

Markova, E. (2010). Optimising migration effects: A perspective from Bulgaria. In R. Black, G. Engbersen, M. Okólski, & C. Pantîru (Eds.), *A continent moving west? EU enlargement and labour migration from central and eastern Europe* (pp. 207–230). Amsterdam: Amsterdam University Press. IMISCOE Research.

Martiniello, M., & Rath, J. (Eds.). (2010). *Selected studies in international migration and immigrant incorporation.* Amsterdam: Amsterdam University Press. IMISCOE Textbooks.

Mazzucato, V. (2011). Reverse remittances in the migration-development nexus: Two-way flows between Ghana and the Netherlands. *Population, Space and Place, 17*(5), 454–468.

Mintchev, V., Kalchev, I., Goev, V., & Boshnakov, V. (2004). External migration from Bulgaria at the beginning of the XXI century: Estimates of potential emigrants' attitudes and profile. *Economic Thought, XIX*(7), 137–161.

Mintchev, V., & Boshnakov, V. (2010). Return migration and development prospects after EU integration: Empirical evidence from Bulgaria. In R. Black, G. Engbersen, M. Okólski, & C. Pantîru (Eds.), *A continent moving west? EU enlargement and labour migration from central and eastern Europe* (pp. 231–248). Amsterdam: Amsterdam University Press. IMISCOE Research.

Morawska, E. (2008). *East European Westbound income-seeking migrants: Some unwelcome effects on sender- and receiver- societies* (Working Paper Series of the Research Network 1989, Working Paper 16/2008).

Mountz, A. (2011). Specters at the port of entry: Understanding state mobilities through an ontology of exclusion. *Mobilities, 6*(3), 317–334.

Napierała, J., & Trevena, P. (2010). Patterns and determinants of sub-regional migration: A case study of polish construction workers in Norway. In R. Black, G. Engbersen, M. Okólski, &

C. Panţîru (Eds.), *A continent moving west? EU enlargement and labour migration from central and eastern Europe* (pp. 51–71). Amsterdam: Amsterdam University Press. IMISCOE Research.

NSI. (2002a). *External and internal migration of population in the late 90s.* Sofia: National Statistical Institute.

NSI. (2002b). *Territorial mobility of population. Population and Housing Census 2001, 6(3).* Sofia: National Statistical Institute.

NSI. (2011). *Population of country according to census.* Sofia: National Statistical Institute. Retrieved November 27, 2015, from http://censusresults.nsi.bg/Census/Reports/1/2/R1.aspx.

Okólski, M. (2001). Incomplete migration: A new form of mobility in central and eastern Europe. The case of polish and Ukrainian Migrants'. In C. Wallace & D. Stola (Eds.), *Patterns of migration in central Europe* (pp. 105–128). Basingstoke: Palgrave.

Østergaard-Nielsen, E. (2011). Codevelopment and citizenship: The nexus between policies on local migrant incorporation and migrant transnational practices in Spain. *Ethnic and Racial Studies, 34*(1), 20–39.

Pecoraro, M. (2005). Les migrants hautement qualifiés. In W. Haug & P. Wanner (Eds.), *Migrants et marché du travail: Compétences et insertion professionnelle des personnes d'origine étrangère en Suisse* (pp. 71–110). Neuchâtel: Bundesamt für Statistik.

Polese, M. (1981). Regional disparity, migration and economic adjustment: A reappraisal. *Canadian Public Policy/Analyse de Politiques, 7*(4), 519–525.

Portes, A., Guarnizo, L. E., & Landolt, P. (1999). The study of transnationalism: Pitfalls and promise of an emergent research field. *Ethnic and Racial Studies, 22*(2), 217–237.

Rangelova, R. (1995). Divergent and convergent processes in integrating Europe: Where are the Balkans. In B. Dallago & G. Pegoretti (Eds.), *Integration and disintegration in European economies* (pp. 163–180). Aldershot: Dartmouth.

Rangelova, R. (2008). Convergence in the Neo-classical model of economic growth. *Economic Thought, XXIII*(7), 3–20.

Ravenstein, E. G. (1885). The laws of migration. *Journal of the Royal Statistical Society, 48,* 167–227.

Ravenstein, E. G. (1889). The laws of migration. *Journal of the Royal Statistical Society, 52,* 214–301.

Riaño, Y. (2011). Barrieren aufbrechen: Erfahrungen und Strategien von qualifizierten Migrantinnen beim Zugang zum Schweizer Arbeitsmarkt. *Berichte zur deutschen Landeskunde, 85*(1), 25–48.

Riaño, Y., & Baghdadi, N. (2007). Understanding the labour market participation of skilled immigrant women in Switzerland. The role of class, ethnicity and gender. *Journal of International Migration and Integration, 8,* 163–183.

Richter, M. (2011). Topographien der Ungleichheit. Dequalifikation als ein weibliches Phänomen? *Berichte zur deutschen Landeskunde, 85*(1), 49–59.

Ruspini, P. (2011). Conceptualising transnationalism: East-west migration patterns in Europe. In C. Allemann Ghionda & W. D. Bukow (Eds.), *Orte der Diversität: Formate, Arrangements und Inszenierungen* (pp. 115–127). Wiesbaden: VS Verlag.

Ruspini, P. (Ed.) (2010). South-Eastern Europe and the European migration system. East-West mobility in flux. *The Romanian Journal of European Studies,* No.7-8/2009, Special Issue on Migration and Mobility.

Ruspini, P. (2008a). Report from Switzerland. In J. Doomernik & M. Jandl (Eds.), *Modes of migration. Regulation and control in Europe.* Amsterdam: Amsterdam University Press.

Ruspini, P. (2008b). The post-enlargement migration space. In C. Bonifazi, M. Okólski, J. Schoorl, & P. Simon (Eds.), *International migration in Europe: New trends, New methods of analysis* (pp. 179–196). Amsterdam: Amsterdam University Press. IMISCOE Research.

Sandu, D. (2005). Emerging transantional migration from Romanian villages. *Current Sociology, 53*(4), 555–582.

Schweizerisches Rotes Kreuz (2006). *Sans-Papiers in der Schweiz. Unsichtbar—unverzichtbar.* Zürich: Seismo.

Shopov, G., Yankova, N., Ivanov, S., & Kirilova, Y. (2011). *Regional disparities in Bulgaria—Tendencies, factors, policies.* Sofia: Marin Drinov Publishing House.

Stola, D. (2001). Two kinds of quasi-migration in the middle zone: Central Europe as a space for transit migration and mobility for profit. In C. Wallace & D. Stola (Eds.), *Patterns of migration in central Europe* (pp. 84–104). Basingstoke: Palgrave.

Swiss Federal Statistical Office, SFSO. (2014). Retrieved December 31, 2014, from http://www.bfs.admin.ch/bfs/portal/en/index.html.

Tangram. (2011, December). *Città-Campagna. No. 28*. Bern: Federal Commission against Racism, p. 143.

Totev, S., & Kalchev, I. (2000). *Emigration process and the socio-economic development in Bulgaria. Migration studies*. Roma: Estratto.

Totev, S. (2004). Regional economic differences in Bulgaria and the other countries applying for membership of the EU. *Economic Thought, 2*, 3–17.

Totev, S. (2006). Comparative analysis of the processes of regional specialization and concentration in EU. *Economic Studies, 1*, 67–89.

Totev, S. (2011). Regional differences and regional policy in Bulgaria. *Economic Studies, 3*, 33–52.

United Nations. (1998). *Recommendations on statistics of international migration*. Revision 1. New York: United Nations.

Wanner, P., Pecoraro, M., & Fibbi, R. (2005). Femmes étrangères et marché du travail. In W. Haug & P. Wanner (Eds.), *Migrants et marché du travail. Compétences et insertion professionnelle des personnes d'origine étrangère en Suisse* (pp. 17–38). Bundesamt für Statistik: Neuchâtel.

Wessendorf, S. (2008). Culturalist discourses on inclusion and exclusion: the Swiss citizenship debate. *Social Anthropology, 16*(2), 187–202.

Wicker, H.-R., Fibbi, R., & Haug, W. (Eds.). (2003). *Migration und die Schweiz. Ergebnisse des Nationalen Forschungsprogramms Migration und interkulturelle Beziehungen*. Zürich: Seismo.

Wimmer, A., & Glick Schiller, N. (2002). Methodological nationalism and beyond: Nation-state building, migration and the social sciences. *Global Networks, 2*(4), 301–334.

Yankova, N., Shopov, G., Ivanov, S., Hristoskov, I., Tchkorev, N., & Kirilova, Y. (2003). *Socio-economic disparities between the municipalities in Bulgaria*. Sofia: Roll Publishing House.

Yankova, N. (2007). *Statistical study of structural changes*. Sofia: Marin Drinov.

Yeoh, B. S. A. (2013). 'Upwards' or 'Sideways' Cosmopolitanism? Talent/labour/marriage migrations in the globalising city-state of Singapore. *Migration Studies, 1*(1), 96–116.

Zincone, G., Penninx, R. & Borkert, M. (Eds.) (2011). *Migration policymaking in Europe: The dynamics of actors and contexts in past and present* (IMISCOE Research). Amsterdam: Amsterdam University Press.

Chapter 2
Determinants of Migration and Types of Migration and Mobility

Vesselin Mintchev, Venelin Boshnakov, Marina Richter, and Paolo Ruspini

2.1 Introduction

When studying migration, it is important to ask why and in which way migrants decide to leave their country for shorter or longer periods of time. These two questions, the first one about the determinants of migration and the second one about the types of migration, are intensely linked, as different types of migration might also have different determinants. We therefore start the book with a chapter that in a double sense frames the analysis: on the one hand, it provides the background to understand the migration processes we will analyse in detail and, on the other hand, it also provides a description of the data that will serve for the subsequent chapters.

Why people migrate or in more technical terms, what the determinants of migration are, has long preoccupied migration research. Various migration theories try to explain what factors are characteristic for migration and how—with statistical means—migration can be explained. They can be largely grouped into functionalist and structuralist approaches (De Haas 2010). *Functionalist approaches* seek to explain migration as a function of market processes. For instance, *neoclassical*

V. Mintchev (✉)
Economic Research Institute at the Bulgarian Academy of Sciences, Sofia, Bulgaria
e-mail: v.mintchev@abv.bg

V. Boshnakov
University of National and World Economy, Sofia, Bulgaria
e-mail: venelinb@unwe.bg

M. Richter
Social Policies and Social Work, University of Fribourg, Fribourg, Switzerland
e-mail: marina.richter@unifr.ch

P. Ruspini
Faculty of Communication Sciences, University of Lugano (USI), Lugano, Switzerland
e-mail: paolo.ruspini@usi.ch

© Springer International Publishing Switzerland 2017
M. Richter et al. (eds.), *Migration and Transnationalism Between Switzerland and Bulgaria*, DOI 10.1007/978-3-319-31946-9_2

theory (Lewis 1954; Todaro and Maruszko 1987) explains international migration at the macro level by geographical differences in labour supply and demand. Wage differentials are the main driver for labour force participants to search for options to relocate from depressed regions with excessive labour supply to destinations with encouraging labour demand at higher wage levels. At the micro level, neoclassical migration theory views migrants as individual, rational actors, who decide to move on the basis of a cost-benefit calculation. As they are free in their decision about migration and have full access to information, they are expected to go to places offering the highest wages. Todaro (1969) and Harris and Todaro (1970) elaborate the basic two-sector model of rural-to-urban labour migration. Their model is considered to be a basis of the neoclassical migration theory. Empirical analysis, though, has found a low responsiveness of migration to wage differentials in the industrial countries (Bentivogli and Pagano 1999).

In the 1980s and 1990s, the so-called *New Economics of Labour Migration (NELM)* emerges as a critical response to, and improvement of, neoclassical migration theory (Massey et al. 1993: 436). According to NELM, decisions are often made by household members together and for the well-being of the family as a whole. Households also do not migrate together but rather send one or more household members off as migrants. NELM also explicitly links the migration decision to the impacts of migration by stressing the importance of remittances (Hagen-Zanker 2008). According to NELM, a household maximizes joint income and status, and minimizes risks. All three aspects contribute to the migration decision of the household resulting in the actual migration of certain household members.

The *historical-structural theories* claim that international migration is caused by an unequal distribution of political and economic power in the world economy. They have criticized a key aspect of neoclassical migration theory: the free choice of individuals in their decision to migrate. Historical structuralists emphasize that migrants are subjected to structural constraints. From this structural perspective, migration has above all an increasing effect on regional disparities and constitutes therefore a negative phenomenon that further hinders the economic development of sending societies (De Haas 2008). An example is the *Model of migration transition* by Zelinsky (1971) who argues that migration is part of the economic and social changes inherent in the modernization process.

A recent development in migration theory by Hein De Haas (2010, 2011, 2014) aims at bridging the shortcomings of both functionalist and structuralist approaches. He proposes to analyse the determinants of migration according to migrants' aspirations, capabilities and opportunities. De Haas builds his approach on Sen's (1999) by arguing that aspirations for migration as a desired state of being or condition can be economic, sociocultural and political and can exist at various levels, such as the individual and the household or family. These aspirations are not sufficient, as potential migrants also need to have the capabilities—those factors that expand people's freedom to migrate, such as education, health, social security and equality—as well as personal and political freedoms.

And finally, the structural context (the nation state and its policy) needs to provide the opportunity, for example through visa conditions. We will base our further elaborations on the three conceptual approaches proposed by de Haas. In particular, this chapter will deal with the aspirations and the capabilities, whereas the third focus—the opportunities—will be the topic of Chap. 5.

There are various definitions of who qualifies as a migrant and what different types of migration exist. As shortly discussed in the book's introduction, the United Nations (1998) defines an international migrant as a person who leaves his country of birth and stays in another country for more than a year. While this definition has for long been widely acknowledged, there are two reasons to broaden it. The first reason is that migration research has dealt in many cases with forms of migration that do not strictly match the common UN definition. For instance, in the Swiss context, from the 1960s until the 1980s there existed a migration policy that encouraged people through treaties between states (most importantly Italy, but also Spain and Portugal), to work in Switzerland for 9 months, return home and after 3 months return back to Switzerland (Piguet 2005). The so-called guest worker regime encouraged people to engage in circular migration because it suited seasonal work and because the policy aimed at having *guest* workers but not people who would stay in the country.

The second reason applies to recent developments in migration. When we look at various regions in the world, but in particular also at the region we are focusing on with this book, i.e. South-Eastern Europe, migration is strongly characterized by movements of people that do not fall under the UN migration definition. We know from other studies (Marchetti 2013; Sandu 2005; Skeldon 2012), and our data confirms this, that there is much circular and short-term migration. Therefore we propose to frame our analysis by the notion of transnationalism which encompasses different forms of physical mobility—among other forms of contact and connection—between two countries, linking these countries and the diaspora group with their community in their place of origin (see also Chap. 1). Not in vain is there a new interest arising in migration studies for topics such as mobility. In this regard, "traditional" definitions of migration are not applicable anymore to different forms of mobility. This growing mobility has become possible because of improved means of travel and communication (Glick Schiller and Salazar 2013). In the European context, similar patterns of mobility are also the result of economic factors and the impact of regional migration regimes like the European Union on migrants' behaviours, directions and flows (Ruspini 2010, 2011; Glorius et al. 2013; Ruspini and Eade 2014).

The fall of the Iron Curtain and the EU east-enlargement also brought with it a discussion about the potential migration that might be induced by the opening of the borders inside the EU. As mentioned earlier in Chap. 1, the inclusion of new member states from Central and Eastern Europe led to several studies that estimate the potential migration from these countries to the Western European countries at between 2 and 4 % of the population (Bauer and Zimmermann 1999; Boeri et al. 2000; Straubhaar 2001; Zaiceva 2006). As it is a difficult task to estimate, the amount of people who will actually migrate, potential migration is calculated on the basis of people's intention to migrate—in the conceptual terms of De Haas (2011) this represents the migration aspiration (see also Wallace and Stola 2001; Kaczmarczyk 2004; Wallace 2008; Fassmann et al. 2009; Fuchs-Schundeln and Schundeln 2009; Kahanec and Zimmermann 2010).

An inclusion of potential migrants in a survey on migration allows the comparison between the people who have the intention (aspire) to leave and those who have actually migrated. The rich information we have allows us to track key characteristics of the potential migrants as well as the individuals with recent migration experience in Bulgaria, and the actual Bulgarian migrants living in Switzerland. It also allows us to discuss what determines their future plans.

In general we will base the categorization of the studied groups on their aspirations regarding migration. We have opted for this categorization because we can in most cases only be certain about people's aspirations, as this is what they state in the survey or in the interviews. Whether their aspiration is realized at some later stage is not predictable in most cases. This is easily understandable in the case of potential migrants who just state their willingness to migrate. But it is also the case, for instance, for return migrants who express their will to stay in the country of origin. However, an option for them to migrate again cannot be excluded and the category of return migrant remains therefore a controversial category in this respect. In the end, these aspirations are described in view of the actual capabilities for migration of the categories of Bulgarian migrants studied.

The groups outlined in Table 2.1 represent the major aspirations of potential and actual migrants. Among potential migrants we did not diversify further than distinguishing between long-term and short-term migrants, as the aspiration to migrate is still far from becoming a real plan at this stage and further categorization seems futile. Among the actual people with migration experience the differentiation between people who have returned to their country of origin and people who are still living abroad leads to differing categories of aspirations. Among both groups we find the aspiration to return home and stay there (return migration) and the aspiration to engage in circular migration. Among the group living currently abroad there exist also aspirations regarding the desire to stay in the current country of residence or to move to a third country.

Table 2.1 Categorization of migrants according to their aspirations regarding migration

Potential migrants		People with migration experience					
		In country of origin		Abroad			
Long-term	Short-term	Return migrants	Circular migrants	Settled migrants	Secondary migrants	Return migrants	Circular migrants
Intending to go abroad for more than a year	Intending to go abroad for less than a year	Planning to stay in the country of origin	Planning to go abroad again	Staying in the same country	Leaving for another (third) country	Returning (to the country of origin)	Living between the two countries

As we noted in the beginning, the questions of why and how people migrate are at the core of this chapter. With reference to the groups of people with aspiration to migrate and actual migrants, we can detail the leading questions for further analysis as follows:

- What characterizes the groups of potential migrants and of actual migrants (settled, return and circular migrants)? In other words: what is their profile?
- What are the determinants for the aspiration to migrate?
- What are the determinants for the actual migration?
- What are the determinants for the different groups of migrants (for instance, settlers, circular and return migrants)?

After discussing methodological and definitional issues (Sect. 2.2), the chapter addresses these questions by describing the profile of the groups defined above (Sect. 2.3). The statistical data that provides the basis for the profiles is enriched with material from our qualitative interviews conducted in Bulgaria and Switzerland. The following Sect. (2.4) discusses the determinants of the aspiration to migrate, the determinants of circular vs. return migration and finally the determinants of various aspirations regarding future plans once migrated abroad. A last section sums up the chapter and concludes with a discussion of the findings presented.

2.2 Definitions and Methodology

As explained in the Introduction (Chap. 1), we base our analyses on two quantitative data sets collected in Bulgaria and in Switzerland, as well as qualitative interviews conducted similarly in both countries. In particular the quantitative data sets require some additional information regarding the usage of the data and the construction of the various subgroups representing types of migrants according to their aspirations.

Both questionnaires include a set of overlapping questions in order to make them comparable. These items comprise:

- Outmigration attitudes, drivers and motives.
- Economic activity, socio-economic shifts, inequalities and other details about the last period of stay abroad.
- Social networks, transnational practices and attitudes of Bulgarian citizens.
- Impact of migration policies.
- Demographic, social and economic profile of the respondent and his/her household.

Apart from the overlapping items, both questionnaires differ in the way the data was collected and in the necessary data processing as explained in the following sections.

2.2.1 Bulgarian Survey

The sample design of the Bulgarian survey is a version of the two-stage cluster model (Eurostat 2008) typically used by the National Statistical Institute and professional agencies in Bulgaria. First, census enumeration clusters of households are used as primary sampling units and, second, a fixed number of randomly drawn households are interviewed in each selected cluster. The questionnaire contained five separate sections targeted at the following topics: A—Migration experience: filled in by any respondent who has recent migration experience ("mobile" respondent); B—Potential migration: filled in by all respondents; C—Transnational practices, relations with Diaspora: filled in by non-mobile respondents; D—Socio-demographic status: both person-level and household-level attributes. For the purpose of differentiating the types of migration outlined above (Table 2.1) we used two main criteria: (1) the migration experience and (2) the aspiration to migrate. The combination of both criteria allows us to identify people with migration experience and distinguish among them according to their aspirations regarding further migration plans—thus to delineate return from circular migrants. As "migration experience" we apply a threshold of minimum 1 month during the last 5 years for the period of stay abroad. We consider this the shortest period of stay that could be related to a temporary job or a short-term visit with a purpose other than tourism (Mintchev and Boshnakov 2006). The individuals without migration experience—considered as non-mobile population—are also differentiated according to their aspirations into potential migrants or non-migrants.

The instrument for identifying the types of potential migrants is adapted from previous studies (e.g. Kaltchev 2001; Mintchev et al. 2004; Mintchev and Boshnakov 2006, 2007, 2010). In the survey, the following set of items is designed to capture both the duration of the intended move and its main goal:

How likely is for you in the near future to:

1. *Emigrate* to another country to live there?
2. Go abroad to work for *more than a year*?
3. Go abroad to study for *more than a year*?
4. Go abroad to work for a *few months* (up to 1 year)?
5. Go abroad to study/specialize for a *few months*?

Answers to *each question* are required from respondents applying a scale of likelihood. The potential migrants (short- and long-term) are identified based on the answers to these questions, by following the subsequent steps:

- Step 1: any respondent who has indicated a likelihood: (1) to leave for good (emigrate) or to leave for a period over 1 year (2) to work or (3) to study is defined as "potential long-term migrant".
- Step 2: after extracting the first subset of respondents, *from the rest* a second subset is separated including anyone who has indicated a likelihood to leave for a period of less than 1 year (4) to work or (5) to study. These are defined as "potential short-term migrants".

Table 2.2 Structure of the sample in respect of migration typology (%)

Aspirations	Long-term	Short-term	Non-migrants	Total sample	
Without migration experience	12.4	4.9	82.7	100.0	
	57.1	62.9	93.0		84.5
With migration experience	50.6	15.7	33.7	100.0	
	42.9	37.1	7.0		15.5
Total sample	18.3	6.6	75.1	100.0	
	100.0	100.0	100.0		100.0
Within people with migration experience					
Circulars	74.4	25.6	–		9.0
Returnees	–	–	100.0		6.5

Note: The numbers in the *upper left* corner of each field represent the *horizontal* distribution; the numbers in the *lower right* corner represent percentages in the group (*vertical*)

- Step 3: all others are categorized as "potential non-migrants": these are respondents who did not indicate a high likelihood of engaging in any of the suggested migration options.

This algorithm produces three non-overlapping subsamples by delineating the category of "potential non-migrants" from those who intend to leave the country. The rationale behind this approach is the initial focus on those who are willing to leave for a long time and who have the intention of changing the country of residence (i.e. potential long-term migrants). The short-term migrants might in many cases enter a circular migration although this does not become clear directly from people's intentions and might often not be their initial purpose. This is why we only differentiate the aspirations of potential migrants by the time horizon.

Table 2.2 summarizes the sample structure in respect of the typology presented above and allows us to assess aspirations across the categories of migrants. The share of individuals with migration experience is estimated at 15.5 % in the total sample. From all respondents, with and without migration experience, 18.3 % of the respondents have aspirations to migrate for long term and 6.6 % for short term. On the other hand, 75.1 % of all those interviewed did not express any intentions to migrate at all (or to leave Bulgaria again if they have migration experience). From the individuals who have aspirations to leave for the long term, a large share (43 %) has recent migration experience. It goes without saying that the aspirations expressed will not completely match the actions which some of these respondents will actually take in the near future, but they provide us with a picture to assess future migration plans of Bulgarians. Having this kind of partitioning of the total sample accounting for different aspiration perspectives (e.g. potential migrants or non-migrants; return or potentially circular migrants) and the exploration of the demographic and socio-economic profiles of each subsample in a comparative manner provides further insights into the analysis of the types of migration of the Bulgarian population.

Table 2.3 Registered Bulgarians in Switzerland and coverage in the sample

Permit	Registered (2013)		Sample	
Short-term (L)	1186	23.9%	181	15.9%
Midterm (B)	2943	59.3%	698	61.4%
Residence (C)	805	16.2%	239	21.0%
Rest	28	0.6%	19	1.7%
Total	4962	100%	1137	100%

2.2.2 Swiss Survey

The Swiss survey was designed as a post mail survey and was sent to all Bulgarian citizens living officially in Switzerland. The State Secretariat for Migration (SEM) provided us with the postal addresses of 4962 Bulgarian citizens with either long-term residence (C), a midterm permit of more than a year (B), a short-term permit of less than a year (L), or other permits including those for refugees but in numbers too small to be looked at in detail (see the distribution in Table 2.3).

The questionnaire was sent out to all available addresses. Completing the questionnaire and collecting the filled-in forms was possible via normal mail or via an online version of the questionnaire. A data collection based on face-to-face interviews with trained interviewers was too expensive for Switzerland so we relied on people's readiness to fill in the questionnaire. In order to stimulate respondent participation, the questionnaire was reduced to cover the key issues selected from the one used in Bulgaria. The comparison of the distribution of the permits of officially registered Bulgarians in Switzerland with our sample distribution of permits points to a quite acceptable representation of the various groups in the survey. Nevertheless, respondents with short-term permits are under-represented because often such individuals do not live at the registered address any more and maybe even have left the country. Accordingly, people with midterm permits and in particular residence permits are over-represented.

In the questionnaire we asked, just as in the Bulgarian survey, about their migration experience as well as future aspirations regarding migration. The following aspirations were included:

- To stay in Switzerland
- To return to Bulgaria
- To continue travelling back and forth
- To move to another country
- I don't know/I cannot say

As the questions were answered as single answers, they provided us with discrete groups according to migrants' future aspirations. These groups will later be portrayed and analysed.

2.3 Demographic Profiles, Aspirations and Capabilities

The descriptive part of the chapter is organized along the main groups we find in our data: potential migrants in Bulgaria, people with migration experience in Bulgaria, and the specific group of Bulgarian migrants living in Switzerland. The groups are further subdivided along their aspirations regarding future migration desires.

2.3.1 Potential Migrants in Bulgaria

Demographic Characteristics Potential migrants can be differentiated into people with long- and short-term migration aspirations. The comparison with people without aspirations to migrate provides the background to draw a profile of the group of people willing to leave the country, as Table 2.4 shows. In general, the potential migrants are predominantly male and are more strongly represented among the population of a younger working age (21–40 years). They also tend to be single rather than married or in any other type of familial relation. Finally, though the ethnic distribution is near to the distribution in society, the minority groups, in particular Roma, are only slightly over-represented.

In East–West-European migration the *gender ratios* of outmigrants vary according to different countries (see, for instance, the results of the SEEMIG project (SEEMIG 2015)). Our results show a higher propensity for men to migrate since their share within the group of long-term migrants is 58 %, as compared to 48 % among the non-migrants. Furthermore, the share of long-term potential migrants within Bulgarian men (21 %) is 1.5 times higher than this share among the female respondents (15 %). This is however not valid for short-term migration aspirations — the shares of short-term potential migrants estimated separately within men (7 %) and women (6 %) do not differ substantially.

As far as *the age of potential migrants* is concerned, 45 % of all respondents aged up to 20 declare intentions to leave — 34 % and 11 % for a long and short term, respectively. These shares decline when the age increases — for example, only 38 % of those aged 21–30 are potential migrants (28 % long-term and 10 % short-term); the next age group, 31–40, records less frequent intentions (22 % and 8 %, respectively). The age structures of potential migrants' subsamples provide an additional perspective in the analysis. Here the youngest individuals (aged up to 20) within the non-migrants are just 6 % which is more than two times lower than the same share within the long- and short-term potential migrants (15.5 % and 14 %, accordingly).

Albeit not so notable, similar effects are observed for the next two age cohorts whose shares in the non-migrants are 17 % and 20 % (for age intervals 21–30 and 31–40) whereas their shares within the potential long- and short-term migrants are, respectively, 30 % and 26 % on average. As a natural result, the share of the oldest (age 50+) among the non-migrants reaches 35 % which is 3–4 times higher than this share within the long (9 %) and short-term (12 %) potential migrants subsamples.

Table 2.4 Types of potential migrants—demographic characteristics (%)

	Long-term		Short-term		Non-migrants		Total	
	18.3		6.5		75.1		100.0	
Gender								
Male	21.2		7.0		71.9		100.0	
		58.20		53.70		48.20		50.40
Female	15.4		6.1		78.5		100.0	
		41.80		46.30		51.80		49.60
Age groups								
Up to 20	34.3		11.1		54.6		100.0	
		15.5		14.1		6.1		8.3
21–30	27.6		10.0		62.4		100.0	
		30.2		30.5		16.7		20.1
31–40	21.9		8.0		70.1		100.0	
		26.2		26.6		20.4		21.9
41–50	16.8		5.3		77.9		100.0	
		19.4		17.2		22.1		21.3
Above 50	5.6		2.7		91.7		100.0	
		8.7		11.7		34.8		28.5
Marital status								
Married/cohabiting	14.1		5.2		80.8		100.0	
		46.8		48.0		65.7		61.0
Single	28.7		10.7		60.6		100.0	
		42.6		44.5		22.0		27.3
Divorced	20.7		5.1		74.1		100.0	
		8.5		5.9		7.4		7.5
Widowed	9.3		2.5		88.3		100.0	
		2.1		1.6		4.9		4.2
Ethnic group								
Bulgarian	17.6		6.6		75.8		100.0	
		83.8		87.1		87.9		87.1
Turkish	21.7		6.4		71.9		100.0	
		9.9		8.2		8.0		8.4
Roma	25.2		7.6		67.2		100.0	
		4.6		3.9		3.0		3.4
Other	25.5		4.3		70.2		100.0	
		1.7		0.8		1.1		1.2

Note: The numbers in the *upper left* corner of each field represent the *horizontal* distribution; the numbers in the *lower right* corner represent percentages in the group (*vertical*)

All this supports the widely spread statements about the adverse demographic trends, e.g. the irreversible negative growth rate of the Bulgarian population during almost two decades caused by a substantial negative natural growth rate combined with a persistent outmigration process (see, for instance, MLSP 2012).

As expected, the *marital status* also interacts with migration intentions, however, to a somewhat lower extent. Married individuals are the modal group in the total sample (61 %) and within the non-migrants subsample (66 %)—however, their share declines notably within both long- and short-term potential migrants (47–48 %). The opposite effect is observed for the singles (22 % within the non-migrants) that hold quite high shares within the two potential migrant types (44 % on average). This can be related to a higher willingness to move expressed by singles as compared to married individuals. Generally, the divorced respondents diverge from the married in a manner similar to that of the singles (e.g. 21 % of the divorced express intentions for a long-term move).

The ethnical affiliation of respondents does not show any substantial relation to the outmigration intentions studied here. For example, the shares of Turkish respondents within the potential long-term, short-term and non-migrants subsamples are 10 %, 8 % and 8 %; similar low variation is observed also for the Roma (5 %, 4 % and 3 %, respectively)—in both cases, these shares reflect the ethnical composition of the total sample with 8.4 % Turkish and 3.4 % Roma respondents. Slight divergence is worth noting when comparing the outmigration intentions of the different ethnical groups. For instance, the share of long-term potential migrants within the Bulgarian ethnicity is 17.6 % whereas this share among the Turkish and Roma communities reaches 21.7 % and 25.2 %, respectively. As a general conclusion, the migration attitudes of the traditional ethnical communities in Bulgaria do not differ substantially according to the analysed sample data.

Capabilities Characteristics Three attributes describing the capabilities for migration, as earlier presented in this chapter according to the De Haas (2010, 2011, 2014) classification, are incorporated hereafter—education level, social status and the level of income of respondents (see Table 2.5). The scope of these characteristics is expanded by one additional variable—mostly related to networks (see also Chap. 6) which support the perpetuation of outmigration—namely, the availability of household members abroad. These variables are typically expected to act as drivers of migration aspirations since they concern the social and economic capacity of migrants or their respective households.

The largest group of respondents has declared a secondary vocational education (45 %) followed by those with higher education (25 %). When comparing *the educational distributions* of the two types of potential migrants, no substantial differences are observed. Nevertheless, the share of potential long-term migrants who have basic or lower education (18 %) is higher than the share of lower educated, potential short-term migrants (12 %). On the contrary, those with secondary general and vocational education among the short-term migrants have a somewhat higher share than the same educational groups within long-term migrants (19 % and 47 % vs. 15 % and 43 %, respectively). And finally the share of university graduates among long-term potential migrants is slightly higher than the respective share among the short-term ones.

Interestingly, the distributions of the respondents by their *social status* within each group of potential migrants also do not diverge substantially. The main group of respondents in the total sample consists of hired employees (33 % private and

16% public) followed by the unemployed (20%). However, the shares of the unemployed within the two types of potential migrants are substantially higher — 32% within the long-term and 29% within the short-term ones (contrasted to 16.5% for the non-migrants). A remarkable disparity is also observed for the employed in the public sector — the share of these respondents within the long- or short-term migrants (8–9%) is more than two times lower than the share within the potential non-migrants group (18%) — this could be explained by the security of public sector jobs in reducing migration aspirations. Moreover, such an effect is not observed for the group of privately hired employees. From another perspective, 29% and 9.5% of the unemployed respondents have expressed a willingness to leave for a long- or short-term period which confirms the expected impact of unemployment on the formation of outmigration attitudes. In addition, similar attitudes have been expressed by the students in the sample — almost half of them have indicated a strong likelihood to leave for a long (36%) or short (11%) term period.

The exploration of *the income distribution* also does not provide evidence for any unambiguous disparities between the types of potential migrants and non-migrants. The modal income group in each subsample consists of respondents from households with income per capita of 150–300 BGN (between one half to one minimum wage in Bulgaria) — their shares vary from 35% within the long-term migrants to 42% within the short-term ones. It is interesting to note that the so-called "top-income" respondents hold the highest share within the long-term potential migrants (13%) as compared to about 9% within short-term and non-migrants subsamples. In relation to this, the incidence of long-term outmigration intentions among the "top-income" respondents is highest (25%) as compared to the lower income groups (17–20%). This provides some ground to suggest that the long-term migration intentions are related to the "ability to be funded" — supporting the understanding that "emigration is an expensive endeavour" (Clemens 2014).

Last but not least, *the availability of a household member as a current migrant abroad* provided clear evidence for a disparity between potential migrants and non-migrants. About every tenth respondent in the sample originates from a household having at least one of its members abroad. However, this share calculated for potential long- and short-term migrants subsamples reaches 18% and 14%, respectively — by contrast, the fraction of these respondents within the non-migrants is just 8%. In line with this, the share of long-term potential migrants among all respondents with family members abroad is almost two times higher than this share among those who do not have such members (31% vs. 17%).

2.3.2   People with Migration Experience: Bulgarian Return and Circular Migrants

This section describes the characteristics of individuals with migration experience. This group represents 15.5% of the population aged 15–65 — the others 84.5% are considered hereafter as "non-mobile population" (at least during the period of the

Table 2.5 Types of potential migrants—capabilities characteristics (%)

	Long-term		Short-term		Non-migrants		Total	
	18.3		6.5		75.1		100.0	
Education								
Basic or lower	22.2		5.3		72.5		100.0	
		18.0		12.2		14.4		14.9
Secondary general	17.9		8.0		74.1		100.0	
		15.4		19.2		15.5		15.7
Secondary vocational	17.6		6.9		75.5		100.0	
		43.2		47.1		45.1		44.9
Higher	17.5		5.7		76.7		100.0	
		23.5		21.6		25.1		24.6
Social status								
Employed—private	17.4		6.3		76.3		100.0	
		31.3		31.8		33.6		33.0
Employed—public	9.8		3.9		86.3		100.0	
		8.4		9.4		18.2		15.8
Own business	12.0		5.0		83.0		100.0	
		3.4		3.9		5.7		5.1
Self-employed	19.2		6.4		74.4		100.0	
		2.1		2.0		2.0		2.0
Agricultural producer	12.5		12.5		75.0		100.0	
		0.6		1.6		0.8		0.8
Student (sec/ter)	36.1		11.1		52.8		100.0	
		17.8		15.3		6.4		9.0
Unemployed	29.1		9.5		61.4		100.0	
		31.9		29.0		16.5		20.1
Pensioners	2.6		1.7		95.7		100.0	
		1.5		2.7		13.6		10.7
On maternity leave	16.1		8.0		75.9		100.0	
		2.5		3.5		2.9		2.9
Other	21.1		10.5		68.4		100.0	
		0.6		0.8		0.4		0.5
Groups by income per capita (BGN)								
Up to 150 BGN	19.6		6.4		74.0		100.0	
		16.2		16.2		14.9		15.2
150–300 BGN	16.5		6.5		77.0		100.0	
		34.6		41.6		39.4		38.6
300–450 BGN	17.2		5.9		76.9		100.0	
		22.8		23.8		24.7		24.3
450–600 BGN	19.8		4.8		75.4		100.0	
		13.1		9.7		12.1		12.1
Over 600 BGN	25.4		5.4		69.2		100.0	
		13.4		8.6		8.9		9.7

(continued)

Table 2.5 (continued)

	Long-term		Short-term		Non-migrants		Total	
Household member currently abroad								
No	16.8		6.3		76.9		100.0	
		82.1		86.3		91.6		89.5
Yes	31.1		8.5		60.3		100.0	
		17.9		13.7		8.4		10.5

Note: The numbers in the *upper left* corner of each field represent the *horizontal* distribution; the numbers in the *lower right* corner represent percentages in the group (*vertical*)

Table 2.6 Types of people with migration experience—demographic characteristics (%)

	Returnees	Circular/repeat	Non-mobile
	3.8	9.0	84.5
Gender			
Male	60.5	62.6	48.5
Female	39.5	37.4	51.5
Age groups			
Up to 20	0.7	3.4	9.1
21–30	26.0	33.8	18.1
31–40	28.8	30.9	20.5
41–50	19.2	20.6	21.5
Above 50	25.3	11.2	30.8
Marital status			
Single	25.7	37.0	26.2
Married/cohabiting	58.1	52.4	62.3
Divorced	10.1	9.1	7.2
Widowed	6.1	1.4	4.3
Ethnic group			
Bulgarian	85.9	81.1	87.9
Turkish	7.4	12.3	8.1
Roma	4.0	5.7	2.9
Other	2.7	0.9	1.1

last 5 years). If they intend to stay in the country of origin after returning, they are considered as "return migrants". If they express a wish to leave again, they are considered as "circular" (or repeat) migrants (see, for instance, Constant et al. 2012). As with all other types of migrants discussed here, these categories are based on the aspirations stated during the surveys. It should be noted that two additional constraints have been implemented for the subgroups of individuals with migration experience by excluding those who: (a) have declared a permanent residence not in Bulgaria and (b) those who have indicated "guest" as a reason for their stay abroad. This way, the total share of people with migration experience shrinks to 12.8–3.8 % returnees and 9 % circular (see Table 2.6).

Demographic Characteristics The group of people with migration experience that were surveyed in Bulgaria is characterized by being more male and of a younger age, in particular when it comes to circular migration aspirations. Singles are over-represented among circular migrants and married people dominate the returnees. The ethnic distribution is quite even compared to the general population; nevertheless, there is a slight ethnical bias towards circular migration.

Regarding *gender structure* there is a distinctive majority of men within both types of mobile respondents (about 62 % on average) which resembles the potential long-term migrants' gender distribution. This provides a hint for a conclusion that gender (to a great extent) clearly influences the profile of the temporary migration from Bulgaria.

The *age distribution* confirms the common assumption that younger individuals are more active in international migration processes. For example, almost two thirds of those wishing to move again (i.e. the circular/repeat migration type) are aged 21–40 whereas this share within the returnees and non-mobiles decreases to 55 % and 39 %. In line with this, the age group of 50+ holds only 11 % within the circular type compared to 25 % and 31 % for the returnees and non-mobiles, respectively. Again, the age structure of the people with migration experience appears to be similar to that of the potential migrants discussed above. In any case, the presence of a relatively young Bulgarian population abroad "narrows" the potential of the age cohorts from which migrants are usually recruited and increases the share of the elderly (by definition, non-migrant) population in the country. It is not a coincidence that in the last two decades Bulgaria has been considered as a "migration exhausted" country from the purely demographic point of view (see MLSP, p 28).

The *family status* of the mobile respondents diverges from that of the non-mobile, however, not so distinctively in comparison with the disparity between potential migrants and non-migrants groups. Still, the share of singles within the circular migrants (37 %) is over 10 % points higher than this share among returnees and non-mobiles. Moreover, married people dominate among the returnees (58 %) so the family commitment can be considered as an important driver of return migration.

Ethnic distribution does not show any notable differences between the actual and potential migrants. Nevertheless, one can notice the relatively lower share of Bulgarians as well as somewhat higher fractions of Turkish and Roma individuals among the circular type (18 %) as compared to the returnees (11 %). Bearing in mind that these ethnical groups hold minor shares within each subsample, there is no considerable evidence supporting the alleged expansion of the international mobility of the ethnic minorities in Bulgaria.

Capabilities Characteristics When exploring the capabilities of the people with migration experience, we found that their distribution by educational level does not differ significantly from the one observed for the non-mobile individuals. The social status and in particular the employment status show a distinct pattern: employees in the public sector are clearly represented among the non-mobile population, whereas employees in private enterprises are rather over-represented among the returnees. Besides, unemployment acts as a strong driver for migration. At the same time the top-income strata tend to be well represented among the people with migration

Table 2.7 Types of people with migration experience—capabilities characteristics (%)

	Returnees	Circular/repeat	Non-mobile
Education			
Basic or lower	12.2	11.7	15.2
Secondary general	17.7	14.5	15.8
Secondary vocational	46.3	45.9	44.6
Higher	23.8	27.9	24.4
Current activity			
Employed—private	43.2	30.4	32.9
Employed—public	6.1	4.6	17.6
Own business	6.8	2.9	5.4
Self-employed	2.7	3.2	1.9
Agricultural producer	0.7	1.1	0.8
Student (sec/ter)	4.1	5.4	9.5
Unemployed	25.0	46.7	17.1
Pensioners	8.8	1.4	11.8
On maternity leave	2.0	3.4	2.9
Other	0.7	0.9	0.3
Groups by income per capita			
Up to 150 BGN	12.9	17.0	15.3
150–300 BGN	31.9	32.6	39.9
300–450 BGN	24.1	20.7	24.8
450–600 BGN	16.4	13.8	11.8
Over 600 BGN	14.7	15.9	8.3
Household member currently abroad			
No	85.0	83.7	91.2
At least 1	15.0	16.3	8.8

experience. Not surprisingly, people with migration experience twice as often have members of their family living abroad in comparison to those without such experience (Table 2.7).

The two types of mobile respondents do not differ substantially in respect of their *educational structure* and they appear to be quite similar to the non-mobiles. The share of tertiary educated individuals is estimated at 24 % for the returnees and non-mobile respondents whereas it slightly goes up to 28 % amongst the circular migrants. The modal group here is the secondary vocational education, which holds a share of 45–46 % for the three groups. In fact, the education structure of the returnees is almost identical to the one of the non-mobile population as well as the short-term potential migrants. A contrast with the long-term potential migrants is observed regarding the unexpectedly high share of individuals with basic or lower educational level among them (18 % compared to 12 % of the mobile persons).

When considering the *social status* of each group, several indicative facts are worth noting. The modal category here is "employed in private enterprises" with one third of the non-mobile respondents. In the same time, this share reaches 43 %

within the returnees which indicates the main area of occupations taken after the return. By contrast, the share of privately employed within the circular migrants is only 30 %. The employment in the public sector is more frequently met among the non-mobiles (17.6 %) as compared to the two other groups (4–6 %) which is in line with the result obtained for the potential migrants.

On the opposite side of the labour market, unemployment brings a clear distinction between the non-mobile and the individuals with migration experience. This is especially harsh for the circular migrant type where almost half of the individuals (47 %) are unemployed whereas this share among the non-mobile is only 17 %. Nevertheless, every fourth person among the returnees has declared him/herself to be unemployed at the time of the survey which could possibly induce willingness for a subsequent move in the foreseeable future. After all, the unfavourable labour market position of the circular/repeat migrants clearly encourages their motivation to go abroad again. Another issue is whether they are interested at all in the local labour market or just currently looking for the next job abroad. These findings get confirmation in the qualitative work carried out in Bulgaria in which the aspiration for circular/repeat migration seems to prevail among the individuals with migration experience. Many persons interviewed stated the possibility of leaving again soon or if the financial situation gets worse. Those who came back for good, or at least stating this intention, have either fulfilled their goals (such as paying back credit) or were able to establish themselves in Bulgaria by finding a job or setting up a business.

The exploration of *income distributions* evaluated for the different migrant types does not show any clear divergence between the two mobile groups. Still, some interesting peculiarities are observed when contrasting them to the non-mobile persons. The modal income group within the latter is 150–300 BGN (one half to one minimum wage per household member) containing 40 % of this subsample; however, this share diminishes to 32 % for returnees and circular migrants. In the same time, the fraction of the top-income group (over 600 BGN) is estimated at 15 and 16 % for these mobile categories unlike the non-mobile individuals where this share is just 8 %. When combined with income group "450–600 BGN", the non-mobile persons are less frequently observed here (a total of 20 %) in comparison with the individuals who have a recent migration experience (30 %). In any case, this income differentiation—slightly biased toward the top-income intervals—does not fit somehow with the findings about employment status, especially considering the high unemployment rate estimated for the subsamples of the two mobile types.

Quite as expected, the availability of a *household member abroad* supports the result found regarding the potential migration. Within the non-mobile subsample the share of respondents from households with a current migrant is about 9 % (with 10 % for the total sample)—by contrast, this share for the returnees and circular migrant is considerably higher (15–16 %). Although this result is just slightly indicative, one may expect that the mobile individuals have more or less strong ties with any existing migration networks (see also Chap. 6) as compared to the non-mobile ones.

2.3.3 Socio-Demographic Profile and Future Plans of Bulgarians in Switzerland

Bulgarians in Switzerland appear to be a select community compared to the potential migrants and the people with migration experience described above. Firstly, 64 % of them are female, most of whom are married, with a relatively high level of education—e.g. the share of women with tertiary education reaches 65 % and that of men 54 %.

Obviously, this specificity reflects the interaction between a strictly selective immigration policy (see also Chap. 5) and the scarcity of the targeted segment within the potential migrants' pool. On the other hand, the immigration policy of Bulgaria also makes its mark—at least concerning citizenship granting which is attractive in many countries like Macedonia, Moldova or Ukraine (especially after the accession of Bulgaria to EU in 2007). This is a natural reason for which, among the Bulgarian residents in Switzerland, individuals originating from other countries number more than those from the traditional minorities in Bulgaria (i.e. Turks and Roma).

The socio-demographic profile of the Bulgarian residents in Switzerland— regarding their demographic and capabilities characteristics—is explored in relation to their future plans declared during the quantitative survey. This profile is reviewed separately for several subsamples depending on their intentions, where the main group (48 %) consists of those who definitely wish to stay in Switzerland. The other three groups have clear migration intentions, namely, those who prefer to return to Bulgaria (4.2 %), to circulate between the two countries (11 %) and to move to another country (3.7 %). A rather large group of respondents (33 %) did not express any particular intention, so we further denote them as "hesitating" (see Fig. 2.1).

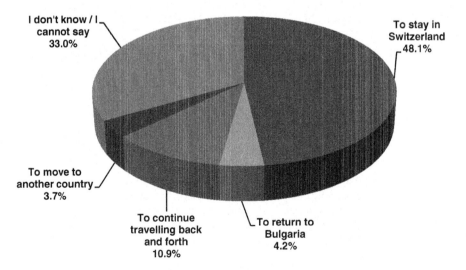

Fig. 2.1 Aspirations of Bulgarians living in Switzerland

Finally, the qualitative work enriches the above perspective concerning the future aspirations of Bulgarians in Switzerland. For some of the interviewed persons, a mixed sample in the 26–69 age range of men and women, comprising highly skilled and less skilled people as well as students, the future is still very unclear. Their future plans depend on their working situation and their permit of stay (particularly for the ones with L-permit as per the following exception resulting from the quantitative sample). The majority of our interviewees do not want to return to Bulgaria either because of the local political and economical situation which seems very unstable to them or because they have settled for good in Switzerland.

Demographic Characteristics of Bulgarians in Switzerland A particular gender effect is observed concerning the future plans of respondents—over half of the women (51 %) prefer to stay in Switzerland, as compared to 42 % of the men wishing to stay (see Table 2.8). On the other hand, 39 % of men still hesitate about their future whereas the share of women who do not have any clear plans is notably lower (30 %). Regarding the other options, despite the significantly lower frequencies of observation, it is found that the shares of those choosing one alternative over another are similar within men and women, e.g. 11.2 % of the men and 10.8 % of the women prefer to circulate between the two countries. From another perspective, among all those wishing to stay in Switzerland the share of women is two times higher than that of men; similar gender discrepancies are observed also within those who are willing to move to another country (70:30) or to circulate (63:37).

The *age distribution* of respondents does not suggest any particular surprise regarding the migration intentions of Bulgarians. The so-called "young adults" (aged 31–40) are the modal group in the sample (40 %) and along with those aged up to 30 (26 %) they comprise about 2/3 of the Bulgarian community in Switzerland. The young adults (aged 31–40) are most willing to stay (53 %) as contrasted to those aged over 50—among the latter only one third (34 %) express such intentions. On the other hand, the inclination to return to Bulgaria or circulate between the two countries is most frequently observed among the older respondents (aged over 50) and least frequently among those aged 31–40. According to the initial expectations, the intentions to move to another country among the youngest are notably more widespread as compared to the older cohorts (8.2 % of those aged up to 30, and only 2 % on average among the other age groups).

Regarding the *marital status* of respondents, married individuals are the majority (about 58 %) whereas the singles, divorced, and widowed have much lower shares (29 %, 11 % and 2 %). This is the main reason for married persons predominating in almost every profile considered here, especially among those who wish to stay in Switzerland (62 %). Just one exception should be mentioned here: among those who intend to move to other countries the singles hold the highest share (65 %).

Interesting findings are observed in respect of the link between migration intentions, *ethnic affiliation*, and *the country of origin* of Bulgarians in Switzerland. Surprisingly, the representatives of the Bulgarian ethnic group least frequently express intentions to stay (48 %) as compared to individuals from other communities (53 % and 67 % for Turkish and Roma groups). Along with this, those who indicate a plan to return are only ethnic Bulgarians (albeit only 4.5 % of them have

Table 2.8 Bulgarians in Switzerland according to their future plans—demographic characteristics (%)

	Stay in CH		Return to BG		Circulate BG-CH		Move to another country		Hesitate		Total	
	48.1		4.2		10.9		3.7		33.0		100.0	
Gender													
Male	42.2		4.8		11.2		3.1		38.7		100.0	
		31.7		41.3		37.0		30.0		42.3		36.2
Female	51.4		3.9		10.8		4.0		29.8		100.0	
		68.3		58.7		63.0		70.0		57.7		63.8
Age groups													
Up to 30	43.1		5.0		10.7		8.2		33.1		100.0	
		23.3		30.4		25.4		57.5		26.1		26.0
31–40	53.2		2.3		9.4		3.2		31.8		100.0	
		44.4		21.7		34.7		35.0		38.8		40.2
41–50	51.2		4.7		11.0		0.4		32.7		100.0	
		25.0		26.1		23.7		2.5		23.3		23.5
Above 50	34.2		9.0		17.1		1.8		37.8		100.0	
		7.3		21.7		16.1		5.0		11.8		10.3
Marital status													
Single	38.0		3.8		12.1		8.3		37.7		100.0	
		23.0		26.1		31.9		65.0		33.0		29.0
Married/ cohabiting	51.7		4.0		10.4		1.9		31.9		100.0	
		62.2		54.3		54.6		30.0		55.6		57.6
Divorced	55.8		5.8		7.5		1.7		29.2		100.0	
		12.9		15.2		7.6		5.0		9.8		11.1
Widowed	40.0		8.0		28.0				24.0		100.0	
		1.9		4.3		5.9				1.7		2.3
Ethnic group													
Bulgarian	47.8		4.5		11.0		3.8		33.0		100.0	
		92.3		100.0		92.4		95.0		93.5		93.1
Turkish	53.3				13.3		6.7		26.7		100.0	
		3.1				3.4		5.0		2.3		2.8
Roma	66.7								33.3		100.0	
		0.4								0.3		0.3
Other	53.7				12.2				34.1		100.0	
		4.2				4.2				4.0		3.8

Note: The numbers in the *upper left* corner of each field represent the *horizontal* distribution; the numbers in the *lower right* corner represent percentages in the group (*vertical*)

such plans). The intentions to "circulate" between Switzerland and Bulgaria are most evident among the Bulgarian Turks (13 %) and among the so-called "others" (12 %)—the latter by itself is an interesting phenomenon since most of the individuals in this category originate from Macedonia.

Capabilities Characteristics of Bulgarians in Switzerland The distributions of respondents by several capability variables evaluated for each type of migration

Table 2.9 Bulgarians in Switzerland according to their future plans — capabilities characteristics (%)

	Stay in CH	Return to BG	Circulate BG-CH	Move to another country	Hesitate	Total
	48.1	4.2	10.9	3.7	33.0	100.0
Education						
Basic or lower	50.0		19.6		30.4	100.0
		4.4	7.6		3.9	4.2
Secondary general	47.8	3.7	13.4	2.2	32.8	100.0
	12.3	10.9	15.1	7.5	12.3	12.3
Secondary vocational	49.4	4.4	12.4	1.2	32.5	100.0
	23.6	23.9	26.1	7.5	22.6	22.9
Higher	47.5	4.6	9.3	5.2	33.5	100.0
	59.8	65.2	51.3	85.0	61.3	60.5
Current activity in Switzerland						
Work	48.8	4.0	10.2	3.9	33.1	100.0
	74.0	68.9	68.1	75.0	73.2	72.9
Education	35.3	6.9	10.3	7.8	39.7	100.0
	8.0	17.8	10.3	22.5	13.1	10.9
Care for family	56.7	3.3	15.8		24.2	100.0
	13.3	8.9	16.4		8.3	11.3
Other	46.2	3.8	11.5	1.9	36.5	100.0
	4.7	4.4	5.2	2.5	5.4	4.9
Groups by income per capita (CHF)						
Up to 2100 CHF	49.3	4.3	10.9	3.4	32.1	100.0
	45.5	48.6	47.4	36.8	44.3	45.1
2100–4200 CHF	48.1	3.2	12.0	4.1	32.6	100.0
	33.9	27.0	40.0	34.2	34.3	34.4
4200–6300 CHF	46.3	6.5	6.5	6.5	34.3	100.0
	11.2	18.9	7.4	18.4	12.3	11.8
Above 6300 CHF	52.5	2.5	6.3	5.0	33.8	100.0
	9.4	5.4	5.3	10.5	9.0	8.7
Type of permit in Switzerland						
L: Short-term	46.1	10.2	11.4	3.0	29.3	100.0
	15.4	37.8	16.5	12.8	14.0	15.9
B: Midterm	45.1	3.4	10.4	4.5	36.5	100.0
	58.0	48.9	58.3	74.4	67.3	61.4
C: Residence	55.9	2.3	13.2	0.9	27.7	100.0
	24.6	11.1	25.2	5.1	17.5	21.0
Other	60.0			20.0	20.0	100.0
	1.8			7.7	0.9	1.4
No Swiss permit	33.3	33.3			33.3	100.0
	0.2	2.2			0.3	0.3

Note: The numbers in the *upper left* corner of each field represent the *horizontal* distribution; the numbers in the *lower right* corner represent percentages in the group (*vertical*) plan provide a variety of findings (see Table 2.9). No substantial distinctiveness is observed regarding the groups by education level—the aspirations to stay are most frequently met at each level. This is inevitable bearing in mind the substantial homogeneity of the general sample, at least as far as it concerns the education level of the respondents (over 60 % with tertiary education in the total sample). However, some divergence is found between the groups with lowest and highest educational level in respect of the willingness to circulate between the two countries (20 % and 9 %, respectively). It is important to note that university degree holders form a substantial majority in some of the groups considered here, namely, among those intending to return to Bulgaria (65 %), and to move to another country (85 %).

The current activity of Bulgarian respondents is dominated by a quite high share of employed people (73 %) and does not vary substantially between the subgroups (68–75 %). At the same time, only half of the working individuals (49 %) clearly intend to stay in Switzerland. About 1/9 of the respondents are students (11 % in the total sample); however, only 35 % of them wish to stay in Switzerland and another 40 % still hesitate about their future. Also, students hold a relatively higher share among those who intend to move to other countries (22.5 %) or among those who plan to return to Bulgaria (18 %). Another 11 % of respondents declare caring for family as their current activity—the majority of them (57 %) wish to stay in Switzerland and a further 16 % express a wish to circulate.

A specific finding of our study presents itself from the distribution of respondents by their *financial status* which was expected to provide evidence about the importance of economic arguments in making a decision to stay or move (Clemens 2014). However, the empirical results do not show substantial differences between low and high income groups in respect of their future plans. For example, the share of individuals from households with highest income per capita (above 6300 CHF monthly) that wish to stay in Switzerland is 52.5 %—though, this share calculated for those with lowest income level (up to 2100 CHF) is not much lower (49 %). The share of the two highest income level groups in the total sample are about 12 % and 9 % (the other 79 % declare a lower income level)—the only subsample which slightly diverges from this total sample structure is observed for those wishing to "circulate" where the two intervals below 4200 CHF contain 87 % of the respondents. The expectation about the low income groups having clear stimuli for leaving Switzerland did not find support, albeit among the two low income groups the share of those willing to "circulate" is about 11–12 % whereas this share among the two higher income groups is two times lower (6.4 %).

The exploration of profiles of Bulgarians finally considers also the possible interaction with *the types of permits* held by these respondents. Three main permit types are recorded in the survey: L (short-term), B (midterm) and C (residence). The largest share is observed for the B-type holders (61 %) followed by C-type (21 %) and L-type (16 %); the remaining minor share is held by those with other kinds of administrative status. No substantial differences between the subsamples formed according to the future plans of Bulgarians are found regarding the types of permits held by them. The most notable divergence is observed for those who wish to return to Bulgaria: 38 % of them have a short-term permit (L)—at the same time, only 11 % of the returnees have the most secure (i.e. residence) permit. Unlike them, a share of about 25 % for the C-permit holders is observed for those who wish to stay or to circulate between the two countries. This is related also to the fact that 56 % of all C-permit holders express a clear wish to stay—however, this share among the modal group (midterm permit holders) is somewhat lower: 45 %.

2.4 Determinants of the Aspirations to Move: A Logistic Regression Analysis

The explorative analysis of the socio-economic profiles provided in the last sections can be enriched by analytic statistics. In particular we apply binary logistic regression that utilizes sample microdata to estimate a multivariate causal model. The variables involved in the analysis are treated as determinants as per earlier definition. In order to facilitate the interpretation of the empirical results each determinant variable is represented by a set of binary indicator variables using a traditional coding scheme. All quantitative variables have been transformed into ordered categories by defined numerical intervals. For each variable a choice has been made about the reference category of individuals (serving as a basis for interpreting the marginal effects of this variable). The strategy for choosing the reference category is related to the general expectation about how each variable is linked to the aspiration to move. In this way, the reference category for each attribute is chosen to be the value which is expected to have a "holding" (pull-down) effect towards the outmigration aspiration of the individual.

2.4.1 Potential Migrants vs. Potential Non-migrants

The categorization of respondents who participated in the Bulgarian survey provides an opportunity to build a logistic regression model with dependent variables (DV) of specific interest. In order to identify the main determinants of the aspiration to migrate, two main migration types have been chosen as target groups:

- Potential long-term migrants—all those who have expressed a clear aspiration to leave for a period of over 1 year (either for work or study).
- Potential short-term migrants—those who have expressed an aspiration to leave only for a few months, *without* assuming the alternative for long-term involvement.

On this basis we derive two separate discrete dependent variables—for the long-term and the short-term potential migrants. This strategy provides an opportunity to estimate marginal effects of the independent variables on the aspiration to move, however, *separately* for the two types of migration aspirations. For both cases, the comparison group is the potential non-migrants—this way we can distinguish between the target group (coded by DV = 1) and the base group (coded by DV = 0) in respect of the attributes considered as determinant variables.

Thereafter we present the selection of independent variables along with the categories for which indicator variables have been defined. The variables' scope covers mostly the demographic and capability attributes discussed in the previous sections.

Variables of the demographic profile of the individual (personal and family) are traditionally considered as facilitators of migration behaviour. Four major demographic attributes are selected as independent variables:

- *Gender* (reference category: females; one indicator variable: male = 1 for a man, 0 otherwise).
- *Age* (reference category: 51 or higher; four indicator variables: (1) age up to 20, (2) age 21–30, (3) age 31–40, (4) age 41–50; each of them takes 1 if the individual's age is in the respective interval; otherwise 0).
- *Marital status* (reference category: married; one indicator variable: single = 1 for a respondent who is single or divorced, including the widowed ones, 0 otherwise).
- *Ethnicity* (reference category: Bulgarian; one indicator variable: minority = 1 for a respondent who is Turkish or Roma, including also "Other", 0 otherwise).

According to De Haas (2011: 18), individuals can make a move only "if they have the capabilities to do so". Such a capability could be enhanced through capital accumulation — human, social and economic — which can make the choice possible. Here we include three main variables of this category:

- *Educational level* (reference category: basic or lower; 3 indicator variables: (1) secondary general, (2) secondary vocational and (3) higher; each of them takes 1 if the individual has the respective degree, 0 otherwise).
- *Income level* (reference category: individuals from a household with income per capita over 600 BGN monthly; 4 indicator variables: (1) income up to 150 BGN, (2) income 150–300 BGN, (3) income 300–450 BGN, (4) income 450–600 BGN; each of them takes 1 if the household income per capita is in the respective interval, 0 otherwise).
- *Social status* is included as a model determinant by a detailed set of 7 indicator variables for the categories: (1) self-employed; (2) freelance job; (3) employed in the private sector; (4) agricultural producer; (5) unemployed; (6) social beneficiary (individual under some regime of social support: pensioners, on temporary leave, social assistance, etc.); (7) students at secondary or tertiary level. Each variable takes a value of 1 if the individual falls within the respective category and 0 otherwise (in this case, the reference category is respondents employed in the public sector).

Since our analysis is conceptualized at a micro level, the "sense of structure" is plausibly incorporated — in so far as migration behaviour is stimulated or constrained by "structurally determined resource and information limitations" (De Haas 2011: 17). Thereafter we consider a migration network variable treated as a determinant of the aspiration to move:

- *Current migrant* (reference category: respondents from households without members currently abroad; one indicator variable: current = 1 for a respondent whose household has at least one of its members residing abroad, 0 otherwise).

A particular dimension of the migrant networking is approximated by this variable, namely the potential informal support abroad. More generally, the availability of close relatives or friends is expected to generate substantial confidence for a successful outmigration move, due to the effective operation of informal migration networks.

The following categories of respondents constitute a synthetic profile of the "reference individual", each of which is expected to have a pull-down effect on the aspiration to move:

- Gender: female.
- Age: over 50.
- Marital status: married.
- Ethnicity: Bulgarian.
- Education level: basic or lower.
- Income level: income per capita over 600 BGN monthly.
- Social status: employed in the public sector.
- Household member abroad: no.

Table 2.10 presents the results for the estimated models for both dependent variables as defined above. Possible adverse effect of multicollinearity could have caused the loss of significance for some of the parameters, in so far as many of the independent variables included together are highly correlated. This way, only part of the indicator variables showed the expected impact on the probability for an individual to be classified as a potential migrant with a longer or shorter horizon of migration aspirations.

Gender differentiates between potential migrants and non-migrants only as regards the long-term intentions. As expected, the sign of the coefficient is positive (+0.358) and this parameter is statistically significant at 1 % level. The positive sign supports the initial hypothesis that men have a higher propensity to leave for a long time (including emigration for good) than women. A gender effect is instead not found to be significant for the short-term migrants.

The most significant results were obtained regarding the *age* variables—the expectation of younger people's high aspiration to leave Bulgaria was confirmed. The net effects of the indicator variables for the youngest respondents were highest but not much different from the estimates about the next age group, as compared to the reference category (age 51+)—the odds ratios are 5.2 and 4.9 for the age groups "up to 20" and "21–30". Similar results for age are obtained also for the short-term aspirations model, albeit with slightly lower odds ratios (4.8 and 4.1, respectively).

Considerable effects are also observed related to the *marital status* that confirmed the hypothesis for a much stronger attitude of the singles towards long-term outmigration, as compared to the reference category (married). The estimated odds ratio for the short-term type is instead almost the same as the one for the long-term type. Obviously, the family is a stable deterrent factor when forming the individual

Table 2.10 Binary logistic regressions for the likelihood to have migration aspirations

	Model-1. Long-term		Model-2. Short-term	
	B	Exp(B)	B	Exp(B)
Gender (male)	0.358***	1.430	0.167	1.182
Age up to 20	1.639***	5.150	1.574***	4.827
Age 21–30	1.582***	4.864	1.411***	4.099
Age 31–40	1.544***	4.682	1.330***	3.781
Age 41–50	1.162***	3.197	0.810***	2.247
Single	0.298***	1.347	0.292*	1.339
Ethnicity	0.326**	1.385	0.151	1.163
Secondary general	0.206	1.229	0.735***	2.085
Secondary vocational	0.466***	1.594	0.818***	2.265
Higher education	0.604***	1.829	0.766**	2.151
Income p.c. up to 150 BGN	−0.179	0.836	−0.160	0.852
Income p.c. 150–300 BGN	0.042	1.043	0.079	1.083
Income p.c. 300–450 BGN	0.084	1.088	−0.079	0.924
Income p.c. 450–600 BGN	0.244	1.277	−0.257	0.773
Self-employed	0.061	1.063	0.226	1.253
Freelance job	0.838**	2.312	0.695	2.004
Employed in the private sector	0.485***	1.625	0.392	1.480
Agricultural producer	0.501	1.650	1.418**	4.128
Unemployed	1.358***	3.889	1.105***	3.021
Social beneficiary	−0.018	0.983	0.152	1.164
Student	1.324***	3.758	1.001***	2.721
HH member abroad (yes)	0.949***	2.583	0.642***	1.900
Intercept (beta-0)	−4.154***	0.016	−4.914***	0.007
No. of observations	3652		3191	
Nagelkerke R square	0.201		0.111	

Notes: Wald test significance levels: *0.10; **0.05; ***0.01
Exp (B) estimates the odds ratios

intentions for any type of migration. On the other hand, the two types differ in respect of the *ethnicity* of respondents—a significant positive effect is observed only for the long-term potential migrants contrasted to the non-migrants but not for the short-term ones. This result plausibly indicates that the inclination to short-term (seasonal or circular) movement is not related substantially to the ethnical affiliation.

The expectations about greater migration attitudes of the better-educated individuals—as compared to the reference category (basic or lower educational level)—are clearly supported by the regression results from both models. The parameters for the *education* variables in model-1 are strongly significant which shows that potential long-term migrants evidently differ from the non-migrants in respect of their education level. This is also valid for the short-term potential migrants where respondents with both types of secondary education (general and vocational) express undoubtedly higher willingness to leave for a short period.

In general, *income* (as a capability determinant) did not show any significant impact—for neither long- nor short-term types of potential migrants, with no significant difference between the individuals with highest household income per capita (the reference category) and those in any lower income stratum. With these regression results we cannot assert that the willingness to move is systematically concentrated mainly in low-income social strata—yet, many individuals with favourable social status and medium to higher income level do not see their future in the country and would opt to out-migrate.

Interesting results are found in respect of the *social status* variables where several categories were found to differ substantially from the reference category (i.e. the employed in the public sector) regarding their aspiration to migrate. Along with this, the results are not identical for the two migration types considered here. The two perspectives show common features for both the students and unemployed respondents who express a much higher aspiration to migrate as contrasted to public employees. At the same time, divergence is observed regarding the freelance job holders and the privately employed individuals—model-1 suggests that they have a stronger aspiration to leave for a long term than the public employees, which is however not supported by model-2 results. Contrariwise, the parameter for the agricultural producers' variable is estimated as significant in model-2 but not in model-1, which shows that this social group aspires much more frequently to leave only for a short-term period, as compared to the employed in the public sector.

Migration networking has proved to have the expected direction and strength in its effect. This is confirmed by the estimated regression models in respect of the variable introducing the *availability of family members abroad* in the analysis. Here both models provide evidence for a clear distinction of migration aspirations between individuals from households with and without a current migrant abroad. On this basis we can postulate that those who can potentially count on relatives abroad express aspirations to move about two times more often than those who cannot rely on networks abroad.

2.4.2 Circular Migrants vs. Returnees

This section focuses on the determinants of the aspiration expressed by the individuals with recent migration experience to make a subsequent move abroad. We deal now with actual migrants who have returned to Bulgaria and express either an aspiration to move again (potentially circular/repeat migration) or to stay (return migration).

For this purpose, a binary logistic regression model is estimated similar to the one applied for the determinants of the attitudes of potential migrants. Here the binary dependent variable takes two values: 1 for those who have been categorized as circular (i.e. potential migrants) and 0 for the returnees. Again, the logistic function evaluates the predicted probabilities for classifying any observation in the target group "1" as a function of a set of independent variables.

One minor modification of the previous two models has been introduced, namely the derivation of the dummy variables capturing the social status of respondents. First of all, those on maternity leave and undefined occupations ("other") have been excluded from the analysis. The reference category here is comprised by those who are less expected to remigrate—pensioners and business people. Further, dummy variables have been constructed for each of the following five categories: unemployed; student; freelance job; public employee; private employee. The selection of attributes along with the categories for which indicator variables have been defined is as follows:

- Gender: male (reference category: female).
- Age (4 levels; reference level: age over 50).
- Marital status (1 category: singles, divorced, widowed; reference group: married).
- Ethnicity (Turkish, Roma, or other; reference category: Bulgarians).
- Education level (3 levels; reference level: basic or lower).
- Socio-economic status (5 categories; reference group: running own business plus pensioners).
- Income level (4 levels; reference level: over 600 BGN monthly income per capita).
- Current household member abroad (1 category; reference group: respondents from households without any members currently residing abroad.

When we compare circular migrants to returnees, most of the demographic and capability variables exhibit analogous results (see Table 2.11). Neither *gender* nor *marital status* nor *ethnicity* shows any significant impact on the aspiration of individuals with recent migration experience to remigrate. Moreover, the *economic status* does not correlate with the aspiration to move which is also observed for the variable accounting for the availability of household members currently abroad. However, a positive and significant impact on the aspiration to move is estimated for the *age* and *educational level* variables since the younger and better qualified (tertiary or secondary vocational degree holders) among the people with migration experience express a higher aspiration to leave again.

It is worth noting that quite a high odds ratio has been estimated for the lowest age group (up to 20) indicator variable (7.3) as well as the *unemployment* variable (6.3)—this clearly shows that any adverse labour market position of the youngest induces a strong aspiration for a subsequent move. Another high ratio has been estimated for the *freelance job takers*—the freelancers have five times higher likelihood to move again than to stay, as compared to those who are running their own business or pensioners. Furthermore, relatively high odds ratios—accompanying statistically significant and positive parameters—are estimated also for the *students* (3.1), *public* (2.8) and *private* (2.2) *employees*. These results for the social status variables provide evidence that—unless they are entrepreneurs—the options provided by the local labour market are not attractive enough for the individuals with migration experience to keep them in Bulgaria.

Table 2.11 Binary logistic regressions for the likelihood to remigrate

Variables	B	Exp(B)
Gender (male)	0.227	1.254
Age up to 20	1.993*	7.336
Age 21–30	0.796**	2.216
Age 31–40	0.630*	1.878
Age 41–50	0.876**	2.401
Single/divorced	0.267	1.306
Ethnicity	0.316	1.372
Secondary general	0.192	1.212
Secondary vocational	0.685*	1.983
Higher education	0.852**	2.344
Income p.c. up to 150 BGN	0.124	1.132
Income p.c. 150–300 BGN	0.207	1.230
Income p.c. 300–450 BGN	0.079	1.082
Income p.c. 450–600 BGN	0.037	1.037
Unemployed	1.837***	6.280
Student	1.130*	3.097
Freelance job	1.609**	4.997
Public employee	1.035*	2.816
Private employee	0.791**	2.206
HH member abroad (yes)	0.330	1.391
Intercept (beta-0)	−1.974***	0.139
No. of observations		477
Naelkerke R square		0.150

Note: Wald test significance levels: *0.10; **0.05; ***0.01

2.4.3 Bulgarians in Switzerland

This section considers the determinants of the aspirations estimated for Bulgarians residing in Switzerland to make a cross-border move. Applying the same method as in the former two sections we targeted our interest on the future plans of Bulgarians. The majority (about 48 %) of them declared a wish to stay in Switzerland. Minor shares of respondents (4 %) expressed an aspiration to return to Bulgaria and even less (3.7 %) thought about moving to another country. Relatively larger shares of Bulgarians aspired for a circular pattern (11 %) or expressed a lack of clear orientation about their future plans (33 %).

On this basis we derive *three separate dependent variables* in a manner similar to the potential migrants' differentiation. Each potential migrant type is contrasted to the group of "potential non-migrants" — in this case: all those willing to stay in Switzerland. These respondents are chosen as a base group of each of the three logistic regression models and the respective dependent variable is coded by "0". The target categories for each dependent variable are as follows:

- DV1 is coded by "1" for each respondent aspiring to *return to Bulgaria*.
- DV2 = 1 for those who aspire to *circulate* between Switzerland and Bulgaria.
- DV3 = 1 if the respondent aspires to *migrate to another country*.

In the same way as the models in the previous sections, similarly this strategy allows an estimation of the net marginal effects of each independent variable on the likelihood to form one or another orientation towards migration moves. The independent variables comprise a selection of main demographic and capability characteristics of the sampled Bulgarian residents in Switzerland. However, some new variables have been introduced because of the specificities of the survey instrument and the target population.

1. The social status is introduced by two indicator variables — (1) for the students and (2) for those who take care of family members. The reference group here comprises the working individuals.
2. Income level is included in the analysis after the calculation of the "household monthly income per capita in CHF" using the size of respondent's household (all members currently living in Switzerland). Income intervals are obtained using thresholds calculated as percentages from the mean monthly wage in Switzerland. The highest interval (defined as monthly income above the mean wage) is chosen as a reference category and three indicator variables are derived for the first, second and third income interval.
3. Two important features of the Bulgarian residents in Switzerland are included as determinants which are expected to correlate with the future migration plans. They were selected in order to account for aspects of transnational practices of Bulgarian migrants in Switzerland. Indicator variables are defined for those who: (1) *send money to Bulgaria* (1 = yes; 0 = no) and (2) *travel to Bulgaria* (1 = "yes, at least once a year", 0 if "don't travel" or "less than once a year").

The estimated models provide the following empirical results for the three types of migration orientation and their net correlation with any of the independent variables involved in the analysis (Table 2.12).

Gender does not appear as a significant variable in any of the regression models so there is not any differentiation between Bulgarian men and women residing in Switzerland in respect of their future migration aspirations. Similar results are obtained for *income* — the "stayers" cannot be differentiated from any of the other migrant types by their income level. Just one exception is observed in model-3 (estimated for those who aspire to move to another country) where individuals with income per capita 4200–6300 CHF differentiate from the top-income stratum. A plausible explanation for this is a relatively high aspiration of these individuals to relocate to another country, in as much as their income level (and most likely their professional status) provides them the necessary "capability" to act this way.

Interesting results are obtained about the *age* in any of the three models, however, with some specificity regarding the respective migrant types. For instance, the eldest respondents show a higher willingness to return to Bulgaria or to continue travelling between the two countries. On the other hand, the youngest individuals (age up to 30) are differentiated from the modal group by their aspiration to consider a possible return back home or a move to another country. This could be due to a perceived wider range of alternatives for the youngest different from the only option of staying in Switzerland — the latter is found to be typical for the middle age groups (i.e. aged 31–50).

Table 2.12 Binary logistic regressions for the aspiration to a consequent move of Bulgarian migrants residing in Switzerland

Variables	Model-1. Return to BG		Model-2. Circulate		Model-3. Move to another country	
	B	Exp(B)	B	Exp(B)	B	Exp(B)
Gender (male)	0.419	1.520	0.277	1.319	0.087	1.091
Age up to 30	0.870*	2.386	0.221	1.247	1.042**	2.835
Age 31–40	Ref		Ref		Ref	
Age 41–50	0.660	1.935	0.093	1.098	#	
Age 50 plus	1.934***	6.915	1.014***	2.757	#	
Single/divorced	0.275	1.316	0.385*	1.470	0.968**	2.632
Basic or lower	#		0.996**	2.708	#	
Secondary general	−0.232	0.793	0.250	1.284	Ref	
Secondary vocational	−0.007	0.993	0.242	1.274	−0.083	0.920
Higher	Ref		Ref		1.340**	3.818
Income p.c. up to 2100 CHF	−0.087	0.916	−0.108	0.898	0.393	1.481
Income p.c. 2100–4200 CHF	−0.514	0.598	0.006	1.006	0.548	1.730
Income p.c. 4200–6300 CHF	0.243	1.275	−0.574	0.563	1.047*	2.849
Student	0.979*	2.661	0.442	1.555	0.505	1.656
Take care of family	−0.062	0.940	0.397	1.488	#	
Sends money to BG	0.491	1.635	0.614***	1.848	−0.092	0.912
Travels to BG	2.012***	7.479	0.850***	2.341	0.14	1.150
Intercept (beta-0)	−5.321	0.005	−3.084	0.046	−5.093	0.006
No. of observations	564		6317		558	
Nagelkerke R square	0.149		0.089		0.185	

Notes: Wald test significance levels: *0.10; **0.05; ***0.01
Exp (B) estimates the odds ratios
"#" for redundant variables (due to lack of cases)
"Ref" indicates the chosen reference group

A significant parameter is estimated for the *marital status* variable in models 2 and 3 when differentiating between the "stayers in CH" and those who consider a "circulation" or a move to another country. In both cases those who are married (or cohabiting) are found to be more prone to stay in Switzerland than to look for other options. Similar results are obtained also for *educational level*. For example, the respondents with the lowest educational level tend to have aspirations towards circular migration two times more frequently than towards staying in Switzerland. Furthermore, the higher educated respondents express almost four times higher willingness to relocate to another country than to stay in Switzerland.

The two *social status* groups considered explicitly in the models—namely, students and individuals taking care for their families in Switzerland—did not diverge substantially from the working respondents (reference category). One exception needs to be emphasized: students show some higher aspiration to return to Bulgaria. This by itself can be motivated by optimistic perceptions of adequate employment and remuneration opportunities after their graduation at a Swiss educational institution.

The first of the two variables related to transnational behaviour of Bulgarians in Switzerland—namely, the regular practice of *sending money* home—showed the expected effect when comparing those aspiring to circulate with the stayers (model-2). Obviously, this is a clear strategy of a relatively small part of Bulgarians residing in Switzerland to gain from some temporary but revolving employment. The estimated effect of the second variable accounting for regular direct contacts with the home country is even stronger. The fact of travelling to Bulgaria at least once a year clearly differentiates those aspiring to return (model-1) or to circulate (model-2) from those aspiring to stay. Obviously, those with aspirations of returning to Bulgaria or to continue circulating actually keep such a contact more frequently than the stayers.

2.5   Conclusions

What can we learn from the Bulgarian-Swiss case in terms of patterns of migration and mobility between the two countries and their determinants? Can we call for distinctive features compared to the East–West well-known migration configurations as far the different migrant types, their aspirations and actual capabilities to migrate?

As far the general lessons learned, one should recall, first of all, that potential migration remains a controversial issue since the resulting estimations need always to be treated with care and they may be subject to data misuse or even manipulation for political purposes, as the recent EU enlargement processes have historically demonstrated. Wrongly estimated migrant stocks and flows can provide fertile ground for supposedly "massive migration" configurations and instil fears of invasions and the resulting xenophobic and populist reactions. If correctly interpreted, potential migration's forecasts can, however, furnish some useful indications for the economic and demographic analyses and assist different migration stakeholders in preparing adequate policy and legislative frameworks for their own country's development.

Secondly, the actual process of migration resulting from the aspirations and capabilities analysis inevitably requires some "second thought" since different methods and selected samples might lead to different outcomes. In the context we have investigated, the logistic regression analysis is indeed useful in checking for different variables, acquiring additional information and contrasting the outcomes provided by the survey instruments. A mixed method approach, which includes also a few sketches of our qualitative work, assisted in better framing the migration aspirations of Bulgarian migrants and starting a preliminary process of understanding the determinants of migration between Switzerland and Bulgaria.

Thirdly, this thorough analytical multivariate statistical exercise gives us the first foundation to build and guide the following work presented in this book pertaining to the different concepts that we aim to investigate, i.e. social inequalities, regional disparities and last but not least the migration policy determinant. Their interrelations are represented by the findings contained in different chapters. Moreover, the transnational approach mentioned further assists us in framing the determinants of migration and mobility between Switzerland and Bulgaria as the former East–West migration constellations in Europe have historically proved.

In the following paragraphs, a collection of different potential and actual Bulgarian migrant profiles resulting from our analysis are summarized and contrasted. This outcome was one of the main aims originating from the research questions described earlier in this chapter.

Potential migrants included in our sample, either long or short term, share a common demographic profile. Men, younger individuals, and persons without family commitments tend to express a higher aspiration to migrate, which is also confirmed by the regression analysis. The outmigration aspirations of the youngest Bulgarians are widely spread; however, bearing in mind that their share in the total population is quite low, it can be expected that the actual migration will gradually decrease in the near future.

The comparison of capability characteristics of the two types of potential migrants reveals, in particular, if one combines the descriptive and the analytical statistics, that migration aspiration is driven to a great extent by education, it being the higher educated people who aspire more for long, as well as for short-term migration. Regarding the income level it seems that Bulgarians from all income ranges aspire at migrating. Migration, in the Bulgarian context, therefore does not represent a phenomenon that is linked to certain social strata. The differentiation lies rather in the type of occupation. Whereas students and unemployed people aspire to a high degree to migrate, either long or short term, working in the public sector seems to hold people back from migration, as these jobs represent fairly stable and secure positions. People occupied in agriculture have again a strong aspiration to migrate, which seems to be linked to low earnings and little security in these positions.

Not surprisingly, having networks that reach to other countries represents a strong determinant of migration aspiration. This is also a reason why we dedicate a full chapter (Chap. 6) to this issue.

In general, the fact of having once migrated may be a strong determinant of having aspirations again to migrate for good, or engage in *circular migration*. As the data records people's aspirations and former experiences regarding migration, it is hard to say whether the aspiration to migrate again results in circular migration or in a migration for the long term or even for good.

The data on the aspirations of people with migration experience points in particular to the labour market context in Bulgaria for people who have returned from migration. Younger respondents and unemployed people are very likely to express an aspiration to migrate anew. The same applies to people working freelance in comparison to people who have obtained a more stable position after their *return*. Having experienced migration, it is the young and better qualified who express a strong aspiration to leave the country again, which points towards the unsatisfactory absorption in the Bulgarian market, which drives people again to search for better job opportunities elsewhere.

Finally, *Bulgarians in Switzerland* represent a very specific component of Bulgarian migration. Women are over-represented and in general they also tend to be highly qualified, with secondary or even tertiary diplomas.

The regressions correct some of the findings discussed in the descriptive part, for instance we could not confirm a gender difference in the aspirations to return or to stay in Switzerland. Instead, the fact of being married results in a strong determinant to prefer to stay in Switzerland. This is also linked to the age group: whereas young individuals opt for either returning to Bulgaria or moving to another country, older groups tend to prefer to return to Bulgaria. People in the middle range (the ones who potentially are also married) tend instead to state the aspiration to remain in Switzerland.

This results in a group of predominantly married people of a middle age group that prefers to stay in Switzerland and settle, whereas younger individuals seem more mobile and also opt for migration to another country. The group of potential migrants to a third country is further categorized by higher incomes which provide them with the capabilities to consider a secondary movement. The last group, people aiming at circulating between both countries or even returning to Bulgaria, is also distinguished by transnational practices such as sending money or travelling frequently to Bulgaria (see also Chap. 6).

The extent of circular migration between the two countries remains an open issue for further investigation with important implications for the sending country in terms of opportunities for skills transfer and local development as well as for the receiving country as far the functioning of the labour market and immigrant integration framework is concerned. The following discussion will try to elucidate the role of inequalities, regional disparities and migration policies in this regard.

Ultimately, the recent East–West migration experience indicates a high level of unpredictability of any potential and actual migration forecast. East–West migrants remain "free-riders" and temporary and circular migration seems historically to prevail where the borders are open and the local labour markets provide attractive conditions for these fluid migration patterns. Bulgaria with an exhausted demographic situation and Switzerland, a non-EU member, with a highly selective admission policy seem, however, to represent a special case in this regard.

References

Bauer, T., & Zimmermann, K. F. (1999). *Assessment of possible migration pressure and its labour market impact following eu enlargement to central and Eastern Europe* (IZA Research Report No. 3). Retrieved November 30, 2015, from www.iza.org/en/webcontent/publications/reports.

Bentivogli, C., & Pagano, P. (1999). Regional disparities and labour mobility: The euro-11 versus the USA. *Labour, 13*(3), 737–760.

Boeri, T., Brücker, H., et al. (2000). *The impact of eastern enlargement on employment and labour markets in the EU member states.* Brussels: European Commission.

Clemens, M. (2014). *Does development reduce migration?* (Working Paper 359). Center for Global Development. Retrieved November 30, 2015, from http://www.cgdev.org/section/publications.

Constant, A. F., Nottmeyer O., & Zimmerman, K. F. (2012). *The economics of circular migration* (IZA Discussion Paper No 6940). Retrieved November 30, 2015, from www.iza.org/en/webcontent/publications/papers.

De Haas, H. (2008). The complex role of migration in shifting rural livelihoods: A Moroccan case study. In T. van Naerssen, E. Spaan, & A. Zoomers (Eds.), *Global migration and development*. New York: Routledge.

De Haas, H. (2010). *Migration transitions: A theoretical and empirical inquiry into the developmental drivers of international migration* (International Migration Institute Working Paper 24). University of Oxford. Retrieved November 30, 2015, from http://www.imi.ox.ac.uk/publications/wp.

De Haas, H. (2011). *The determinants of international migration: Conceptualising policy, origin and destination effects* (International Migration Institute Working Paper 32). University of Oxford. Retrieved November 30, 2015, from http://www.imi.ox.ac.uk/publications/wp.

De Haas, H. (2014). *Migration theory Quo vadis?* (International Migration Institute Working Paper 100). University of Oxford. Retrieved November 30, 2015, from http://www.imi.ox.ac.uk/publications/wp.

Eurostat. (2008). *Survey sampling reference guidelines: Introduction to sample design and estimation techniques*. Luxembourg: Office for Official Publications of the EC.

Fassmann, H., Haller, M., & Lane, D. (Eds.). (2009). *Migration and mobility in Europe: Trends, patterns and control*. Cheltenham: Edward Elgar.

Fuchs-Schundeln, N., & Schundeln, M. (2009). Who stays, who goes, who returns? East-West migration within Germany since reunification. *Economics of Transition, 17*(4), 703–738.

Glick Schiller, N., & Salazar, N. B. (2013). Regimes of mobility across the globe. *Ethnic and Migration Studies, 39*(2), 183–200.

Glorius, B., Grabowska-Lusinska, I., & Kuvik, A. (Eds.). (2013). *Mobility in transition. Migration patterns after EU enlargement*. Amsterdam: Amsterdam University Press. IMISCOE Research.

Hagen-Zanker, J. (2008). *Why do people migrate? A review of the theoretical literature* (Working Paper MGSoG/2008/WP002). Maastricht: Maastricht Graduate School of Governance, Maastricht University.

Harris, J. R., & Todaro, M. P. (1970). Migration, unemployment and development: A two-sector analysis. *American Economic Review, 60*, 126–142.

Kaczmarczyk, P. (2004). Future westward outflow from accession countries: The case of Poland. In A. Górny & P. Ruspini (Eds.), *Migration in the new Europe: East-West revisited*. Basingstoke: Palgrave-Macmillan.

Kahanec, M., & Zimmermann, K. (Eds.). (2010). *EU Labor markets after post-enlargement migration*. Berlin: Springer.

Kaltchev, I. (2001). *External migration of Bulgarian population*. Sofia: Dunav Press.

Lewis, W. A. (1954). Economic development with unlimited supply of labour. *Manchester School of Economic and Social Studies, 22*(2), 139–191.

Marchetti, S. (2013). Dreaming circularity? Eastern European women and job sharing in paid home care. *Journal of Immigrant and Refugee Studies, 11*(4), 347–363. doi:10.1080/15562948.2013.827770.

Massey, D. S., Arango, J., Hugo, G., Kouaouci, A., Pellegrino, A., & Taylor, J. E. (1993). Theories of international migration: A review and appraisal. *Population and Development Review, 19*, 431–466.

Mintchev, V., & Boshnakov, V. (2006). The profile and experience of return migrants: Empirical evidence from Bulgaria. *South East Europe Review for Labour and Social Affairs, 9*(2), 35–59.

Mintchev, V., & Boshnakov, V. (2007). Stay or leave again? New evidence for Bulgarian return migration. *Economic Thought, XXII*(7), 107–126.

Mintchev, V., & Boshnakov, V. (2010). Return migration and development prospects after EU integration: Empirical evidence from Bulgaria. In R. Black, G. Engbersen, M. Okólski, &

C. Pantîru (Eds.), *A continent moving west? EU enlargement and labour migration from central and eastern Europe* (pp. 231–248). Amsterdam: Amsterdam University Press. IMISCOE Research.

Mintchev, V., Kalchev, I., Goev, V., & Boshnakov, V. (2004). External migration from Bulgaria at the beginning of the XXI century: Estimates of potential emigrants' attitudes and profile. *Economic Thought, XIX*(7), 137–161.

MLSP (2012). *Updated national strategy for demographic development of the population in Republic of Bulgaria, 2012–2030.* Sofia: Ministry of Labour and Social Policy (in Bulgarian). Retrieved November 30, 2015, from https://www.president.bg/docs/1352302457.pdf.

Piguet, E. (2005). *L'immigration en Suisse depuis 1948.* Une analyse des flux migratoires vers la Suisse. Zürich: Seismo.

Ruspini, P. (Ed.) (2010). South-Eastern Europe and the European migration system: East-West mobility in flux. *The Romanian Journal of European Studies*, No. 7–8/2009, Special Issue on Migration and Mobility.

Ruspini, P. (2011). Conceptualising transnationalism: East-West migration patterns in Europe. In C. Allemann Ghionda & W. D. Bukow (Eds.), *Orte der Diversität: Formate, Arrangements und Inszenierungen* (pp. 115–127). Wiesbaden: VS Verlag.

Ruspini, P., & Eade, J. (Eds.). (2014). A decade of EU enlargement: A changing framework and patterns of migration. *Central and Eastern European Migration Review, Special Issue, 3*(2).

Sandu, D. (2005). Emerging transnational migration from Romanian villages. *Current Sociology, 53*(4), 555–582.

SEEMIG (2015). *Managing migration and its effects in South-East Europe—Transnational actions towards evidence based strategies.* Retrieved October 10, 2015, from http://seemig.eu/index.php/mediamenu.

Sen, A. (1999). *Development as freedom.* New York: Anchor Books.

Skeldon, R. (2012). Going round in circles: Circular migration, poverty alleviation and marginality. *International Migration, 50*(3), 43–60. doi:10.1111/j.1468-2435.2012.00751.x.

Straubhaar, T. (2001). *East-West migration: Will it be a problem?* Inter-economics, July/August, 167–170.

Todaro, M. P. (1969). A model of labor migration and urban unemployment in less-developed countries. *American Economic Review, 59*, 138–148.

Todaro, M. P., & Maruszko, L. (1987). Illegal migration and US immigration reform: A conceptual framework. *Population and Development Review, 13*(1), 101–114.

UN. (1998). *Recommendations on statistics of international migration.* Revision 1. New York: United Nations.

Wallace, C. D. (2008). New patterns of East-West migration. In T. van der Naerssen & M. van der Velde (Eds.), *Migration in a new Europe: People, borders and trajectories* (pp. 1–12). Rome, Italy: Home of Geography, Società Geografica Italiana.

Wallace, C. D., & Stola, D. (Eds.). (2001). *Patterns of migration in central Europe.* Basingstoke, United Kingdom: Palgrave Macmillan.

Zaiceva, A. (2006). *Reconciling the estimates of potential migration into the enlarged European Union* (IZA Discussion Paper No. 2519). Retrieved November 15, 2015, from http://www.iza.org/en/webcontent/publications/papers.

Zelinsky, W. (1971). The hypothesis of the mobility transition. *Geographical Review, 61*, 219–249.

Chapter 3
Linking Social Inequalities and Migration

Dotcho Mihailov and Michael Nollert

3.1 Introduction

Nowadays, it is impossible to determine the social status of migrants exclusively based on their position in a singular society defined by political borders (Weiss 2005; Amelina 2010). But let us remember: migrants who left their homeland in the nineteenth century also left a social space in which they occupied a more or less distinct position which was determined by a specific set of cultural, economic, and social capital (Bourdieu 1986; Lin 2001; Savage et al. 2005). Although many migrants returned or retired back home, migration then meant a loss of social capital and acquiring a new (not necessarily better) social position in a another society.

This change from one state-defined society to another is no longer a definitive break with the homeland. Modern transportation and communication technologies help to preserve the social ties to friends and relatives back home and facilitate sporadic or definitive returns to the home country. In addition, migrants are no longer even forced to transfer their assets to the host country. On the contrary, now migrants are able to enlarge their assets in their home country and to remit money to their relatives.

However, the motives for migration have remained similar. In addition to political reasons, economic motives still prevail, even though the reason is not only economic hardship but simply the wish to get a better income, the dream of a different lifestyle or life project. In consequence, there are no longer only poor and low-skilled people, but also well-trained and highly qualified people who leave their home country.

D. Mihailov (✉)
Agency for Socioeconomic Analyses, Sofia, Bulgaria
e-mail: dmihailov@asa.bg

M. Nollert
Social Policies and Social Work, University of Fribourg, Fribourg, Switzerland
e-mail: michael.nollert@unifr.ch

© Springer International Publishing Switzerland 2017   61
M. Richter et al. (eds.), *Migration and Transnationalism Between
Switzerland and Bulgaria*, DOI 10.1007/978-3-319-31946-9_3

These highly skilled migrants constitute a major challenge both in sociology and migration research. On the one hand, they often still have property in their country of origin. On the other hand, they don't any longer automatically form the "underclass" in the target country. On the contrary, many migrants — as the example of Switzerland shows — are much wealthier and get higher salaries than the natives. In consequence, a "migration background" is not necessarily a disadvantage any more.

Although there are still countries whose emigrants are either low or highly skilled, there are more and more countries in which low and highly skilled people migrate to the same country. This seems to be a characteristic of the migration from Eastern to Western Europe. Thus, we find in Western Europe a big variety of migrants from Eastern Europe, ranging from construction or agricultural workers through nurses, to doctors, to computer scientists, and to managers. Therefore, it would not be wise to expect that Bulgarian migrants in Switzerland concentrate in certain social positions, especially since the bilateral agreement on free movement has been extended with the European Union in 2009 (see Chaps. 1 and 5).

This chapter focuses on economic inequalities as a key driver of migration, the migrants' use of social capital and experiences of discrimination, occupational and income mobility, and the social inequalities between migrants in the host and origin country as well the occupational and social shifts, resulting from migration. After sketching out a theoretical framework, we present empirical findings provided by our qualitative and quantitative analyses (see Chap. 1).

3.2   Theoretical Remarks

Social inequalities and migration are manifoldly interwoven. On the one hand, social inequalities between and within countries are important drivers of migration. On the other hand, migration influences both the inequalities in the country of origin and the destination country. The following are some theoretical remarks which structure the subsequent analyses.

There is no doubt that global social inequalities are a key driver of international migration flows. It requires no great explanation that migration from poor countries to rich countries is more frequent than migration from rich countries to poor. However, this does not mean that emigrants are a priori among the losers in their countries of origin. Of course, we know well enough from research that, first of all, people migrate who experience material hardship or at least a gap between what they expect and what they get in their home countries. With the opening of the European labour markets, more and more highly skilled people tend to move from the poorer to richer countries, where they often develop a transnational habitus (Guarnizo 1997; Kelly and Lusis 2006).

From a sociological point of view, it is obvious that education, gender, and the ethnic affiliation of the migrant primarily determine which social status he/she reaches in the destination country (Gans 2007; Papademetriou et al. 2009). Thus, highly educated males with sufficient language skills and without marks of discredit (stigma) can easily transfer their social status from the country of origin to the host country. Vice versa, low-skilled females with a Roma background, for example, run the risk of only getting a job in the low-wage sector (Gans 2009). However, many lower-skilled people nonetheless stay if they compare themselves not with the natives but with their peer group back home.

It is important to note that sociology has always stressed that beside education, qualifications, and ascriptive characteristics such as milieu of parents, gender, and ethnic affiliations, the social network resources (social capital) determine the social status. Thus, at least since the studies by Granovetter (1973), we can assume that the success of migrants also depends on their social capital (Anthias 2007). Especially for migrants with little economic and cultural capital, the social networks in the destination country are extremely important for job searching and for finding cheap accommodation. Of course, social networks are also important after having settled down. And it remains an open question in which areas *weak ties* tend to matter more than *strong ties*.

Just as social capital helps immigrants integrate into the society of destination, discriminatory practices and processes of social closure (Collins 1979; Parkin 1979) are a major hurdle for successful integration. The most important legal discrimination to protect the native workers from foreign competition is educational certificates. In other words, for many positions in the labour market, the laws require that the candidate has a recognized certificate. Also, the demand, segmentation, and ethnicization of the host country's labour market restrict the access to jobs. Therefore, especially low-skilled migrants suffer from a rigid qualification regime unless they find jobs for which no natives apply for (e.g. Fullin and Reyneri 2010). In consequence, due to the protection of native workers with recognized certificates, many migrants may not work in jobs for which they are qualified. Migrants, however, are not only faced with closure processes, they often also suffer from cultural prejudices (D'Amato 2001; D'Amato and Fibbi 2007; Girard and Bauder 2007; Mountz 2011; Pecoraro 2005; Riaño and Baghdadi 2007; Wessendorf 2008).

Of course, every migrant is aware that establishment in the foreign context does not grant a higher quality of life. However, the loss of social relations and the lack of cultural habits are often offset by the extra income provided by the job in the host country. Hence, many migrants even take jobs for which they are overqualified (Haug 2006; Jaccard Ruedin and Weaver 2009; Richter 2011). With the opening of national labour markets in Europe, this situation has changed in so far as the companies can focus on foreign workers with recognized qualifications. In other words, we expect that we can observe both Bulgarian migrants who preserve or even ameliorate their occupational status in Switzerland and Bulgarian migrants who experience downward mobility. Concerning the return migrants, we expect a further polarization.

The extent to which migration affects the *inequalities between countries* is a controversial topic. On the one hand, it seems plausible that the host country benefits from the import of cheap low-skilled workers and highly skilled workers whose training costs are covered by the home country. On the other hand, the active promotion of emigration in certain poor countries suggests that poor countries primarily benefit from the export of unemployment (for Bulgaria, see Markova 2010). Nevertheless, emigration can also imply that expensively trained workers leave the economy. The economic harm of this "brain drain" (for Bulgaria see Glytsos 2010 and Markova 2010) can only be limited if the well-paid migrants sufficiently transfer money home (remittances, see León-Ledesma and Piracha 2004).

However, the impacts of migration on the economy of the sending country may alter when seen through the prism of various migration segments, ranging from low-skilled mobile workers to high-skilled specialists and managers, residing in the host country. Additionally, seasonal workers who are getting back home may incur new social costs in terms of unemployment benefits and new public insurance costs for the sending country.

Besides *international* inequalities, we should be aware of *interpersonal* inequalities *between all world citizens*. According to Milanovic's (2011) calculations, 80 % of these global income differences are due to the mean income differences between countries. Hence, he anticipates migration as the great twenty-first century "adjustment" mechanism for reducing global inequality and global poverty (p. 21).

Of course, migration not only affects international and global inequalities, it also influences economic inequalities, not only at home, but also in the host country. Thus, it can be assumed that inequality in the poorer home country decreases if the members of the lower-income quintiles leave the country (Black et al. 2005). The expansion of the lower class due to immigration tends instead to result in an increase in inequality in the destination country, though it decreases the poverty among the migrants. It is more difficult to assess the impact of mobility of highly skilled workers. If we assume that these migrants are members of the middle-income quintile we could expect the inequality in the home country to increase, whereas the inequality in the destination country decreases (Kahanec and Zimmermann 2009).

Of major interest, however, is the question of how the inequality among migrants changes from the home country to the destination country and then back in the home country. If we assume that lower skilled migrants have more trouble than highly skilled ones preserving their former professional status in the host country, one would expect that inequality, as measured by the distribution of income, would increase in the receiving country. However, if the poorest sections of the population stay at home (see Chap. 2), the income gap among migrants will be lower in Switzerland than in Bulgaria.

Furthermore, we can assume that highly skilled migrants primarily return if they can improve or at least preserve their status in their origin country. By contrast, lower skilled migrants are supposed to return when they fail economically or become unemployed. In short, whereas it is difficult to predict how the economic gap among Bulgarians changes after emigration, we expect that economic inequality is highest among the return migrants.

However, inequalities in sending and receiving countries are also influenced by capital transfers of migrants. Thus, we also consider remittances. In contrast to the transfer of capital from wealthy to rich countries, which increases international inequality, remittances are rather assumed to reduce international inequalities (Faist 2008). This expectation is again supported by the fact that many poor countries actively promote emigration (Mazzucato 2011).

In terms of inequality in the home country, however, the impact is not clear, because it is hard to assess which peers and which regions profit most from these money transfers. Based on a sample of 80 developing countries, Ebeke and Le Goff (2011) suggest that inequalities are fostered if most of the migrants are comparatively wealthy and well-educated. By contrast, if the majority of the migrants have a poor background, remittances reduce income inequality back home. Therefore, we can at least presume that the remittances of the lower-class migrants reduce economic inequalities in Bulgaria. However, the analysis of inequality at lower (community) level may bring other results, as remittances may imply, for example, new economic gaps in poor Roma neighbourhoods.

Based on our theoretical considerations, the following research questions can be formulated:

- What are the social background characteristics of the migrants?
- What are the major economic motives to migrate?
- How do migrants use their social capital?
- Do immigrants experience discrimination?
- Do migrants improve or downgrade their occupational position?
- Do migrants improve their economic situation?
- How do inequalities, income, and property change with migration?
- How important are remittances for the various social groups?

For each of these questions, a section is reserved. To answer the research questions, we rely on data provided by the quantitative and qualitative research in Switzerland and Bulgaria, see Chap. 1.

3.3   Social Background Characteristics of the Migrants

Concerning social inequalities among the Bulgarian migrants in Switzerland, the first important finding from the quantitative survey carried out in Switzerland is that the number of female respondents in the Swiss sample is 63.1 % compared to 35.9 % male. Secondly, in terms of age, the sample is comprised of comparatively young people with a median age of 36 years. It is remarkable that only 3 % of the sample are above 60 years, while only 1.7 % are at or above the retirement age of 64 (for women/65 for men). In comparison, at the end of 2005, just under 22 % of the permanent population in Switzerland were aged less than 20, and nearly one sixth were aged 65 and over. Thirdly, the majority of the sample are predominantly married or cohabiting (57.7 % compared to only 29.2 % who are single). Nevertheless, only 4.5 % of the respondents report having children.

Most of the Bulgarian migrants in Switzerland originate from big settlements: 28.0 % come from Sofia and 27.0 %, from district centres, while only 8.6 % from villages. The ethnic structure of the sample is dominated by people of Bulgarian ethnic identity (92.9 %). The Roma minority, which is the most marginalized in terms of education and employment in Bulgaria, constitutes only 0.4 % of the respondents. Similarly, the Turkish minority is represented by a very small proportion (2.8%). These shares correspond to the religious affiliation, comprising 73.8% Orthodox and only 3.2% Islam. It is interesting that 2.8% of the Bulgarian ethnic group report being Catholic (1.0%) and 1.8% Protestant. According to the census (2011), the number of Catholics back in Bulgaria is 0.8% while the Protestants are only 1.1%. Thus, the comparatively bigger number of catholic and protestant affiliation among Bulgarians in Switzerland in the sample (if not due to statistical errors) is most probably related to marriages, cohabitations, or other reasons for shifts in faith affiliation. In terms of citizenship, the majority of the migrants keep their Bulgarian status—89.5% are Bulgarian citizens compared to only 0.4% Swiss, 4% holding double citizenship, and 6% other citizenship.

The qualification level of the Bulgarian migrants in Switzerland is comparatively high. More than half (51.2%) of the sample are university graduates, who are mainly female (55.2%) and largely younger people. In terms of residence permit, the data verifies the findings from the Bulgarian "return migrant" survey. Short-term migration is typical for the less qualified return migrants. According to the Swiss survey, 47.1% of people with secondary education hold a short-term permit (L), compared to only 39.3% among the people of residence type. On the other hand, 55.9% of the mid-term residents (B) are university graduates, compared to 44.8% of the short-term migrants.

The mid-term level of residence type among the university graduates suggests that these comparatively highly qualified migrants have come to Switzerland lately, e.g. they are not from the first migration wave immediately after the changes in Bulgaria in 1989. According to additional tabulations, 51.9% of the university graduates have come after 2007 (when Bulgaria entered the EU) compared to 49% before that. At the same time, these recent years have brought to Switzerland Bulgarians of very low (basic) education (5.7% after 2007 compared to 1.7% before). Contrariwise, the number of middle-level education migrants has decreased during these last years after Bulgaria entered the EU.

Generally, the socio-demographic profile of the Bulgarian migrants in Switzerland suggests a higher social stratum, compared to the migrant profile of the returnees from other countries, described in Chap. 2. These Bulgarian returnees are more mobile, less educated, and hold lower professional competencies in comparison to the migrants in Switzerland.

3.4 Inequality as a Driver of Migration

Prior research suggests that the desire to improve the economic situation is the major motive to migrate (e.g. Winchie and Carment 1989; Milanovic 2011; see also Chap. 2). Hence, migrants hope to elevate their social status in the host country. In fact, according to the survey carried out in Switzerland, the main reasons for leaving the country are the improvement of the occupational and income situation, followed by the general perception of a missing development perspective in Bulgaria (see also Chap. 2). The main peculiarity concerning social inequalities is the comparatively high ranking of the reason related to career development "Better professional realization in Switzerland", which is topping the hierarchy of motivations.

The career accent in the migration incentives is determined by the comparatively high professional and educational profile of the Swiss survey sample. This fact is confirmed by the significant differences within this leading reason according to education: professional realization is a migration reason for 55.6 % of the PhD graduates, compared to 21.3 % of the migrants who have basic education. This dominating motivation is also significantly salient for the groups of men (49.4 % vs. 38.7 % female), the middle age group (44.1 %), and mid-term residence permit (47.1 %).

Regarding the main occupation, career reasons are distinctive for students (better professional realization—52.1 %), while the immediate gains from this realization (higher payment—37.2 %) are more indicative for workers. The immediate financial advantages and benefits of being in Switzerland are acknowledged most commonly by those in medium qualification and social strata, including migrants engaged in middle-level elementary occupations such as technicians 41.2 % and machine operators (64.3 %). On the other hand, career development is the main migration motivation largely for managers (66.0 %) and professionals (62.0 %).

According to the qualitative interviews in Switzerland, aspirations to leave Bulgaria can be summarized by the search for a different life (not necessarily "better") and more adequate labour and economic conditions than those in Bulgaria. In general, Bulgarian migrants tend to capitalize as much as possible on their migration experience, in the same way as other patterns of recent Eastern Europeans circular migration to Europe which resemble an "income-seeking, opportunistic or overly exploitative" mode (Morawska 2008). The majority of those interviewed across the different linguistic regions tend to think about their migration experience as something that will last as long as the benefits of migration are much larger than the costs involved. Obviously, the margin of benefits compared to the psychological and social harm of being a migrant has been high enough because only few have aspirations of returning home. The pull return factors therefore are still not that relevant and their time in Switzerland has led to them feeling ambivalences in identity and belonging (see Chap. 6).

The economic situation, as well as political instability, was mentioned as a strong reason to leave Bulgaria.

> *The situation was critical to (decide) to come here after the set in of our pseudo democracy, the state was sold, the people were driven on the streets (without a job), so people were unemployed, on the other hand they had to seek a way to feed their families.* (female, 55, working as housemaid in Switzerland).
>
> *Bulgaria I decided to leave from purely financial reasons. A friend of my mother worked here in Switzerland and she needed help. She worked in a restaurant and they needed help for a few months during the summer, actually, (they were searching) for someone to come here for 2-3 months for someone to work instead of her temporarily. And she asked me to come and try.* (female, 26, working in a coffee shop in Switzerland).

On the other hand, Switzerland is still perceived by some Bulgarians as "a country of luxury" because of its tidy and affluent way of living, which offer first-hand opportunities to work and to run a decent life.

The people we interviewed in Bulgaria mostly left Bulgaria because of financial reasons. In general, their living was not secured by the labour market opportunities in Bulgaria.

> *In Bulgaria the salary is just not enough. 300–350 Lv., it is nothing, you take a credit from one bank and a credit from another to pay back the first credit. One month you balance the situation, then the next month you have to balance again. You are tricked by the system.* (female, 49, working as care taker for elderly people in Switzerland).

> *Before (maybe 20 years ago), they had no financial problems. She was taking care of her children and his husband had a good job in the police. He lost the job and since then they have financial problems* (female, 57, working as a care taker for elderly people in Cyprus).

In some cases (in particular the middle class cases with education), particular aggravating factors, such as losing their job or having to pay back credits, made them leave the country in order to provide quick funding for their needs.

We only met one case of a woman who went to study abroad and then came back, because she felt that the work opportunities were better for her in Bulgaria than abroad (Austria). It seems that with her training as a medical doctor in Austria she would still be in education for a long time, whereas in Bulgaria she is accepted as a full doctor and has access to more interesting positions. Nevertheless, this rather looks like a very specific case related to the training and work opportunities of medical doctors.

Finally, there are some people who are very mobile because of their current working situation. Their work as a sales representative or controller imposes a high degree of mobility on them. Whether this is migration or rather mobility remains an open question. For instance, there is the case of a 26-year-old man who has a job that requires a high degree of mobility. He has been in many places in Europe, in Latin-America, and soon he will go to Asia. He works for a British company that has representatives all over the world.

A final remark applies to the Roma population's motives to migrate. A common argument was related to the way people treat Roma. They all supported the opinion that they receive much more respect abroad than in Bulgaria. They feel discriminated in Bulgaria and understand that they are excluded from the labour market because of their ethnicity. Nevertheless, they work abroad under very exploitative conditions.

> *There is a lot of discrimination in Bulgaria. When you are a bit darker, then you don't get the job. Also at the municipality (municipal social services) it is the same. When there is a job opportunity and a Roma presents himself, they tell him, that the job is already taken.* (male, 60, various jobs in the Netherlands).

He gives two examples: a Roma woman went to a shop where they were searching for a vendor and she was told that the job was already taken. But another woman had just heard before that they were still searching for somebody and did not take her because of being Roma. Another example is about two men who were applying for a job at a factory. The employer first made inquiries to know whether the men had white skin and blue eyes. At the end, they didn't get the job.

3.5 Social Capital as a Resource for Migration

Social capital indicated by the availability of information and assistance provided by social networks is very important for finding jobs and for information about how to deal with administrative issues such as health insurance and the authorities. Hence, social capital can substitute a lack of economic and cultural capital.

The survey carried out in Switzerland suggests that the migrants have received less support for moving to Switzerland from friends (21.7 %) and relatives (19.2 %) than from Swiss employers (35.7 %). Although the support given by *strong ties* (Granovetter 1983) accounts to above 40 %, the support given by the Swiss employers is quite specific for the migrants in Switzerland compared to the migrants from Bulgaria in general. By contrast, returnees and circular migrants were supported basically by local friends, relatives, and workers from the same regions, who are already established there. The high level of employers' support means that migration has been "arranged" or "negotiated" in advance by the employer and the potential migrant.

The demand and interest of the employers obviously focus on migrants with specific qualification and skills (see also Sect. 6.2.2). In fact, the "employer's" support rises up to 43.8 % for the university graduates and surges up to 55.1 % for the PhDs, compared to only 17.0 % of people with basic education. Thus, employers' support increases with the skills and the qualification of the potential employees. So, employers' support is given for the initial migration to 60 % of the current managers and 56.3 % of the current professionals, compared to only 35.7 % of the machine operators and 9.4 % of migrants (consequently) occupied in elementary jobs.

Alternatively, support given by "friends" is the highest among migrants with basic education (12.8 %) and nearly missing for the PhDs (0.9 %). Another significant factor of the employer's support is "age", being highest for the middle or rather the active older young age groups (45 % aged 31–40 years, compared to 35.2 % above 40).

The employers' support is distinctive for the high profile of migrants (managers and professionals), while the networking route, facilitated by previously settled friends, relatives, and colleagues, is typical for the lower strata of migrants. By contrast, the "managerial" and "professional" profile migrants rely on the support from employers.

Settling down in terms of finding work, finding a place to live, and dealing with the administration is again supported mainly by the employers (37.8 %), followed by friends who are already based there (32.4 %) and the family (25.6 %) (see Sect. 6.2.2).

By contrast, most of the *return migrants* have found a job via acquaintances and friends — 34.7 %. This number together with the *people from my home town/region* (13.3 %) makes up almost half of the sample (48 %). The *networking* channel is more effective than the services of a *recruiting company based in Bulgaria* (10.4 %) or *Internet engine* 2.2 %, which is surprisingly low. Alternatively, the "family" pattern of finding a job is less effective and less frequent. There are only 2.2 % who

Table 3.1 First job and perceived financial status according to return migrants*

	Much better	Better	Average	Worse	Much worse	Total
Through..........-My spouse was there		2.4	3.5	0.9		2.6
My relatives/family were there	16.5	19.9	21.3	24.0	43.9	22.1
People from my home town/region were there	14.5	12.5	15.7	17.2	32.7	16.0
Bulgarian colleagues/acquaintances, working there	23.2	28.6	43.4	46.0	55.2	41.1
Bulgarian employer there	2.8	1.7	5.7	7.8	5.6	5.4
Recruiting company in Bulgaria	19.5	16.9	11.6	12.1		12.5
Labour office in Bulgaria		5.5	1.5	2.2		2.1
Local labour office/institution there		8.5	4.3	1.5	7.8	4.3
Internet job search engine	5.7	4.2	2.9			2.6
Applying for a "green card"						
Marriage/cohabitation						
In another way	24.6	13.2	10.0	6.4	8.3	10.4

Tabulated questions: How did you find work abroad the first time?/How do you evaluate your financial status compared to most people in Bulgaria?
* *Base*: Multiple response analysis of cases

have found a job through her/his spouse being already abroad and only 18.7% who have found a job via relatives.

According to Table 3.1, networking via colleagues is similar to networking via relatives when it comes to finding a job. It is the low socio-economic profile of people with low incomes, coming from villages, having lower education. Thus, there are 55.2% of migrants self-estimating their financial situation as "worse than others" who have found a job via colleagues compared to 23% of the "better off". Alternatively, the number of "better off" migrants finding a job via Internet increases with financial welfare. A similar correlation is found for the channel of finding a job *through relatives*, but the correlation there is less distinct.

According to the survey of the return migrants, *weak-ties* networking is typical for jobs requiring middle and lower qualifications (see Sect. 6.2.1). In summary: there are two main types of networking—*strong tie* networking via close relatives and friends and *weak ties* networking via colleagues/acquaintances and people from the home town. In line with Granovetter (1973, 1983), the latter seems more effective for finding a job, but is typical for lower social strata and generally results in finding low-qualification occupations (see also Sect. 6.8).

3.6   Experiences of Discrimination

Many migrants suffer in the host country not only from economic and social insecurities, but also from experiences of discrimination. According to the qualitative interviews in Switzerland, most Bulgarians don't experience much discrimination (with the exception of the reported cases in Southern Switzerland which fall either in the category of discrimination or self-perceived discrimination). They are very careful in mentioning cases of discrimination and they tend to refer to other people, stating that they did not experience any direct discrimination. For instance, it could happen in low-skilled professions, or then they limit it to the salary (as a structural thing) and not to people discriminating them directly.

Nevertheless, there is the problem for people who enter the country and start searching for a job, once they are in Switzerland. This happens in particular for people who follow their spouse (Bulgarian or Swiss). Without work experience in Switzerland, it becomes very difficult to find a suitable job.

Cases of discrimination and self-discrimination are reported in Southern Switzerland and they are usually connected with deskilling processes, the original lack of competence in the local language, or the still persistent Eastern European accent. As for the whole of Switzerland, they affect those working in the lower segments of the labour market notwithstanding the educational qualifications acquired in Bulgaria.

> *Not because I am 'Bulgarian' but because I am a foreigner... I noticed it for the others as well, even for Russians and Serbs is like that. They think we are a bit more stupid and we do not understand things or that we are not capable. There are ridiculous times when they say, for example: 'Now I will teach you how to make coffee' (...) but where do they think we are from? I am a graduate. In this sense, yes, there is discrimination. But it is more in the workplace, but I do not listen to them and usually speak with everyone.* (female, 37, working as a care taker in Switzerland).

For highly skilled, students or Bulgarians married to Swiss or resident foreigners, discrimination does not take place because either they don't look foreign from a somatic standpoint or because of the social environment where they work. Sometimes forms of institutional discrimination are minimized by these very same Bulgarians as isolated cases or described as inevitable "disadvantages".

> *This is actually a question we Bulgarians are often talking about. I am the only one who says no. Other Bulgarian women, the age of my mom say yes, but because they have expected it. I do not ever expect to be considered a foreigner. I am different because of my origin, but I have never personally suffered any kind of discrimination. Only when I am in the office of foreigners I feel a bit discriminated when they say 'Miss, you do come from Bulgaria, we cannot...'.* (23, female, studying in Switzerland).

According to the survey carried out in Switzerland, the majority of the migrants have not faced any specific difficulties at work that result from the foreign status of the worker (see also Chap. 5). The most commonly indicated difficulty is "a lower chance to get a job compared to the local people". In terms of the socio-demographic profile, this difficulty significantly varies only on gender (42.5 % women, compared to 34.1 % men), suggesting a cumulative form of discrimination adding discrimination against migrants to gender discrimination. Otherwise, there are no differences in discrimination at work by age, education, income, or other socio-demographic variables, including ethnicity, suggesting that, if any, discrimination is horizontal by these groups. There are, however, some differences by position linked to level of qualification. Less qualified workers (service and sales workers, 45.0 %) more frequently perceive lower access to work compared to managers (36.0 %).

Other difficulties at work such as *lower payment for the same job, compared to local people* (18.3%), *job and a position lower than my qualifications and skills* (15.9%), and *bad/rude attitudes of the employers/superiors at work* (7.2%) are rarely reported and are typical again for women and workers in lower positions.

The survey on various return migrants carried out in Bulgaria confirms that *getting a lower payment for the same job compared to local people* is the most frequent discrimination practice at work. The data on return Bulgarian migrants from various countries, however, shows higher levels of discrimination, indicating that 58% of the sample had been paid less than local people, compared to 18% for the current migrants in Switzerland (based on the Swiss survey). It should be remembered that the return-migrants survey has sampled migrants of lower qualification and educational status compared to the current Bulgarian migrants in Switzerland. So, the data verifies that discrimination practices at work are rather typical for the lower qualification segment. In fact, the cross-tabulations by education in both quantitative surveys prove this hypothesis. The number of return migrants getting lower payment when working abroad surges up to 68.5% among people of up to secondary education compared to 52.1% among university graduates.

Employment practices in Switzerland which unequivocally abuse the work code are rarely reported in our data. If any, they are related most often to *increased working time/overtime/shift work/night work without compensation* (16.1%) or *working without a contract* (9.0%). Again, the Bulgarian survey shows that discrimination at work among return migrants is higher than among current migrants in Switzerland. Working with increased *working time/overtime/shift work/night work without compensation* is reported by 40.7%, again being more typical of lower education return migrants—60.1% of up to secondary education, compared to only 26.9% among university graduates.

Discrimination *in access to education services* is also nearly not found. There are only 6.1%, rising to 7.4% among women, who have looked for and been rejected access to any university services or educational opportunities because of being a foreigner. Ethnic identity here adds some fuel to the perception of discrimination. Such difficulties in access to education services could be related to some language deficiencies as reported by 28.0% of the Bulgarian students with Turkish identity, compared to 5.5% of the ethnic Bulgarians. This suggests a perception of cultural and religious discrimination rather than discrimination merely based on the status of a foreign student. Similarly, more than 95% of the entire sample deny experiencing any forms of discrimination while studying in Switzerland. However, for all reported discrimination practices, the values for women and ethnic minorities (Turks and Roma) are higher than for men and ethnic Bulgarians.

These discrimination levels according to the Bulgarian survey among return migrants are again higher, though closer compared to discrimination at work (11.1% for return Bulgarian migrants, compared to 7.4% for the current students in Switzerland).

In short: discrimination among Bulgarian migrants in Switzerland is rare and generally lower, compared to data provided by the Bulgarian return-migrants survey. The main reason for this discrepancy is probably the generally higher level of social status (qualification and education) of the current migrants in Switzerland in comparison with the return migrants surveyed back in Bulgaria. This is related to various reasons, including the circumstance that return migrants are normally former (or current) mobile workers who are exposed to higher risks of discrimination, being engaged in short-time or seasonal jobs. Alternatively, one can imagine that a resident migrant would be more adapted to the host cultural environment and would be therefore less critical of the local employers, compared to someone who has decided to leave the country and return back to Bulgaria. On the other hand, it could be exactly the discrimination practices, or rather, the perception of such practices that forces migrants to return back home. In general, the findings are more about misperceptions, self-perceptions, and attitudes (both among Swiss and Bulgarians) rather than about actual discrimination practices.

3.7 Social Mobility Abroad and Back Home

Now, we turn to the question as to whether the migrants experienced social mobility. Thus, although migrants usually hope to improve their economic situation, both emigration and remigration do not necessarily prevent downward mobility. According to the qualitative analysis, there are three different types of occupational mobility:

1. Persistence or upward mobility: There are migrants who enjoyed in Bulgaria a rather comfortable position, middle class with jobs and resources such as property, and a family network to rely upon. They came either as professional workers (banks, industry, etc.) or as students. They manage to establish themselves, to find jobs at their levels and to be successful in their jobs (for instance, measured through salary increases).
2. Downward mobility: People who migrated without proper planning or who got caught up in the pitfalls of migration: not knowing about the official ways and being trapped in some type of smuggling or at least illegal border crossing; not planning for a job in Switzerland before migrating and finding difficulties in getting a job at their level once arrived in Switzerland, etc.
3. Unstable status: There are a few people from lower social strata who work under very irregular, precarious, sometimes even illegal conditions in Switzerland. Their stay in Switzerland is geared towards financing the family back home in Bulgaria. Their situation is maybe not worse than in Bulgaria and their earnings help to support their families.

According to the survey carried out in Switzerland, the *"working" status of the migrants improves* with the migration process from Bulgaria to Switzerland. While the number of workers back in Bulgaria had been 57.4%, it goes up to 61.1% at the moment of "first activity in Switzerland", and surges up to 72.9% for those in a "current position". Similarly, the frequency of activities related to taking care of family members increases, shifting from 6.1% in Bulgaria to about 11% in

Table 3.2 Main activity shifts

	In Bulgaria before migration (%)	First activity in Switzerland (%)	Current activity in Switzerland (%)
Work	57.4	61.1	72.9
Education	28.3	22.4	10.9
Taking care of family members	6.1	11.6	11.3
Other	8.3	4.8	4.9

Table 3.3 Shifts in positions

	In Bulgaria before migration (%)	First activity in Switzerland (%)	Current activity in Switzerland (%)
Managers	12.9	7.8	9.6
Professionals	35.7	26.5	30.3
Technicians and associate professionals	14.1	15.3	16.3
Clerical support workers	8.3	3.9	5.7
Service and sales workers	16.4	25.1	21.3
Skilled agricultural and forestry workers	.2	.2	.2
Craft and related trade workers	3.9	4.6	3.8
Plant and machine operators and assemblers	3.5	2.5	2.7
Elementary occupations	5.1	14.2	10.2

Switzerland. Alternatively, the number of students falls from 28.3 % down to 10.9 % in the current status.

This finding suggests a transition from "education" to "work", but it also emphasizes the process of searching and acquiring employment in Switzerland. The return migrant survey verifies this data because migration provides a substantial shift from "unemployment" to "employment" activity status.

Three conclusions can be derived from Table 3.2 regarding occupations and qualification level related to positions.

Firstly, the level of occupational competence and position is comparatively high, comprising mainly middle-level occupations, such as professionals (30.3 %, current position), service and sales workers (21.3 %), and technicians and associate professionals (16.3 %). Unlike the return migrants, only a few migrants are occupied in elementary jobs (10.2 %) and in agriculture (0.2 %), which is a major occupational domain for the return migrants. This finding is quite exceptional as elementary occupations and agriculture are generally among the key destination sectors for the Bulgarians abroad. Alternatively, there are a good number of migrants at managerial level (9.6 %), which is also quite outstanding (Table 3.3).

Secondly, there is an overall trend of a *decreasing* level of competence and position rank at individual level when moving from Bulgaria to Switzerland. However, some of the "lost" competence is recovered during the stay in Switzerland. The number of migrants at managerial positions, for example, shifts from 12.9% back in Bulgaria to 7.8% for the first position in Switzerland, recovering slightly up to 9.6% in the current position in Switzerland. Similarly, the number of professionals falls sharply from 35.7 to 26.5% for the first occupation in Switzerland, but then recovers to 30.3% for the current position.

Finally, the share of people occupied in lower-middle level positions increases when going to Switzerland. This is particularly valid for service and sales workers, but also for the bottom of the occupational hierarchy. Thus, the number of migrants occupied in elementary jobs starts at 5.1% in Bulgaria, rising up to 14.2% and then slightly falling back to 10.2%.

In short, downward mobility prevails. Although the occupational level of the migrants is comparatively high, it decreases sharply with the first job, which migrants acquire in Switzerland. However, during the stay, the level of positions rises mainly up to the level of professionals and technicians, but generally does not regain the level of occupations they had back in Bulgaria.

The data derived from migrants, who have returned to Bulgaria from various countries, gives an opportunity for analysing the occupational shifts and the resulting impact on inequality. What has been the main occupation of the *return migrants* before they went abroad and how does it compare to the social status abroad and the main occupation in the host country once the return migrants have come back?

According to Table 3.4 the most significant shifts are observed among the *former unemployed*, decreasing from 19.6% "before emigration" to only 2.8% abroad, and again increasing even higher up to 36.8% once they have come back to Bulgaria. This finding has outstanding policy implications in at least two ways: firstly it underlines the positive impact of migration. This is generated of course largely by

Table 3.4 Main activity of return migrants

	In Bulgaria before migration	Abroad	In Bulgaria after migration
Employed in private company	45.1%	64.4%	33.8%
Employed in state/municipal company or organization	7.5%	1.6%	5.7%
Running/Managing a business (owner/co-owner/manager of a company)	4.3%	2.1%	4.2%
Freelancer (self-employed)	1.4%	3.3%	2.6%
Agricultural producer	1.0%	3.1%	0.9%
Student (High school/College/University)	16.5%	6.5%	6.8%
Unemployed	19.6%	2.8%	36.8%
Pensioner	3.5%	0.4%	4.7%
On maternity leave	0.6%	0.2%	3.1%
Other	0.2%	1.1%	1.5%
Caring for close people	0.2%	5.1%	
Guest/vacation		9.4%	

the private sector which absorbs 64 % of the migrants "abroad", compared to 45.1 % in the host country "before" migration and respectively 33.8 % after migration.

However, this data outlines the difficulties in re-entering the home labour market, when returning to Bulgaria—the ratio of unemployment (36.8 %) is actually twice as high as the ratio of unemployment among migrants before going abroad. The difficulties in re-entering the home labour market are also seen from the increase in occupations related to other social transfers. Pensioners for example are 3.5 % before migration, coming down to only 0.4 % "abroad" and increasing even more than before to 4.7 % after returning to Bulgaria. A similar, even stronger surge of dependency on social benefits after returning to the home country is found for maternity benefit—it increases from 0.2 "abroad" to 3.1 % "back in Bulgaria" after migration.

From the point of view of the sending country, migration therefore proves, on the one hand, to have a positive impact in terms of lifting some burden from unemployment costs, but, on the other hand, return migration is negative in terms of increasing costs for other social benefits. Once they have come back to the home country, the number of pensioners or women entering maternity leave increases.

There are a number of activities that seriously change their relative shares abroad but recover to similar levels in the activity structure once migrants come back home. Such are the entrepreneurs (running own businesses) who drop from 4.3 % down to 2.1 % when they go abroad and recover to 4.2 %—obviously sustaining their own business when coming back home. Since the figures are similar for agricultural producers and freelancers (self-employed), these activities may be considered as the least risky in terms of occupations that might be recovered if or when the migrant decides to go back home. Surprisingly, a similar opportunity is associated with the position of being employed in a state/municipal company or organization. Understandably, only few of the 7.5 % employed in public organizations succeed in finding a similar job abroad (1.6 %). Nevertheless, when they come back home, a significant proportion (5.7 %) succeed in regaining a state job (5.7 %).

There are differences between the percentages of the various economic activities among return migrants, respectively "before" and "during" their stay abroad. This provides an opportunity to look at the direction in which return migrants apply their working skills. The general tendency is to shift into economic sectors, requiring low qualification when Bulgarian migrants move to work abroad. The biggest increasing shift is in agriculture—while there are only 5.2 % who have been employed in this sector in Bulgaria, there are 21.1 % who work in *agriculture* abroad. Other economic activities experiencing significant increases are respectively "household/family activities helper, caretaker, cook, garden keeping" (13.1 vs. 2.0 % at home) and respectively hotels and restaurants (14.0 % vs. 8.8 % at home). Alternatively, the sectors that lose employment are generally those that require higher education, but the decrease there is much smaller. In the "human health and social-work activities" sector, for example, employment decreases from 3.2 % at home "before migration" to 2.5 % "abroad".

The most increasing economic sectors are agriculture, receiving 21.1 % workforce, followed by construction (19.6 %), hotel and restaurants (14.0 %), and household/family activities (helper, caretaker, cook, garden keeper). Alternatively, the only Bulgarian sectors that lose workforce are mainly construction (18.6%) and "trade, repair and technical service of automobiles and motors" (14.1%), which may be considered as requiring some middle-level technical skills. However, the processing industry, which is the most significant user of technical skills in Bulgaria, loses only 6.5%.

In short, there seems to be a "win-win" situation in which the labour market "abroad" gains low qualified labour, attracting workforce in agriculture, construction, and "people-care services", while the local labour market sheds unemployment. The draining effect in terms of losing highly qualified working force is very limited, but could be negative for some mechanical professions, construction and health services. Despite causing some structural distortions, at individual level, migration provides new job opportunities, dramatically decreasing unemployment.

However, both the receiving and sending countries are gaining from migration at the level of the occupational status in terms of qualification and hierarchical position in the company. The general trend is that *return migrants tend to move to lower qualification groups*. This downgrading in occupation can be seen both on the negative side of the scale in terms of increasing the number of unqualified positions and to a smaller extent at the positive end of the qualification ladder in terms of decreasing qualified positions. The negative shift is particularly apparent from the dramatic surge in the lowest qualification group (elementary occupations requiring no qualification)—there are only 8.7% of the migrants engaged in such professions "before" migration surged up to 26.8% "abroad". Alternatively, at the top end of the occupational hierarchy, there are 9.6% of return migrants who have worked as specialists before migration in Bulgaria and respectively only 3.4% abroad. Similarly, the number of technicians and applied specialists decreases from 5.2 to 2.8%.

According to Table 3.5, two opposite tendencies suggest a polarization between lower and highly skilled migrants. On the lower level of the occupation scale, there

Table 3.5 Occupational status of return migrants

Qualification groups	In Bulgaria before migration	Abroad	In Bulgaria after migration
Managers and team leaders	4.7	3.3	8.3
Specialists	9.6	3.4	19.3
Technicians and applied specialists	5.2	2.8	4.1
Assistants and administrative personnel	2.9	1.6	6.3
Employees in services for the population, trade, and security	29.0	26.2	21.6
Qualified workers in rural, forestry, fishery and hunting, etc.	5.7	10.6	4.3
Qualified workers and craftsmen	32.4	24.2	26.0
Machine operators and assemblers	1.9	1.0	1.0
Elementary occupations requiring no qualification	8.7	26.8	9.1

is the negative news for the sending country, described by an incomplete recovery of the pre-migration situation. In other words, after coming back home, many return migrants, who have been employed in low qualification jobs abroad, are not able to recover their former "higher" occupation and continue to work in underqualified jobs. These persons are obviously losing from the migration experience.

However, at the other pole there is some positive news for the sending country. There are only 4.7 % managers and team leaders before migration, compared to 3.3 % abroad and respectively surging up to 8.3 % after coming home. Apparently, these are the winners from migration. These are the ones for whom migration has opened new opportunities at home, the ones that have accumulated experience and skills which have promoted their careers. This positive scenario is particularly typical for the specialists, who constitute 9.6 % before migration, falling down to 3.4 % abroad, and doubling at 19.3 % after coming back home.

In short, according to the survey in Switzerland among the Bulgarian migrants, downward mobility prevails, which fits the two qualification shifts of downward mobility and unstable status identified in the interviews. Although their positions rise during the stay to the level of professionals and technicians, they do not regain the level of occupations they had back in Bulgaria. This trend is also explained by the interviews with the few cases who manage to take advantage of their skills or improve their situation after an initial process of deskilling. The return migrant data suggest two mobility patterns. On the one hand, returnees experience a decreasing qualification when it comes to comparing occupation at home and occupation abroad. Concerning the opportunity to re-enter the labour market at home, migration has a polarizing impact—the experience abroad increases the promotion chances for the top qualified positions such as managers and specialists, but at the same time sustains the low-qualified labour at the bottom of the occupational hierarchy. The data suggest, however, that the majority of returnees belong to the latter category. On the whole, taking into account all the data sources including the qualitative interviews, migration induces three qualification shifts: downward mobility, which is generally prevailing, upward or persistent mobility, typical for a limited circle of qualified migrants, and unstable status.

3.8 Economic Improvement Abroad

Because the mean income in the host country tends to be higher than in the sending country, downward mobility is often not linked to an economic worsening. In fact, according to the survey carried out in Switzerland, most migrants perceive an improvement of their material status (77.4 %), while only 3.2 % believe it has worsened. This positive attitude is consensual without any demographic fluctuations besides age (highest satisfaction in the middle age group) and, understandably, duration of stay, reaching 83.1 % of perceived positive change for the migrants that arrived in Switzerland before 2007. It is remarkable that there are no significant variations neither among ethnic nor educational groups. By contrast, the improvement is higher, the higher the social position is.

The perceptions about the change of the material status for the *migrants' households left back in Bulgaria*, since they arrived in Switzerland, are not entirely opposite, as could be speculated. The majority of the sample is actually divided between positive self-perceptions (improved, 23.2 %) or neutral ones (23.1 %, no change). Similar to the perceptions for the change *"since arriving in Switzerland"*, there is a minor part of the sample which sees a negative change for the Bulgarian households of the migrants. It should be taken into account, however, that 47 % of the respondents have actually no households in Bulgaria, reconfirming the settled type of migration in Switzerland. As expected, there is a significant correlation between the positive perception of the material status of the migrants' households in Bulgaria and the remittances sent to Bulgaria—37.8 % of the households who sent money to Bulgaria acknowledge the improved material status of their households in their home country, compared to only 11.7 % of those who do not send money to Bulgaria. There are indications that these remittances most frequently improve the material status of the lower strata migrants, such as workers engaged in elementary occupations (77.4 % improved material status in Bulgaria), compared to 19.5 % of the professionals.

It is difficult to immediately derive answers from the qualitative interviews for the question as to whether life quality changed in Switzerland. However, specific questions helped us in tracking life changes over time and support the view that at least the material level improved.

"My life in Switzerland changed at the material level for the better, but on a spiritual level for the worse (since) I had already a little shock, with the marriage, separation, then the fact of having to raise a daughter alone. (…) At the end, I also feel a bit as a foreigner there (in Bulgaria) as I feel here, because I have now adopted something from the mentality here" (female, 45, working as a bar manager in Switzerland).

Also, the return migrants in Bulgaria, such as the live-in care givers for example, often mentioned that the material living conditions were good compared with Bulgaria, but their round-the-clock job meant a great burden for them, if not indeed exploitation. In particular, the workers who went and found a job through an agent, often had to face very difficult conditions or even perceived their job as exploitation.

3.9 Income Inequality Abroad and Back Home

There is lack of research on the question of how economic inequalities among migrants from the same origin country change after emigration and remigration. In other words, if the high-skilled migrants profit more than the low-skilled ones, inequality will increase. Vice versa, presuming that the most poor do not emigrate (see Chap. 2), we expect instead a decrease in inequality.

The monthly median income of the entire household of Bulgarians in Switzerland is CHF 5700, while the median income per capita is CHF 3300. The income for the entire household significantly correlates with all socio-demographic variables. The income is higher in the class of middle age households (31–40 years, 44.2 % above CHF 7400) than younger households (up to 30 years, 25.3 % above CHF 7400). Education is also a strong predictor of income. Thus, 57.1 % of the respondents of university education report household incomes above CHF 7400 compared to only 5.4 % of the respondents with basic education. The income differences by ethnic groups are replicated. 36.4 % of Bulgarians are in the upper third of the income distribution (above CHF 7400), compared to half that number of Turks (16.7 %). The type of settlement in Bulgaria, where the households come from, is also a significant determinant of incomes. Thus, the number of migrants, coming from Sofia and having household incomes above CHF 7400, is 46.1 % compared to only 14.1 % of the migrants coming from villages.

The years spent in Switzerland and the permit type also have a significant impact on incomes. 71.4 % of the respondents whose household incomes are above CHF 7400 hold a residence type of permit, compared to only 12.1 % of the short-term migrants. Similarly, the number of respondents with household incomes above CHF 7400 is 43.4 % for the people who arrived in Switzerland by 2007, compared to 27.9 % of the ones arriving after 2007.

Table 3.6 unveils the distribution of migrants' incomes per capita by occupational level. Professionals and technicians are getting about 2.5 times the pay of the machine operators. Similarly wide is the gap between the pay of service and sales workers compared to the income of the workers engaged in elementary occupations, not to mention managers whose average pay is about three times the pay of the workers.

Furthermore, working migrants have higher incomes (CHF 3700 per capita) than students (CHF 2500 per capita). This is, however, not valid for all occupational groups. The survey data shows that migrants engaged in elementary and low-skilled occupations have even lower average incomes than students. Students get a median income per capita of about CHF 2500 per month, compared to CHF 2000 for the workers in elementary occupations and CHF 1750 for machine operators. Of course, this indicates the revenues of the students' parents rather than the labour incomes of the students. In addition, students' part-time jobs, offered by the students' labour offices in the universities, may provide higher earnings than the low-skilled jobs.

In short, the income gap in Bulgaria seems to be reproduced in Switzerland, if not getting even higher. Thus, the high income of the skilled working force and better educated groups suggest that the income gap between highly and low qualified migrants is even higher than in Bulgaria. However, according to the return migrants survey, both Roma and Bulgarian agricultural workers and former unemployed people are getting similar incomes abroad compared to their unequal incomes back home.

This peculiarity is typical for the lower occupational segment and is supported by data on the financial situation of *return migrants*, surveyed in Bulgaria. Comparing their level of income and financial welfare "before" "during", and

Table 3.6 Monthly income (median) in Switzerland per capita

Last activity: work code

Managers	Professionals	Technicians and associate professionals	Clerical support workers	Service and sales workers	Craft and related trade workers	Plant and machine operators and assemblers	Elementary occupations
6000	4375	4450	4750	2800	3575	1750	2000

Current activity

Work	Education	Taking care of family members	Other
3700	2500	2250	2625

Table 3.7 Income inequality abroad and back home*

Income indicators/BGN	In Bulgaria before migration	Abroad	Per capita after migration	Per capita total sample
Median income	500	2000	400	350
Arithmetic average income	546	2122	1002	529
Low 10 percentile	250	1000	167	150
High 90 percentile	900	3200	1000	750
Decile dispersion ratio (p90/p10)	3.6	3.2	5.98	5

*Based on return-migrants survey

"after" their stay abroad (see Table 3.7), the median income value of the Bulgarian return migrants while abroad is BGN 2000 per month with a mean value of BGN 2122 or about € 1000 in median terms, compared to only BGN 500 received in Bulgaria. The deviance around the median income abroad is comparatively low. The income abroad at the lowest 10 percentile is BGN 1000, while the return migrants located at the highest 90 percentile get BGN 3200, resulting in a decile dispersion ratio equal to 3.2.

This measure of inequality suggests a very low income gap among the Bulgarian migrants' communities abroad, which takes into account the comparatively high concentration of Bulgarian migrants in few low-skilled occupations and sectors. By contrast, the national decile dispersion ratio in the main host countries for the Bulgarian return migrants is much higher—Germany (6.67), United Kingdom (13.57), Spain (10.23), not to mention the countries of highest income inequality such as in Latin America (above 70 for most of the countries).

Of course, the median monthly income received abroad is significantly lower among the return migrants who have up to secondary education degree (BGN 1600), in comparison with those with university education (BGN 2000). Significant differences are also found by gender, revealing a median income for men equal to BGN 2000, compared to 1512 for women. Obviously, men are more often engaged in higher income occupations like construction or mechanical workshops, whereas women are employed in people-care services or "tourism and restaurants" companies. Significant also are differences based on the type of settlement in Bulgaria. Thus, the migrants who come from villages get a median income abroad of 1600 BGN, compared to 2000 for those coming from district centres.

Table 3.7 strongly underlines the importance of income differences as a push factor for migration. The median income increases four times, surging from BGN 500 to BGN 2000 when working abroad. Although the income after migration is not completely comparable, it suggests an insufficient recovery of the income levels once migrants return home. This corroborates our findings on occupational mobility. Low-skilled migrants who have to return home often lose their previous income status.

One of the most important findings, however, is that the income gap among the return migrants decreases abroad, but increases when they return home. The income gap, measured as a decile dispersion ratio, is the lowest when migrants are abroad

(3.2), compared to 3.6 before migration and about 6 after migration. This finding is confirmed by the differences among key socio-demographic groups, respectively, before and after migration. Thus, there are no income differences between Roma and Bulgarians abroad, for example. Both ethnic groups report the same median income amount of BGN 2000. By contrast, the difference between the Roma and the Bulgarians before migration is BGN 500 versus BGN 350 per month. This data corroborates our finding that Roma do not perceive discrimination in Switzerland (see Sect. 3.6).

Also the "settlement type" determinant here in the "before" sample is along the traditional division between Sofia (BGN 700) and country (about BGN 500), while in the "abroad" sample it is rather between villages and towns. Finally, the gender disparities also slightly decrease when migrants move abroad, although there is a clear division in male and female occupations. As shown earlier, women are getting about 75 % of the male income during their stay (about BGN 1500 vs. 2000), whereas before going abroad they received only 69 % of the male income (about BGN 350 vs. 500).

In summary, the data of return migrants, which is based mostly on lower social strata, comprising mostly unqualified and lower education workers, suggest that migration reduces the well-known inequalities among the ethnic groups in Bulgaria. However, we have to be aware that the highly paid managers and professionals probably stay abroad. In consequence, we suggest that—in line with the findings of the Swiss survey—the income gap among the higher social strata migrants is larger abroad than before the emigration.

Regarding insurance status and social benefits, the data indicates that the receiving countries tend to benefit, while the sending countries lose in terms of social welfare costs. According to the return-migrants survey, almost half of the Bulgarian migrants work abroad without a contract, being therefore deprived of any access to social benefits. Actually, only 3.4 % of the migrants had received any social benefits while they were abroad. When back home, return migrants become a burden to the local social assistance system, as unemployed and beneficiaries of social benefits. Once back home, the share of returnees receiving social benefits increased more than ten times soaring to 40.3 % compared to 3.4 % while abroad. Because they are unemployed back home, the health insurance status of the return migrants falls from 62.6 % (while working abroad) to 11.2 % (back home). In short, social insurance should consider a mobility pattern in which migrant workers are occupied abroad without contract and therefore induce no social insurance costs. When they get back home during the winter, they register as unemployed. Therefore, these unqualified migrants become dependent on the welfare system of the sending country.

3.10 Property Inequality Abroad

The survey carried out in Switzerland also provides an opportunity for comparing some key household properties and assets retained by the migrants, respectively, in Bulgaria and Switzerland such as real estate property, vehicles, and financial assets.

Thus, many migrants (51.8%) continue to hold real estate property in Bulgaria, while only 10.7% have acquired such property in Switzerland. These findings outline the fact that many migrants keep "property" bonds with Bulgaria. However, the real estate market in Bulgaria is cheap and affordable in comparison to the one in Switzerland. By contrast, Bulgarian migrants more frequently keep their financial assets in Switzerland (32.3%), than in Bulgaria (15.3%). Also, few Bulgarians in Switzerland keep vehicles in Bulgaria (22.2%), while more than half of them have retained vehicles in Switzerland (50.4%). Finally, real estate property on agricultural land, possessed by the migrants in Bulgaria, is much higher (15.7%) than in Switzerland (0.4%).

The differences in real estate property by occupation groups indicate increased gaps in Switzerland. 74% of the Bulgarian managers and 57% of the professionals possess real estate properties in Bulgaria versus 35.8% of the migrants occupied in elementary occupations. In Switzerland, the gap is bigger—20% for the managers and 14.6% among the professionals versus 3.8% of those with elementary jobs. Therefore, the property ratio of professionals to elementary jobs in Bulgaria is 1.6 rising to 3.8 in Switzerland.

In general, the distribution of high-value assets such as real estate property suggests that wealth inequality increases during the stay in Switzerland. In fact, higher paid Bulgarian migrants can acquire new real estate properties in Bulgaria, which indeed intensifies the inequality in property distribution in Bulgaria.

The impact of educational degrees is associated with smaller property gaps. For example, 60.4% of the university graduates hold real estate property in Bulgaria, compared to 43.1% of the people with secondary education. Real estate property retained in Switzerland is reported by 7.7% of migrants with secondary education versus 10.8% of university graduates, surging up to 23.6% of those with PhDs. Therefore, the ratio of university graduates to migrants of secondary education who hold real estate property in Bulgaria is equal to the ratio of the retained property in Switzerland (1.4).

By contrast, older people hold bigger financial and real estate assets, but the differences in Switzerland are bigger. For example, the number of migrants above 40, holding real estate property in Bulgaria is 60.8% versus 43.3% for the age group, e.g., up to 30, resulting in a ratio of about 1.4. Alternatively, this ratio for Swiss property is 15.9% versus 4.1% or 3.9.

However, the inequality in terms of low-price assets (such as in bank deposits) tends rather to decrease than increase in Switzerland when inequality is measured in financial assets (such as deposits). In Bulgaria the gap is bigger. Twenty four percent of managers and 18.4% of professionals have financial assets in Bulgaria, compared to 3.8% of the low-skilled migrants, which results in a ratio of 4.8 (professionals/unskilled workers). Alternatively, the same ratio regarding financial assets obtained in Switzerland is 1.8.

In contrast to income, focussing on high value assets such as real estate property, there is an increasing inequality among migrants in Switzerland, compared to their property status in Bulgaria. The stay in Switzerland preserves and to some extent aggravates wealth gaps among different professional, educational, and demographic groups. Vice versa, lower cost properties such as vehicles or bank deposits are more affordable than real estate properties. Therefore, inequality there, measured in such assets, decreases.

3.11 Remittances

There is a debate on the question of whether remittances reduce income and wealth inequalities back home (see Chap. 1). In general, especially family and friends in Bulgaria of those migrants interviewed in Southern Switzerland were quite grateful to their dear ones who left, particularly when they perceived the new economic status acquired by them. Thanks to their economic resources, they are able to support their family back home through remittances and occasional gifts (Sect. 6.6.3). All of the return migrants we interviewed sent remittances to their families. Only a few had no family back home and could dispose of their money as they liked (see Sect. 6.6.2). Sending remittances does not always mean that they send money regularly. Often, as the stays abroad are short, they return with all the money they earned.

According to the quantitative data, 44.4 % of the migrants in the survey carried out in Switzerland send money to Bulgaria. Although working migrants are most active, 18.9 % of the students also send money to Bulgaria. Sending money does not vary significantly according to the level of incomes nor the qualification of the migrants and sending remittances depends on the duration of stay (see Sect. 6.6.3).

Due to the low socio-economic profile of the beneficiaries, most of the money received is used either for consumption (61.7 %, multiple response), paying loans (11.3 %, most probably again for consumption), and covering social costs such as education of the children (9.6 %) and medical treatment (9.1 %). There are only 2.2 % beneficiaries who have purchased a vehicle with remittances and just 1.4 % have used the support for starting a small business. This leads, as we could observe with various poorer communities in villages, to a vicious circle (that is often also coupled with circular migration), where migration only suffices for the daily costs and does not secure a living for the family by founding a business.

Remittances along with the sending of goods emerge as social transfers, reducing social contrasts and increasing deep poverty. It is remarkable how precisely remittances are targeted at the most needy social strata. The data on the usage of remittances verifies the social nature of the remittances describing it as "humanitarian" aid and a serious factor for stimulating basic consumption, rather than an investment opportunity in development terms. In general, the data describes remittances and transfer of goods as a factor in reducing social inequalities and welfare contrasts by providing social benefits to the most vulnerable people: almost 20 % of the poorest rely entirely on remittances. By contrast, having a close person abroad, most often a student, implies higher costs for the better-off strata.

3.12 Conclusions

This chapter focuses on economic inequalities as a major driver of migration, the migrants' experience of occupational and income mobility, and the social inequalities between migrants in the home country and in the host country. First of all, the data suggest that most of the Bulgarian migrants in Switzerland are women, are young, and relatively well-qualified, particularly the ones who arrived since the entry of Bulgaria into the EU in 2007. In accordance with the sociological labour market research, the surveys underline the function of social capital in job search and settlement. However, social capital is more important for low-skilled migrants than for high-skilled migrants who are primarily supported by their employers. The central motivation of migrants is primarily the wish to improve their personal economic situation. Although this goal is realized by most migrants, they often admit that they miss their social peers back home. Even though the survey carried out in Switzerland indicates some upward mobility, most migrants experience downward mobility to lower occupational positions and low-skilled economic sectors. Thus, in comparison to Bulgaria, the shares in lower status occupations and in elementary occupations increase sharply in Switzerland. However, many migrants are able to compensate for the status decline in the course of their stay. The data of the return migrants suggests that migration is a "win-win game". On the one hand, migration pays out for the host country as its employers win a highly skilled workforce whose education is paid by the Bulgarian state. On the other hand, Bulgaria profits from the export of unemployment.

If the migrants return home, they are often pushed into lower social positions or even unemployment. The social costs, including those for unemployment benefits and related insurance costs for the unemployed return migrants, weigh on the sending country, which actually reverts into a receiving country for them. While many well-qualified return migrants can preserve or even improve their occupational status, the low-skilled return migrants risk the experience of downward mobility. These "objective" shifts in professional status, downgrading the occupational and respective social status of migrants, often result in inferiority self-perceptions in regard to the local community. However, only few Bulgarian migrants in Switzerland report an experience of discrimination. In the foreground is the fact of either non-existent and non-accredited certificates or unacknowledged skills. In addition, low-skilled migrants as well as Turks and Roma are particularly affected.

The findings on the income of the migrants and on the income gap between the migrants in both countries suggest that the income of the Bulgarian migrants depends on education, gender, and ethnicity. While working abroad increases the incomes of all social strata, income gaps and inequality depend on the level of qualification and occupational status. Income gaps among low qualified workers decrease abroad compared to Bulgaria, narrowing, for example, the incomes of Roma and Bulgarians, pointing to the fact that most of them work in similar fields. Alternatively, the income gaps among the middle and upper qualification groups increase abroad compared to Bulgaria, actually reproducing the inequality patterns of the receiving country and reflecting the differing opportunities available for this group. The survey carried out in Switzerland suggests instead that income inequality increases after migration for the upper social segment comprising highly skilled and well-educated workers and decreases for the low-skilled workers. In summary, this results in a decreased inequality for all Bulgarian migrants at first, whereas some migrants of the upper social segment manage to secure better opportunities which results in an increased social inequality over time again.

The data on distribution of property and financial assets verifies the stratified pattern of inequality. While working abroad increases inequality measured by high value assets such as real estate property, welfare gaps actually decrease abroad compared to Bulgaria if measured with lower value assets such as vehicles or availability of deposits. Therefore, our study suggests that inequality shifts are not universal among all migrants. Changes in inequality are stratified along social strata and are particularly associated with higher occupational skills and professional positions.

Finally, our findings suggest that the inequalities between migrants are generally reproduced in the host country and fostered back home. There are specificities, indicating that higher social segment inequalities, associated with qualified workers and related to high value property assets, increase, while inequalities typical for the lower social strata decrease and become more acute in Bulgaria when they return home. By contrast, the gender and ethnic inequalities tend to decrease rather than increase in the host country. Therefore, the data suggests that migration may be able to combat deep poverty and social contrasts, but it also brings inequality for the upper social layers, while downgrading their occupational level while they are abroad.

Whether migration is a "win-win game" from which both countries profit, the host country due to the import of cheap high-skilled labour and the home country due to the export of unemployment, remains an open question. In any case, future research should be aware that migrants who fail abroad often turn back and might even reinforce current social problems.

References

Amelina, A. (2010). *Scaling inequalities. Some steps towards the inequality analysis in migration research beyond the framework of the nation state* (COMCAD Working papers, No. 91, 2010). Retrieved August 25, 2015, from https://www.uni-bielefeld.de/tdrc/ag_comcad/downloads/Workingpaper_91.pdf.

Anthias, F. (2007). Ethnic ties: Social capital and the question of mobilisability. *The Sociological Review, 55*(4), 788–805.

Black, R., Natali, C., & Skinner, J. (2005). *Migration and inequality*. World Development Report 2006, Background Papers.

Bourdieu, P. (1986). The forms of capital. In J. G. Richardson (Ed.), *Handbook of theory and research for the sociology of education* (pp. 241–258). New York: Greenwood Press.

Collins, R. (1979). *The credential society*. New York: Academic.

D'Amato, G., & Fibbi, R. (2007). Bürgerschaftspolitik statt Neopatriotismus. Zur Debatte über Integration. *Widerspruch, 51*, 75–83.

D'Amato, G. (2001). *Vom Ausländer zum Bürger. Der Streit um die politische Integration von Einwanderern in Deutschland, Frankreich und der Schweiz.* Münster: LIT.

Ebeke, C., & Le Goff, M. (2011). *Why migrants' remittances reduce income inequality in some countries and not in others?* Retrieved August 25, 2015, from https://halshs.archives-ouvertes.fr/halshs-00554277.

Faist, T. (2008). Migrants as transnational development agents. An inquiry into the newest round of the migration-development nexus. *Population, Space and Place, 14,* 21–42.

Fullin, G., & Reyneri, E. (2010). Low unemployment and bad jobs for new migrants in Italy. *International Migration, 49*(1), 118–147.

Gans, H. J. (2007). Acculturation, assimilation, and mobility. *Ethnic and Racial Studies, 30*(1), 152–164.

Gans, H. J. (2009). First generation decline: Downward mobility among refugees and immigrants. *Ethnic and Racial Studies, 32*(9), 1658–1670.

Girard, E., & Bauder, H. (2007). Assimilation and exclusion of foreign trained engineers in Canada. Inside a professional regulatory organization. *Antipode, 39*(1), 35–53.

Glytsos, N. P. (2010). Theoretical considerations and empirical evidence on brain drain grounding the review of Albania's and Bulgaria's experience. *International Migration, 48*(39), 107–130.

Granovetter, M. S. (1973). The strength of weak ties. *American Journal of Sociology, 78*(6), 1360–1380.

Granovetter, M. S. (1983). The strength of weak ties: A network theory revisited. *Sociological Theory, 1,* 201–233.

Guarnizo, L. E. (1997). The emergence of a transnational social formation and the mirage of return migration among Dominican transmigrants. *Identities, 4*(2), 281–322.

Haug, W. (2006). *Migranten und ihre Nachkommen auf dem Arbeitsmarkt: Ein Überblick. Demos Informationen aus der Demographie.* Neuchâtel: Bundesamt für Statistik.

Jaccard Ruedin, H. & Weaver, F. (2009). *Ageing workforce in an ageing society.* Wie viel Health Professionals braucht das Schweizer Gesundheitssystem bis 2030?. Careum Working Papers.

Kahanec, M., & Zimmermann, K. F. (2009). International migration, ethnicity and economic inequality. In W. Salverda, B. Nolan, & T. M. Smeeding (Eds.), *The oxford handbook of economic inequality* (pp. 455–490). Oxford: Oxford University Press.

Kelly, P., & Lusis, T. (2006). Migration and the transnational habitus: Evidence from Canada and the Philippines. *Environment and Planning A, 38,* 831–847.

León-Ledesma, M., & Piracha, M. (2004). International migration and the role of remittances in Eastern Europe. *International Migration, 42*(2), 65–83.

Lin, N. (2001). *Social capital: A theory of social structure and action.* New York: Cambridge University Press.

Markova, E. (2010). *Effects of migration on sending countries: Lessons from Bulgaria* (GreeSE Paper No 35).

Mazzucato, V. (2011). Reverse remittances in the migration-development nexus: Two-way flows between Ghana and the Netherlands. *Population, Space and Place, 17,* 454–468.

Milanovic, B. (2011). *Global inequality. From class to location, from proletarians to migrants* (Policy Research Working Paper 5820).

Morawska, E. (2008). *East European Westbound income-seeking migrants: Some unwelcome effects on sender- and receiver-societies* (Working Paper Series of the Research Network 1989, Nr. 16). Retrieved August 25, 2015, from http://nbn-resolving.de/urn:nbn:de:0168-ssoar-27195.

Mountz, A. (2011). Specters at the port of entry: Understanding state mobilities through an ontology of exclusion. *Mobilities, 6*(3), 317–334.

Papademetriou, D. G., Somerville, W., & Sumption, M. (2009). *The social mobility of immigrants and their children.* Migration Policy Institute. Retrieved August 25, 2015, from http://migrationpolicy.org/pubs/soialmobility2010.pdf.

Parkin, F. (1979). *Marxism and class theory: A bourgeois critique.* New York: Columbia University Press.

Pecoraro, M. (2005). Les migrants hautement qualifiés. In W. Haug & P. Wanner (Eds.), *Migrants et marché du travail: Compétences et insertion professionnelle des personnes d'origine étrangère en Suisse* (pp. 71–110). Neuchâtel: Bundesamt für Statistik.

Riaño, Y., & Baghdadi, N. (2007). Understanding the labour market participation of skilled immigrant women in Switzerland. The role of class, ethnicity and gender. *Journal of International Migration and Integration, 8*, 163–183.

Richter, M. (2011). Topographien der Ungleichheit. Dequalifikation als ein weibliches Phänomen? *Berichte zur deutschen Landeskunde, 85*(1), 49–59.

Savage, M., Warde, A., & Devine, F. (2005). Capitals, assets, and resources: Some critical issues. *The British Journal of Sociology, 56*(1), 31–47.

Weiss, A. (2005). The transnationalization of social inequality: Conceptualizing social positions on a world scale. *Current Sociology, 53*(4), 707–728.

Wessendorf, S. (2008). Culturalist discourses on inclusion and exclusion: The Swiss citizenship debate. *Social Anthropology, 16*(2), 187–202.

Winchie, D. B., & Carment, D. W. (1989). Migration and motivation: The migrant's perspective. *International Migration Review, 23*(1), 96–104.

Chapter 4
Assessing Regional Disparities in Bulgaria and Switzerland

Venelin Boshnakov, Vesselin Mintchev, Georgi Shopov, and Iordan Kaltchev

4.1 Introduction

Regional disparities are closely linked to the issue of divergence of countries and regions, to the extent to which the spread of a particular economic phenomenon differs between the regions of a given country (OECD 2003). This provides a somewhat narrow concept of regional disparity which relates mainly to the territorial divergence in economic activity indicators, e.g. production (GDP per capita) and labour market (employment and unemployment rates). In a much broader context, this concept involves consideration of a variety of aspects of socio-economic, demographic, infrastructure, and human development dimensions.

Traditionally, the issues of regional disparities, development, and convergence are discussed in the specialized literature in a cross-country analytical framework. A major aspect here is whether the initial economic conditions determine the economic disparities regarding countries' development. If not, then in view of the neoclassical postulates, the convergence is in place if certain structural economic indicators are controlled in a similar way. Thus, in their development, countries and regions tend towards one general equilibrium ratio (i.e. a general model of economic development, in the words of Solow 1956). If the initial conditions are key factors, then the countries and regions should follow different development models

V. Boshnakov (✉)
University of National and World Economy, Sofia, Bulgaria
e-mail: venelinb@unwe.bg

V. Mintchev • G. Shopov
Economic Research Institute at the Bulgarian Academy of Sciences, Sofia, Bulgaria
e-mail: v.mintchev@abv.bg; shopov@club2000.org

I. Kaltchev
"Neofit Rilski" South-West University, Blagoevgrad, Bulgaria
e-mail: ikaltchev@abv.bg

© Springer International Publishing Switzerland 2017
M. Richter et al. (eds.), *Migration and Transnationalism Between Switzerland and Bulgaria*, DOI 10.1007/978-3-319-31946-9_4

complying with the specific initial conditions, i.e. the economic development cannot be expected to always lead to convergence.

In the light of these two patterns, the debate on the economic convergence of the European countries becomes an important field of research (Puga 2002; Fischer and Stirböck 2006; Artelaris et al. 2010). The empirical analysis of convergence often involves selected differential approaches between countries as described by Nenovski and Figuet (2006). Initially used for economic growth analysis (Sala-i-Martin 2002), convergence models have been later applied to the study of economic integration of Central and Eastern European Countries. For instance, Mullineux and Murinde (2003) apply this approach to the convergence of the financial sector of post-communist economies and of bank income in particular; Vinhas De Souza and Holschner (2000) to the behaviour of interest rates; and Crespo-Cuaresma et al. (2003) to the study of regional disparities within the EU.

Since the Ravenstein's laws (1885, 1889), the linkage of regional disparities with migration is a core element of the migration theories. Neoclassical functionalists interpret it as an efficient mechanism of resources allocation, while for the historical structuralists migration processes increase the inequalities. In the context of the migration transition approach, it is seen as a common characteristic of development—somehow paradoxically—the more developed country or region, the more involved in human mobility (De Haas 2010).

Thus, the conclusion is twofold. In a static neo-classical world, migration can have an equilibrating effect. Contrariwise, the dynamic approach of historical structuralists (when considering the time dimension, i.e., changing productivity and migrants' behaviour across the years) outlines clear disparity effects of migration.

Other authors underline the low responsiveness of European migration to regional disparities in both per capita income and unemployment rates, in comparison to the United States. Thus, it is not possible to rely on labour force mobility as a mechanism for adjusting to idiosyncratic shocks in the Eurozone, and alternative adjustment mechanisms will be required for this purpose. Bentivogli and Pagano (1999) assessed whether regional disparities in the euro area stimulate labour mobility using migration behaviour in US states as a benchmark. The study shows that the level of United States immigration flows with respect to population is very similar to that in the Euro area, but sensitivity to regional disparities differs considerably. Migration is much more significantly influenced by income disparities in the United States than it is in the Euro-11, both in the short and the long term. Furthermore, the responsiveness of net migration inflows to shocks to the relative unemployment rate is negative in the regions of the United States, but nil in those of the Euro-11. Finally, risk factors are significant determinants of migration decisions in Europe, but not in the United States.

Albeit unemployment rates and average wages indeed affect migration in transition economies, the pattern is only imperfectly consistent with migration facilitating regional adjustment to shocks. Fidrmuc (2004) argues that for the elimination of the consequences of asymmetric shocks, gross and net immigration should be positively correlated with average wages and negatively correlated with unemployment, whereas gross emigration should be positively correlated with unemployment and negatively correlated with wages. He comes, however, to the conclusions that a similar pattern is not observed for migration processes in the Central European economies.

The above-presented judgements differ in their argumentation on how regional disparities affect migration patterns, and even some conflicting conclusions are drawn. In some studies, regional disparities in terms of labour demand, wage, and unemployment are considered to encourage overall migration, while others prove that European migration shows low responsiveness to regional disparities in both per capita income and unemployment.

In any case, the regional disparities in sending countries are expected to affect the attitudes of people who intend to migrate (potential migrants). Potential migrants are of particular importance for demographic, development, and political reasons (see Chap. 2). Accordingly, we expect that the more developed the region, the weaker the migration pressure, and vice versa. However, very often the depressed regions are deficient in young population, considered as the main recruitment contingent of out-migration flows. On the other hand, the spread of return migration depends on the overall involvement of the local population in international migration processes, rather than on regional disparities. Besides, the differentiation in regional development levels at host countries naturally influences the attractiveness of the regions to the immigrant population. Thus, we expect that the more developed the receiving region, the more attractive to migrants.

The main goals of the study in this chapter are focused on:

- The evaluation of regional disparities in a typical sending country such as Bulgaria and in a typical receiving country such as Switzerland.
- The assessment of the interaction between the regional spread of migrants and the main indicators of regional development.
- The regional profiles of potential migrants in a sending country and those of the actual migrants in a receiving country.

The chapter is structured with the following sections:

- Methodological framework
- Regional socio-economic disparities in Bulgaria
- Regional drivers for migration in Bulgaria
- Potential and return migrants in Bulgaria per district ranking
- Regional socio-economic disparities in Switzerland
- Regional drivers for Bulgarian migration in Switzerland
- Profiles of Bulgarians in Switzerland per canton ranking

4.2 Methodological Framework

The assessment of regional disparities through a composite measure seems quite appropriate since it integrates a wide range of relevant indicators and ranks the territorial units by their distance to, e.g., the country-average score. The description of selected individual characteristics of the mobile population (potential or actual migrants) partitioned into homogeneous groups of territorial units in both sending and receiving countries (such as Switzerland and Bulgaria) can show if and how the existing disparities "regionalize" the migration attitudes.

When choosing a methodological framework, we have considered two main alternatives: the taxonomy model and the more popular Morris method (see Harbinson et al. 1970; Isard 1975; Narain et al. 2009). The latter is typically applied for spatial analysis and planning since it ranks regional units by averaging their individual scores on the primary indicators (Morris 1979). This way, the average score is used for ranking of regions or cities by their position as compared to the unit having the best score on each indicator. The Morris index averages the relative scores for each regional unit "i" obtained for all primary variables $(j = 1,\ldots,n)$:

Thereafter, we apply the taxonomic method—also known as Wroclaw taxonomy method—which is a refined approach as compared to the Morris technique. It has been suggested in 1968 by the UNESCO expert Zdzisław Hellwig (1968) for cross-country comparisons; however, it proved to be convenient for quantifying the intra-national territorial socio-economic disparities.

Taxonomic studies treat the territorial units (for example, regions, districts, municipalities) as multi-dimensional objects. The term "multi-dimensional object" is used for the purposes of defining the theoretical basis of this approach. Each multi-dimensional object is defined by a set of expertly selected indicators and can be presented as a point in the corresponding n-dimensional Euclidean space, the number of whose coordinates coincides with the number of analyzed indicators. The essence of the applied method is as follows:

- Each territorial unit is characterized as a set (system) of socio-economic indicators and is treated as a multi-dimensional object.
- On the basis of a set of selected indicators, an "integral score" assessing the level of the development of each territorial unit is calculated.
- All indicators are standardized, which converts them into comparable values.
- All territorial units are presented as points in the corresponding n-dimensional Euclidean space, where n is the number of indicators used.
- The comparison is drawn with a fictional territorial unit—"a benchmark", which is characterized by the most favourable extreme (maximal or minimal) values of the individual indicators of the territorial units, which are subject to analysis.
- The levels of development of the specific territorial unit are assessed via its distance from the "benchmark", and on that basis comparison and ranking are elaborated. The smaller the distance, the higher its level of development, and vice versa (i.e. the lower the value of the calculated integral score, the closer the territorial unit is to the "benchmark").

The regional socio-economic disparities are assessed at NUTS-3 level, as follows: all 28 Bulgarian districts, located in 6 regions (NUTS-2 level), and 26 cantons of Switzerland, grouped in 7 regions. As mentioned earlier in Chap. 1, the so-called "NUTS" (*nomenclature des unités territoriales statistiques*) itself is an EU geocode standard for referencing the subdivisions of countries for statistical purposes.

Fifteen indicators are used for assessing the level of socio-economic development of each of the 28 Bulgarian districts and nine indicators for the 26 Swiss cantons. Their selection is mainly based on the framework of the regional studies of Eurostat applying a wide set of indicators (EC 2012, 2015). In particular, our selection includes standard indicators from the following general areas (e.g. Demography, Economy, Labour market, Infrastructure, Household well-being, Education, and Healthcare), which are typically used for analysis of regional profiles also at country-level studies (Kostadinova et al. 2014; Kutscherauer et al. 2010). The set of indicators is constructed according to the availability and accessibility of data at NUTS-3 level for both countries.

The level of socio-economic development of each territorial unit is assessed by an integral score calculated on the basis of the respective indicators by applying the taxonomic method. In order to provide opportunities for comparison of the territorial units with the mean national level, the average values of the analyzed indicators are combined to constitute a separate country-level unit. Thus, the regional socio-economic disparities are analyzed on the basis of a matrix of 420 indicators for Bulgaria and 243 for Switzerland. The study uses data for the year 2012 from the Bulgarian National Statistical Institute and from the Swiss federal statistical office, available at the end of 2014 (NSI 2014, SFSO 2014).

Following the value of their integrated scores, the territorial units could be divided into three groups applying the following *thresholds*.

1. The first group (well-developed districts) consists of territorial units with scores below the country mean score (threshold 1), i.e. which rank *above* the national average.
2. The second group (medium level of development) includes territorial units whose scores are in the range between the country mean and threshold 2. The second threshold is obtained as the mean plus 50 % of the difference between the lowest and the average score. It is a conditional threshold which should allow for a distinct differentiation of the third group of units—those which lag substantially behind in terms of their socio-economic development.

4.3 Regional Socio-Economic Disparities in Bulgaria

The assessment of the regional socio-economic disparities in Bulgaria is performed using the presented taxonomic methodology and analyzing data for a selection of appropriate indicators. As a result, multidimensional ordering of regional units (districts) is obtained which allows further exploration of the nexus between regional discrepancies and migration. Fifteen indicators are used for assessing the level of socio-economic development of each of the 28 Bulgarian districts (NUTS 3 Level). They are grouped and enumerated (1–15) as follows (see also Table 4.1):

Table 4.1 Grouping of Bulgarian districts according to level of their socio-economic development

Rank	District (NUTS 3 level)	Region (NUTS 2 level)	Score	Rank	District (NUTS 3 level)	Region (NUTS 2 level)	Score
	Group I:			14	Smolyan	SCR	0.7853
1	Sofia (capital)	CWR	0.3889	15	Dobrich	NER	0.7870
2	Bulgaria		0.6173	16	Yambol	SER	0.8090
	Group II:			17	Kurdjali	SCR	0.8261
3	Varna	NER	0.6521	18	Haskovo	SCR	0.8337
4	Gabrovo	NCR	0.6601	19	Shumen	NER	0.8377
5	Stara Zagora	SER	0.6656	20	Pernik	NWR	0.8407
6	Russe	NCR	0.6787	21	Pazardjik	SCR	0.8466
7	Plovdiv	SCR	0.6802	22	Kustendil	CWR	0.8655
8	Sofia (district)	SWR	0.7024	23	Montana	NWR	0.8709
9	Burgas	SER	0.7153	24	Lovech	NWR	0.8712
10	Blagoevgrad	SWR	0.7158	25	Turgovishte	NER	0.8869
11	VelikoTarnovo	NCR	0.7340	26	Vidin	NWR	0.8941
	Group III:			27	Razgrad	NCR	0.8946
12	Vratsa	NWR	0.7578	28	Sliven	SER	0.9091
13	Pleven	NWR	0.7706	29	Silistra	NCR	0.9183

Notation: *NWR* north-western region, *NCR* north-central region, *NER* north-eastern region, *SER* south-eastern region, *SCR* south-central region, *SWR* south-western region

4.3.1 Demographic Conditions

Natural growth rate (the difference between the numbers of births and deaths, standardized per 1000 inhabitants) The indicator characterizes fundamentally the status of the demographic system reflecting the perspectives for natural reproduction in the region.

Migration coefficient (the balance of those who are settled minus those who have left the respective territorial unit, standardized per 1000 inhabitants) This demographic indicator is traditionally considered as highly sensitive to the socio-economic and political environment, reflecting favourable or adverse conditions for career realization, adequate remuneration, and enhanced living standards.

Age dependency ratio (ratio of the number of people aged 65+ and those aged 15–64) The indicator directly characterizes the degree of ageing of the population and the demographic viability of the respective territorial unit.

Share of people with higher education in the total population The indicator reflects the educational attainment of the local population.

4.3.2 Labour Market

Employment rate (ratio of the number of employed and the population aged 15+)
The indicator reflects the degree to which individuals of working age manage to find work in the domestic economy. In more general terms, this rate accounts for the balance between the local economy (the demand for labour) and the economically active individuals (the supply of labour).

Unemployment rate (ratio of the number of unemployed and total labour force)
This is a standard indicator which is expected to represent the local mix of economic and social characteristics.

4.3.3 Local Economy

GDP per capita This is the most common indicator involved in regional analyses and comparisons, which reflects the utilized capacity of the local economic system. The higher the value of the indicator, the stronger and more developed the economy of the respective territorial unit and, respectively, the higher the living standard of the local population.

Labour productivity (ratio between the Gross Value Added and the number of employed in the region) This is another standard macroeconomic measure of the overall efficiency of the local economy.

4.3.4 Transport Infrastructure

Availability of transport infrastructure The indicator reflects the density of transport infrastructure and is measured by the length of railway and road network per 1000 km^2 of a region's area. Under the conditions of intensified economic activity, the degree of local development strongly depends upon the availability and quality of the transport network.

4.3.5 Poverty and Household Incomes

Income per household member This indicator is a classical measure of the living standard applied in regional disparity analyses.

Population at risk of poverty or social exclusion This is a combined indicator which incorporates three sub-indicators: risk of poverty, intensity of economic activity, and material deprivation.

4.3.6   Education and Healthcare

Share of pupils (grades 1–12) in total population This indicator reflects the degree to which the educational system encompasses individuals in school age (up to age of 19) in the respective territorial unit.

Share of university students in total population Availability of higher educational institutions and access to them are considered as factors for enhancing the local pool of human capital.

Doctors per 100,000 inhabitants. The availability of medical doctors is one of the main qualitative indicators which portrays the state of local healthcare system and the overall standard of living.

Number of hospital beds per 100,000 inhabitants This indicator complements the previous one in characterizing the local healthcare system by reflecting the degree of availability of hospital services in the region.

The mosaic of socio-economic disparities in 2012 is revealed on the basis of the integral scores for the level of regional development of the 28 districts in Bulgaria (Tables 4.1 and 4.2). Their analysis suggests particular findings which allow us to emphasize on several main points.

According to their level of socio-economic development, the Bulgarian districts can be differentiated into three main groups:

Table 4.2 Mean indicator levels by groups of socio-economic development of districts

	Socio-economic indicators, 2012	Group I	Group II	Group III	Total BG
1	Natural growth rate (net, per 1000 inhabitants)	−8.57	−7.05	−7.50	−7.40
2	Migration coefficient (net, per 1000 inhabitants)	5.34	−0.94	−3.60	−2.43
3	Age dependency ratio (%)	41.0	49.7	52.7	51.3
4	Share of population with tertiary education (%)	36.8	17.6	13.5	15.6
5	Employment rate (%)	66.9	59.3	54.8	56.6
6	Unemployment rate (%)	7.30	11.03	15.72	13.91
7	GDP per capita (BGN)	23,108	9349	6471	7990
8	Labour productivity (GVA/employed, BGN)	38,688	18,096	13,034	15,577
9	Transport infrastructure (km of roads, per 1000 sq. km)	213	187	180	184
10	Income per household member (BGN)	6403	4066	3677	3899
11	Risk of poverty or social exclusion (%)	39.0	48.6	51.4	50.1
12	Share of pupils (grades 1–12) in the total population of 7–19 age group (%)	76.3	72.2	72.1	72.3
13	Share of university students in total population (%)	8.30	4.64	0.52	2.12
14	Doctors (per 100 thousand inhabitants)	478	372	321	343
15	Hospital beds (per 100 thousand inhabitants)	719	662	548	591

- The first group should consist of well-developed districts whose scores are above the country average. In 2012, this group is represented only by Sofia (capital city), wherein a large share of the country's economic potential is concentrated. It is an unusual situation, since in the studies of the previous years (e.g. Yankova et al. 2010) the first group includes 3–4 districts—however, other recent studies have also outlined the capital city as a separate one-unit cluster (e.g. Kostadinova et al. 2014). Sofia's integral score is considerably different from other districts' scores—40 % beyond the second ranked (district of Varna; its score diverges from the third one by only 1.2 %). The substantial contrast of the capital city for the year 2012 can be explained not only by the concentration of the country's economic potential there (including companies, foreign investors' headquarters, favourable infrastructure, access to qualified labour resources, lowest unemployment and poverty, etc.), but also by the assumed lowest degree of adverse impact of the financial crisis 2009–2010.
- The second group includes nine districts with an average level of development. The leading position in the group is assumed by one of the most dynamic districts of the country—Varna (North Eastern Region—NER): its score is nonetheless close to the average, but too far from the score of Sofia-capital. Otherwise Group II has a higher level of socio-economic development as opposed to those in the third group. The main dimensions of the favourable position of these districts are: GDP per capita (9.6 K. BGN against 6.5 K. BGN), labour productivity (18 K. BGN against 13 K. BGN), unemployment (11 % against 15.7 %), health infrastructure (662 hospital beds per 100 thousand residents, against 548 beds), share of tertiary educated population (17.6 % against 13.5 %), etc. In general, their socio-economic status is relatively balanced, sustainable, and provides comparatively better living conditions contrasted to Group III districts.
- Group III contains twice as many districts (18), however with almost half the average population size. Along with the aforementioned economic and labour market conditions these districts have also notable demographic downfalls revealed by the net migration rate −3.6 (−0.9 for Group II), the share of students in the local population 0.5 % (4.6 %), and to some extent the age dependency ratio 53 % (50 %). The overall living conditions in Group III districts can be described as considerably unfavourable, particularly regarding the bottom-ranked districts (with scores higher than 0.85, which is quite far from the country average score 0.62).

4.4 Regional Drivers for Migration in Bulgaria

The association between the level of regional socio-economic development and the degree of involvement of the Bulgarian population in migration processes is of special interest for our discussion. In this respect, on the basis of the available survey data, we can outline the following facts.

- About 18 % of the total population of the country in 2013 resides in the capital city of Sofia (Level-I of the regional socio-economic development). At the same time, the share of long-term potential migrants (settlers, labour, and educational long-term migrants, as indicated in Chap. 2) located in the city is *two times lower* (9.1 %). This result is indicative in respect of the association between the regional disparities and migration attitudes—the residents in the regional unit with the most favourable living environment have the lowest propensity to engage in migration practices spanning more than a year. Similar misbalance is observed for the share of return migrants located in Sofia (12 %)—a plausible explanation could be the lower rates of re-migration of Bulgarian migrants originating from Sofia, perhaps due to a more stable position abroad.
- These parameters do not diverge so much in respect of the districts in Group II—they host 42 % of the total population, but 48 % of the identified long-term potential migrants are residents of these districts. Comparable, too, is the spread of mobile population considering the share of return migrants located in districts of Group II (47 %).
- About 40 % of the country's population resides in the districts categorized in Group III. The shares of long-term potential migrants (43 %) and mobile residents (about 41 %) are more or less proportional to the total population share, which indicates proportional involvement and attitudes on the part of local residents towards any external migration activities.

Furthermore, the associations between the indicators generating the integral score and the degree of migratory involvement of the district's residents have been explored using the correlation analysis. The following two variables have been constructed and data at district level has been calculated:

- Number of potential migrants (all types) per 100 district residents;
- Number of return migrants per 100 district residents (here the widest definition has been applied: an individual with at least 1 month stay abroad during the last 5 years).

Pearson predict-moment correlation coefficients have been calculated for each of these variables and each of the indicators which constitute the integral score. This provides an opportunity to evaluate any assumed interaction between the regional socio-economic development indicators and the degree of migratory involvement of local residents.

4.4.1 Correlations with the Concentration of Potential Migrants

A positive, albeit weak, correlation of the variable "Potential migrants per 100 district residents" is estimated with the following indicators: natural growth rate (0.23), employment rate (0.26), household income per capita (0.15), and risk of poverty or social exclusion (0.10). Negative but also weak correlation is measured for the following variables: unemployment rate (−0.16), GDP per capita (−0.13), labour productivity (−0.15), transport infrastructure (−0.14), share of the persons with higher education (−0.11), share of pupils (−0.17), doctors per 100 K (−0.13), and hospital beds per 100 K (−0.13). Three variables have correlations less than 0.1 (in absolute values), so we do not consider them to show any notable relation with the potential migrants concentration variable (net migration rate, age dependency ratio, and the share of students in the total population).

Although the estimated measures of association are not high, we observe that the allocation of potential migrants is:

- Slightly more intense in districts with higher natural growth rate, higher risk of poverty, but also higher household income per capita.
- Somehow less intense in districts which are in a better economic position (e.g. higher production level per capita, labour productivity, and educated population), better transport, and health infrastructure.

Some of the results seem contradictory, e.g. regarding the unemployment variable which is (expectedly) negatively correlated with the GDP per capita for Bulgarian districts. Here we have also a slight negative correlation (−0.16) with potential migrants' concentration due to several outliers—districts with peculiar interaction of the two variables. According to Fig. 4.1, Shoumen, Razgrad, and Vidin districts have high unemployment levels (26.6, 21.4, and 17.4 %); however, the estimated potential migration variable shows quite low values there (11.2, 9.4, and 10.2 migrants per 100 district residents). These are typical districts with exhausted migration potential—even with difficult labour market conditions, outmigration intentions are rarely expressed as compared to the other districts.

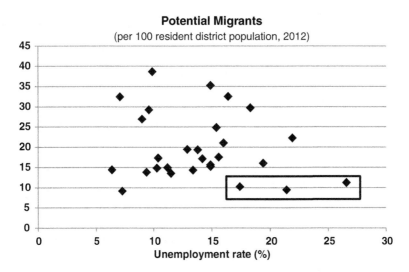

Fig. 4.1 Scatter diagram of the Bulgarian districts based on regional unemployment level and estimated concentration of potential migration

The sign of correlation coefficient with the GDP per capita is negative (−0.13) which was initially expected—i.e. higher GDP per capita weakly associated with lower migration potential. However, this is due to a substantial outlier as the city of Sofia (Fig. 4.2).

If the correlation is calculated without the Sofia city data point, the coefficient value obtains a positive sign (+0.16) which conforms to the estimated positive correlation between the potential migration variable and the regional household income level (+0.15). This provides additional evidence to the assertion met in the literature (e.g. De Haas 2010) that outmigration is related to the funding capability, which is naturally found in relatively higher developed regions.

4.4.2 Correlations with the Concentration of Return Migrants (Mobile Individuals)

A different picture is revealed by the correlations of the variable "Return migrants per 100 district residents" with the indicators:

- Positive: natural growth rate (moderate correlation: 0.35).
- Negative: age dependency ratio (−0.18); share of the persons with higher education (−0.14), transport infrastructure (−0.20), labour productivity (−0.15), and GDP per capita (−0.11).

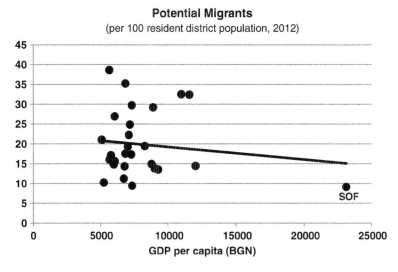

Fig. 4.2 Scatter diagram of the Bulgarian districts based on regional GDP per capita and estimated concentration of potential migration

- All the others have shown correlations less than 0.1 and are not considered hereafter.

This variable does not have any high correlation values with the indicators constituting the integral score, so we can fairly assert that individuals with higher migration experience are relatively:

- More concentrated in districts with higher natural growth rate.
- Less concentrated in districts which are in a good economic position (e.g. higher labour productivity), larger shares of the educated population, and better transport infrastructure.

These results provide some evidence that individuals involved in migration processes, as well as those intending to make any international move, are unevenly distributed to less economically developed districts, with relatively lower density of higher educated labour force, where the transport infrastructure is typically worse. These indicators could be identified as "local drivers" that facilitate the formation of migration attitudes of Bulgarian citizens. In line with this, higher regional risk-of-poverty as well as higher natural growth accompanies relatively more intense out-migration attitudes.

4.5 Potential and Return Migrants in Bulgaria per District Ranking

4.5.1 Profile of Potential Migrants

The profile and characteristics of the potential migrants by districts (grouped by their ranks of development) would orient us if there are some regional peculiarities of the migration attitudes in Bulgaria.

Potential migrants are grouped into two sub-aggregates — potential long-term and potential short-term migrants, respectively. Potential long-term migrants include people declaring that they would settle abroad or would like to stay abroad for more than one year. Short-term migrants include individuals who declare that they prefer to stay abroad for less than a year (see Chap. 2).

The share of the population from Sofia, which would like to migrate, is 9.1% of the total long-term migrants and 25% of the total short-term migrants in the country – in contrast, about 18% of the resident Bulgarian population is concentrated in the capital city (Table 4.3). Obviously, most of the migrants are recruited from the mid-developed and depressed districts — 48% of the long-term migrants are located in Group II and 42.9% in Group III districts. Analogically, the short-term migrants are also recruited mainly from Groups II and III (respectively 39.5% and 35.5%).

Concerning the structure by types of migrants, it is balanced in Sofia (9.1% are long-term versus 8.9% short-term migrants) and unbalanced in the mid-developed and less developed districts, where explicitly prevalent is the share of potential migrants with long-term over short-term intentions (21–6.2% in Group II, and 19.8–5.9% in Group III).

Table 4.3 Potential migrants and potential non-migrants by district groups in Bulgaria (%)

Potential migrants and non-migrants	Group I		Group II		Group III		Total	
Long-term	9.1		48.0		42.9		100.0	
		9.1		21.0		19.8		18.3
Short-term	25.0		39.5		35.5		100.0	
		8.9		6.2		5.9		6.6
Non-migrants	20.1		40.7		39.2		100.0	
		82.0		72.9		74.3		75.1
Total	18.4		42.0		39.6		100.0	
		100.0		100.0		100.0		100.0

The difference in the level of development between the district groups results, on the one hand, in a balance between the intentions for long-term and short-term migration in the well-developed region (Group I). On the other side, things are quite the opposite—there is an unbalance in the mid-developed and depressed districts (Groups II and III) in this respect, which, in general, can possibly restrict the usage of short-term migration as an alternative to the long term in the less developed regions.

A more detailed look into the disaggregated information amplifies the notion of a contrast between Sofia and the rest of the country. 57.2 % of the so-called settlers from the country originate from the mid-developed areas, and 52.4 % of the long-term labour migrants—from the depressed areas. On the contrary, only 6.8 % of the settlers and only 11.4 % of the labour migrants are recruited from Sofia.

In this sense, the effect of the higher regional development level in a typical sending country can be two-sided. First, generally the regional leadership holds down the migration intentions. The so-called "non-migrants" in Sofia are at 82 %, compared to 72.9 % in the districts in Group II and to the 75.1 % non-migrants' share for the country. Second, there are premises for turning the short-term migration into an alternative long-term one. On the other hand, it is more and more difficult for the depressed areas to compensate for the lack of young population, "giving away their leadership" by migration intentions to the mid-developed areas. At the same time, the lower level of regional development seems to be compensated for by the spread of the migration networks (measured as number of acquaintances with Bulgarians living abroad and foreigners living in Bulgaria). Individuals from the depressed areas (Group III) keep many times more such contacts compared to those living in Sofia.

In the next few sections, we will discuss some key demographic and capabilities characteristics of potential migrants in the three district groups.

Demographic Characteristics The demographic structure of the potential long-term migrants from Sofia is similar to the one of the same type in the other two district groups—men and people aged up to 40 are dominant. On the other hand, among the long-term migrants in Sofia, the share of singles (47.7%) exceeds the share of the married individuals (40%), while in the other two district groups this ratio is exactly the opposite—the married persons prevail (47.10–41.9% in Group II and 47.9–42.7% in Group III). It turns out that the well-developed district "supplies" young single men, and the mid-developed and depressed districts—young married men. Of course, in both cases this is a typical labour migration. The nuance is that the single men would probably look for opportunities for professional realization, while the married men would look almost only for ways to support their families back in Bulgaria.

The demographic structure of the short-term migrants by districts seems way more diverse.

First, the percentage of men among the short-term migrants in Sofia remains high (59.4%), while in the mid-developed and less developed districts it drops to 51.5% and 52.3%, respectively.

Second, the share of individuals aged up to 30 decreases from 63.1% in Group I to 43.6% and 31.9% in the next two district groups. Thus, the prevailing age cohorts shift from the 21–30 years old in Sofia to 31–40 and 41–50 years old in the depressed areas.

Third, the contrast in the distributions by marital status is clearer within short-term migrants as compared to the long-term ones. If in Sofia 68.8% are single, in the depressed districts it is quite the opposite—the share of married people reaches 62.2%.

Thus, among the potential short-term migrants in the well-developed district, the prevalence of young single men persists; in the second district group—it is young men and women (both married and single); while in the depressed districts— middle-aged men and women, most of them married.

Capability Characteristics As mentioned earlier in this work, educational structure, social status, and income distribution are among the main factors constituting migration capabilities (De Haas 2010).

The educational structure of the long-term migrants is similar in all three district groups. Individuals with secondary vocational education have the highest share— from 50% for Sofia to 37.8% for the second district group (compared to 47.7% for the third group). Here are at least two peculiarities. Surprisingly, the percentage of university degree holders is highest in the mid-developed districts (28.8%), and not in Sofia (27.3%), dropping to only 16.3% in the depressed districts of Group III. As expected, the share of people with no education is highest exactly in the depressed districts (22.5% compared with 10.6% in the capital city).

Second, the share of unemployed people among the long-term migrants increases from 23.1% in Sofia to 29.4% in Group II and 36.5% in Group III districts. On the other hand, the share of those employed in the private sector follows quite expectedly an opposite trend. It decreases from 44.6% in the well-developed district to 32.3% in mid-developed and 27.4% in the depressed districts.

Third, the income structure of the long-term migrants shifts as well. For example, in Sofia the prevailing share is held by individuals with average monthly income over 600 BGN, whereas the highest share in the other two groups is observed for respondents with monthly income 150–300 BGN. Nevertheless, the depressed districts contrast to the mid developed areas by a high concentration of potential long-term migrants in the lowest income interval (less than 150 BGN).

Thus, the well-developed district "supplies" predominantly long-term migrants with secondary vocational and higher education (a total of 77.3 %), employed mostly in the private sector, with monthly incomes above the country's average. Long-term migrants with the same education degrees have a lower share (two thirds) in the mid-developed districts, both employed and unemployed, with monthly incomes between 150 and 450 BGN. Finally, the depressed districts similarly provide individuals with secondary vocational and higher education (64 %), but also with no education (22.5 %), mostly unemployed (36.5 %), with quite rare low employment in the private sector (27.4 %), having monthly incomes of less than 300 BGN.

A capabilities profile of the short-term migrants, though somewhat similar to the one of the long-term migrants, gives a different region-specific insight. The education structure looks akin to the structure of the long-term migrants. Individuals with secondary vocational education prevail—from 63.5 % in Sofia to the modest 35 % in Group II. The mid-developed districts show some contrasts here. On the one hand, respondents with higher education are most numerous (25 %), compared to the depressed districts (19.8 %) and Sofia (19 %). On the other hand, the share of people with no education again is highest for this group—15 % (compared with only 6.3 % in Sofia and 12.1 % in the depressed districts). Thus, if the percentage of individuals with secondary vocational and higher education reaches a total of 82.5 % in Sofia and 69.3 % in the depressed districts, it is only 60 % in the districts from Group II.

Among the short-term migrants, Sofia and the mid-developed districts seem to have similar employment in the private sector and unemployment rates— 32.8 %/21.9 % for Sofia, and 32.4 %/23.5 %, respectively, for the mid-developed districts. The picture in the depressed districts is diametrically opposite—with the unemployment level at 40.2 %, which is substantially higher than the employment in the private sector (28.3 %).

Generally, the income level of the short-term migrants is below that of the long-term. If in the well-developed districts the highest share of individuals is observed to have a monthly income of 300–450 BGN (43.5 %), in the mid-developed and depressed districts the modal group of individuals is found at the monthly income interval of 150–300 BGN (respectively, 36.7 % in the mid-developed and 50 % in the depressed districts).

Thus, not surprisingly, the highest developed district (Sofia city) provides short-term migrants with relatively higher qualification level. Unexpectedly, the educational level of the short-term migrants in the depressed districts seems better than one of the short-term migrants in the mid-developed districts. Sofia and the mid-developed districts recruit potential short-term migrants with similar social status

(30 % employment in the private sector and 20 % unemployment in the two groups of districts). The depressed districts provide mainly unemployed people—almost every second among the short-term migrants there is unemployed.

4.5.2 Return Migrants

For the purposes of regional analyses hereafter, we define as "return migrants" the individuals who have lived abroad for a period not less than a month during the last 5 years. In this sense, "return migrants" are a subsample of respondents who have recent experience in international migration as opposed to all those not meeting these conditions (considered as "non-mobile" individuals). The general findings provide grounds to assert that the regional leadership of Sofia doesn't proportionately attract return migrants. Almost 88 % of the individuals who ever migrated in the last 5 years return to medium-developed and depressed districts, and only 12 % to Sofia. That's why the proportion of the return migrants estimated for each of these two groups of districts (17.4 % and 16 %) is higher than in the one for Sofia (10.2 %). And vice versa—the proportion of non-mobile is highest in the capital city (Table 4.4).

Furthermore, the data from the survey explored here allows us the possibility of differentiating the return migrants according to their intentions for the future into those planning to stay ("stayers") and those willing to leave again ("movers"). Without any doubt, the overall regional differences reflect on the capacity of the main district groups to retain people at home or, on the contrary, to propel individuals with some previous experience abroad to a consequent out-migration.

In this regard, the contrast between the capital city, on one hand, and either the mid-developed or depressed districts, on the other, is more than obvious. Slightly more than a half of the returnees in Sofia express a will to continue living there (50.7 %). At the same time, the relative share of such attitudes is lower by almost 10 percentage points in the two other district groups (41.8 % in the mid-developed districts and about the same/40.3 %/in the depressed ones). Although the capital city attracts only 12 % of all returnees, it still offers better conditions for their adaptation in the country.

Table 4.4 Return migrants and non-mobile population per district development level in Bulgaria (%)

Return migrants and non-mobile population	Group I		Group II		Group III		Total	
Return migrants	12.0		47.0		40.9		100.0	
		10.2		17.4		16.0		15.5
Non-mobile	19.5		41.1		39.4		100.0	
		89.8		82.6		84.0		84.5
Total	18.4		42.0		39.6		100.0	
		100.0		100.0		100.0		100.0

4.6   Regional Socio-Economic Disparities in Switzerland

A similar evaluation of the degree of regional socio-economic disparities in Switzerland is performed regarding the 26 Swiss cantons. Data at canton level (NUTS 3) for the year 2012 is used from the official regional statistics for Switzerland. However, the range of regional indicators has been reduced in order to perform the ranking on the basis of indicators which are: (1) available at NUTS 3 level; (2) identical for both countries; (3) covering the same areas—demographic conditions, labour market, and so on. This way, the following nine indicators have been used for canton rankings.

Demographic Conditions

1. Natural growth rate (net balance, standardized per 1000 inhabitants).
2. Migration coefficient (net balance, standardized per 1000 inhabitants).
3. Age dependency ratio.
4. Share of population with tertiary education.

Labour Market

5. Employment rate.
6. Unemployment rate.

Local Economy

7. GDP per capita.
8. Labour productivity (Gross value added per employed individual).

Healthcare

9. Hospital beds per 100 thousand inhabitants.

Canton integral scores have been calculated in order to assess the level of socio-economic development of each Swiss territorial unit. This way, the territorial units have been ranked in the same manner as per the Bulgarian districts. In order to determine the thresholds necessary for categorization, the mean national Swiss level has been inserted as a synthetic regional unit and has obtained an integral score. Using this threshold, the cantons were split into three groups:

1. First group—consists of most highly developed units with scores above the country average (T1).
2. Second group—cantons whose integral scores are below the national mean score, but above the conditional threshold (T2) that defines the third group.
3. Third group—less developed cantons which have ranking scores less than T2.[1]

The calculated integral scores provide a basis for general evaluation of the socio-economic disparities at regional level in Switzerland for 2012 (Table 4.5). For each group, the weighted mean levels of the included indicators have been calculated where the canton populations have been used as weights (Table 4.6).

---

[1] See Sect. 4.2. The lowest integral score is actually the highest number in the interval [0, 1] obtained for the score of a particular territorial unit (which ranks the respective unit at the last place in the ranking).

Table 4.5 Grouping of the Swiss cantons by socio-economic development level

Rank	Canton (NUTS 3 level)	Region (NUTS 2 level)	Score	Rank	District (NUTS 3 level)	Region (NUTS 2 level)	Score
	Group I:			13	Vaud	CH01	0.7854
1	Zug	CH06	0.5370	14	Obwalden	CH06	0.7896
2	Zürich	CH04	0.5864	15	Schwyz	CH06	0.7939
3	Basel	CH03	0.6349	16	Nidwalden	CH06	0.7945
4	Geneva	CH01	0.6708	17	Schaffhausen	CH05	0.8115
	Switzerland		0.6959	18	Neuchâtel	CH02	0.8165
	Group II:			19	Solothurn	CH02	0.8401
5	Aargau	CH03	0.7171		*Group III:*		
6	St.Gallen	CH05	0.7280	20	Appenzell Innerrhoden	CH05	0.8612
7	Appenzell Ausserrhoden	CH05	0.7333	21	Glarus	CH05	0.8839
8	Luzern	CH06	0.7533	22	Valais	CH01	0.8901
9	Basel-Land	CH03	0.7656	23	Fribourg	CH02	0.9034
10	Bern	CH02	0.7726	24	Jura	CH02	0.9228
11	Thurgau	CH05	0.7813	25	Uri	CH06	0.9556
12	Graubünden	CH05	0.7831	26	Tessin	CH07	1.0253

Notation: *CH01* Lake Geneva region, *CH02* Espace Mittelland, *CH03* North-western Switzerland, *CH04* Zurich, *CH05* Eastern Switzerland, *CH06* Central Switzerland, *CH07* Ticino region

Table 4.6 Mean indicator levels by groups of socio-economic development of cantons

Socio-economic indicators, 2012	Group I	Group II	Group III	Total CH
Natural growth rate (net, per 1000 inhabitants)	+0.704	+0.391	+0.337	+0.468
Migration coefficient (net, per 1000 inhabitants)	+1.233	+1.174	+1.973	+1.301
Age dependency ratio	0.266	0.283	0.295	0.280
Share of population with tertiary education (%)	37.3	27.7	24.4	29.8
Employment rate (%)	80.4	80.8	77.1	80.2
Unemployment rate (%)	3.67	2.88	3.65	3.20
GDP per capita (thousand CHF)	102.4	64.8	56.9	73.9
Labour productivity (GVA per employed, th. CHF)	132.0	107.4	97.8	112.7
Hospital beds (per 100 thousand inhabitants)	5.36	4.61	4.35	4.78

Group I contains the cantons that have, on average, the most favourable levels for some of the indicators, which results in the highest integral scores. According to 2012 data, this group includes the cantons of Zug, Zurich, Basel, and Geneva, cantons that constitute 27 % of the Swiss resident population. On average, this group shows the highest GDP per capita (102 thousand CHF or 39 % over the national average) and labour productivity (132 thousand CHF)—levels which contrast substantially to the mean levels of the other two groups. Other important indicators that contribute to the configuration of this segment are:

- The level of healthcare capacity (5.4 hospital beds per 100 thousand inhabitants as compared to 4.6 and 4.4).
- The concentration of higher educated population (37 % as compared to 27 % and 24 %).
- The natural growth rate (+7.0 net per 10,000 inhabitants as compared to +3.9 and +3.4 for Groups II and III).

These three indicators naturally correlate with the income level which is revealed by the regional taxonomic analysis.

Group II includes the largest number of cantons (15), which constitute 59 % of the country's population. This group is somewhat heterogeneous in so far as most of the mean levels of its indicators slightly deviate from the national averages. Nonetheless, several indicators which clearly contribute to the estimated distinctions from the other groups (mainly the third one) are:

- The net migration coefficient (+1.17 per 1000 inhabitants, +1.97 for Group III).
- The unemployment rate (2.88 %, 3.65 % for Group III).
- The GDP per capita level (65 thousand CHF, 57 thousand CHF for Group III).

Group III includes 7 cantons constituting 14 % of the Swiss resident population.

Their integral scores are not substantially lower than the scores obtained for the cantons at the bottom of Group II (5 of these 7 cantons have scores deviating by less than 10 % from the lowest score in Group II). The profile of these cantons can be characterized by the following most clearly identified disparities:

- Group III cantons have, on average, the lowest natural growth rates (average of 3.4 per 10,000 inhabitants), the lowest share of persons with higher education (24 %), and the lowest employment rate (77 %).
- At the same time, these cantons have, on average, the highest net migration rate (about 2 per 1000 inhabitants) and the highest age dependency ratio (29.5 persons aged 65+ per 100 persons aged 20–64). Along with the lowest natural growth, these indicators reveal the more unfavourable demographic status of Group III cantons.

As an overall assessment, the applied methodology provides grounds for locating these cantons in the lowest socio-economic development stratum, in so far as the mean GDP per capita for Group III is 23 % lower than the national average.

4.7   Regional Drivers for Bulgarian Migration in Switzerland

The distribution of Bulgarian migrants residing in Switzerland is of particular interest to our study of regional disparities and migration. According to SFSO 2014 data, the total number of Bulgarians officially residing in the country is 5826, which is 0.31 % of the total number of the foreign-born residents in Switzerland (1.87 million). Group I cantons contain 27 % of the total population, 33 % of the foreign born residents, and only 14 % of the Bulgarian residents. Group II cantons have a much more balanced structure (59 % of the total population; 54 % of foreigners; 60 % of Bulgarians), but by contrast—Group III with 14 % of the total population (and 13 % of the total foreigners) contains a disproportionally higher share of the Bulgarian residents: 26 %.

In the light of this, it is informative to further explore the correlations between the indicators of the integral score construct and the degree of concentration of Bulgarian residents by canton. For this purpose, a variable for this concentration level has been defined as "number of Bulgarians per 10,000 of canton population". However, only some of the calculated correlations of this variable with the indicators provide some evidence about any possible interaction between the dimensions of socio-economic development and the location choice of Bulgarian migrants in Switzerland.

In particular, a positive, albeit weak, correlation is found in respect of the following indicators: age dependency ratio (+0.24) and unemployment rate (+0.19). Negative and also weak correlation has been estimated with the variables: share of population with tertiary education (−0.24), GDP per capita (−0.20), and natural growth rate (−0.17). Although not very explicitly, these correlations provide some support for the following propositions;

- The cantonal location of Bulgarians is relatively proportional to that of the total population, with the exclusion of Group III cantons.
- Because of this, the concentration variable correlates negatively with the GDP per capita (i.e. a bit higher concentration in relatively lower income level cantons[2] see Fig. 4.3) and with the share of higher educated individuals (i.e. somewhat higher concentration in cantons with relatively lower density of highly educated residents).

The negative correlation with natural growth rates indicates that, albeit slightly, the settlement of Bulgarians avoids regions with higher-than-average natural growth rates. In support of this, the positive correlation with the age dependency ratio shows that Bulgarians tend to be dispersed towards cantons with a relatively higher share of older population.

Additionally, a correlation coefficient is calculated between the main variable of interest (Bulgarians per 10,000 of canton population) and a similar variable defined as "Foreign residents per 10,000 of canton population". The negative value of this correlation (−0.25) indicates that, to some extent and on average, Bulgarians "tend to avoid" cantons with relatively higher concentration of foreign population.

Finally, the correlation of the Bulgarians' regional concentration variable with the integral scores of the Swiss cantons (+0.31) suggests that the higher the canton score (i.e. the lower the degree of its socio-economic development), the higher the degree of location of Bulgarian residents in the respective cantons. If a very distinct outlier is removed from the calculation (the rural, economically weak canton of

---

[2] The most contrasting four cantons are labelled explicitly in the Scatter diagram—Basel Land and Fribourg (among the lowest GDP per capita level but with a relatively higher concentration of Bulgarian residents) as opposed to Basel and Zug (the highest GDP per capita with a much lower concentration of Bulgarians).

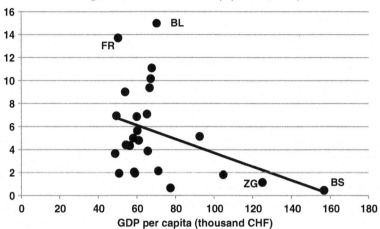

Fig. 4.3 Scatter diagram of the Swiss cantons based on their GDP per capita and the concentration of Bulgarian migrants *(Note: Jura canton is not depicted)*

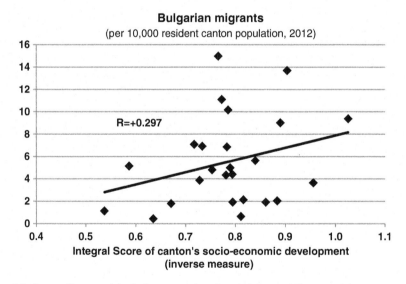

Fig. 4.4 Scatter diagram of the Swiss cantons based on their Integral Scores and the concentration of Bulgarian migrants *(Note: Jura canton is not depicted)*

Jura, with almost 80 Bulgarians per 10,000 canton residents), the correlation coefficient is just slightly reduced to +0.297 (Fig. 4.4). This suggests that, possibly, Bulgarians in Switzerland tend to locate regionally in search of migrant niches in relatively less developed cantons that are yet not fully exhausted by migrants of other origins.

4.8 Profiles of Bulgarians in Switzerland per Canton Ranking

According to the SFSO 2013 data mentioned, the Bulgarian community in Switzerland consists of a little over 6000 people—5153 permanent (having respective permits) and 911 with temporary residents. Of them, 13.6% reside in the first canton group—those having a level of development higher than the country average (Zug, Zurich, Basel, and Geneva). Another 60% are in the second canton group, defined as "mid-developed cantons" with integral scores assessed somewhat below the average—these are 15 cantons with integral scores between 0.7171 (Aargau) and 0.8484 (Solothurn). The last 26.4% of Bulgarian residents live in the less developed cantons—these are 7 cantons with integral scores from 0.8612 (Appenzell Innerrhoden) to 1.0253 (Tessin).

Data from the mail questionnaire survey carried out among the Bulgarians in Switzerland provides a view on the socio-economic profile of the Bulgarian migrants living in the three canton groups: 42.3% of the respondents live in the first group, 44.4% in Group II cantons, and 13.3% in the less developed cantons. The response rate among the Bulgarians living in the Group I cantons is the highest—questionnaires have been received from 55% of the individuals registered there. In the second group (most numerous in terms of the number of cantons), the respondents are about 13% of the registered Bulgarians. The response rate in the third group is the lowest—only 9% of the Bulgarian residents have responded. Despite the mismatch between the regional distribution of the Bulgarians living in Switzerland and that of the respondents to the questionnaire survey, the information received provides a relatively complete view of the social, economic, and demographic features of the Bulgarian residents by canton rankings.

4.8.1 Demographic and Structural Characteristics

Concerning the regional distribution of the Bulgarian population in Switzerland by gender, age, and marital status, no substantial differences have been found. In all three canton groups women, young adults (31–40) and married residents prevail.

The shares of women aged 31–40 (typical of the Bulgarian community in this country) and singles (who are, generally, not frequently met) are highest in Group I (well-developed cantons) as compared to the mid- and less-developed cantons. However, the shares of respondents aged 41–50 and married are most distinct in the mid-developed cantons. The third canton group differs from the others mainly by its relatively high proportion of individuals aged above 50. This provides a hint regarding the assumption that well-developed cantons are more attractive to unmarried women aged up to 40, and the less-developed cantons, contrariwise, to relatively older migrants.

The regional differences by administrative status of the respondents are not particularly distinctive. The residence permit (C) holders, for instance, are equally distributed in all three canton groups (each about 20 % of the Bulgarians living there). Still, in the well-developed cantons the share of people with mid-term permits (B) is comparatively highest (64.9 %). At the same time, in the less-developed cantons (Group III) the percentage of short-term permit (L) holders reaches 22.4 % (compared to only 11.9 % in the first canton group and 17.7 % in the second).

We also consider a distribution of Bulgarian residents by year of arrival in Switzerland (before 2003, between 2004 and 2008, and after 2009). Similar to residence permit (C) holders, people who have arrived before 2003 are evenly distributed in the three canton groups (most likely, these are the same persons). Those who have arrived after 2009 (the year of the extension of EU—Swiss Agreement on the free movement to Bulgaria) are largest in number—about every second Bulgarian who has settled in the country. For one reason or another, the so-called less-developed cantons are most attractive for the newcomers—their share exceeds 60 % of the Bulgarians residing in Group III cantons.

4.8.2   Capability Characteristics

Concerning the distribution by education and occupations of the Bulgarians in Switzerland, clear regional differences are observed in the sample data. They provide a plausible indication that the immigrants' capabilities predetermine their choice of cantons which diverge—to one extent or another—by their level of development.

The divergence between well- and less-developed cantons is most obvious. If in the first group the share of Bulgarians with higher education reaches 74.1 % (compared to 60.6 % average for the country), in the less developed ones it drops to 43 %. Also, in the less developed cantons, people with secondary education prevail (47.2 % compared to only 23.7 % in Group I cantons). On the other hand, in Group III cantons, the share of Bulgarians with basic or lower education is almost 10 % (compared to 4 % average for the country)—it is about 5 times higher than in Group I cantons (2.2 %). The mid-developed cantons occupy an intermediate position—with a larger share of Bulgarian residents with higher education (50.2 %) compared to those with secondary education (43.1 %). Obviously, the most developed cantons attract predominantly educated people, and the less developed ones—individuals with (more or less) modest educational level.

The regional differences in the education structure are naturally related to the professional profile of the employed in the different canton groups.

In general, the regional occupational profiles of the Bulgarian community do not contrast substantially when the structure of current jobs is explored. "Professionals", "Technicians and associate professionals", "Service and sales workers", are clearly present—however in different orders—in all three canton groups. However, the

Table 4.7 Professional profile of Bulgarians per canton group

Group I			Group II			Group III		
1	Professionals	↑	1	Service and sales workers	↓	1	Service and sales workers	↓
2	Service and sales workers	↓	2	Elementary occupations	↓	2	Elementary occupations	↓
							Professionals	↑
3	Technicians and associate professionals	Neutral	3	Professionals	↑	3	Technicians and associate professionals	↑
4	Managers	↑	4	Technicians and associate professionals	↑			

Note: For each group of cantons, the categories of occupations are ordered *top-down* by their shares in the regional occupational profile of Bulgarian residents. Arrows show the change to higher or lower shares of the occupational status from the former to the current job of the respondent

occupation of "Managers" is mostly present in the top-developed cantons, whereas in the other two canton groups, Bulgarians employed at "Elementary occupations" stand out in the regional profiles.

Therefore, a particular contrast is observed between the occupational profile of Bulgarians in the well-developed cantons on the one hand, and in the mid-developed and less-developed cantons on the other. In Group I cantons, the leading occupations are "Professionals" (36.6 %) followed by "Service and sales workers" (18.8 %) and "Technicians" (14.1 %). In the other two canton groups, the most common are "Service and sales workers" (25.5 % in the mid-developed and reaching 44.1 % in less-developed cantons) followed by those employed in "Elementary occupations" (20.7 % in mid-developed and 15.3 % in less-developed cantons) and "Professionals" (respectively 17.6 % and again 15.3 %) (Table 4.7).

The questionnaire survey conducted in Switzerland allows us to assess the prospects facing the different professional communities of Bulgarian residents. The patterns of the shifts are similar in all three canton groups. In general, when changing jobs, the shares of "Professionals" and "Managers" increase and that of "Service and sales workers" decrease. The prospects for "Technicians" seem neutral in the well-developed cantons and positive in the other two groups. On the other hand, the number of people employed in "Elementary occupations" definitely decreases with the job shifts. As a result, (bearing in mind the consequent job arrangements) the professional character of the people in the mid-developed cantons moves to some extent towards the profile of those living in the top-developed cantons—i.e. highest share of "Professionals", followed by "Service workers" and "Technicians". At the same time, the profile of people in less-developed cantons nonetheless maintains the contrast—the so-called "Service worker" remains the most popular occupation there.

However, the income structure still outlines the divergence between the developed cantons and the other two groups. The modal class of individuals in Group I cantons has monthly incomes in the 2100–4200 CHF range (38 %), whereas the modal class in the mid- and less-developed cantons is observed in the interval of monthly income less than 2100 CHF (53 % and 60 % respectively). Besides, Bulgarians from the two high-income groups (respectively, 4200–6300 CHF and over 6300 CHF) residing in the top-developed cantons are about 60 % of all Bulgarians receiving such incomes in the country.

Finally, the future migration plans of the Bulgarians in Switzerland—providing a general assessment of the re-migration potential for Bulgarian residents—reveal another clear contrast between highly and less developed cantons. In the top-developed cantons, the share of the stayers and those with the intention to leave for another country is the highest (respectively, 50.2 % and 4.6 %). Contrariwise, in the less-developed cantons the percentage of those who would like to stay is the lowest (37.8 % compared to 41.3 % for those who still hesitate), as well as the share of those who wish to leave for another country (2.1 %). On the other hand, the percentage of Bulgarians with intentions to circulate between the two countries is the highest exactly in the less-developed cantons (14.7 % compared to 8.6 % in the top-developed ones).

Ultimately, the picture is as follows. Highly developed cantons obviously tend to keep the Bulgarian migrants; however, albeit modest, intentions for a consequent move to another country are not excluded. Living in a less-developed canton is linked to increased hesitation by the Bulgarians toward their future, including in respect of the option to stay in Switzerland. The mid-developed cantons, on the other hand, occupy to some extent an "intermediate position" between those two "extremes".

4.8.3   Regional Inter-linkages

Additional information revealing some patterns of regional location of Bulgarians in Switzerland is derived when the district of migrant's origin is particularly considered. Table 4.8 presents the distribution of survey respondents which takes into account:

• The level of socio-economic development of the district which the migrant has indicated as her/his birthplace.
• The development level of the canton where the migrant currently resides.

It should be noted also that 3.7 % of the respondents who answered the respective question have indicated a birth place out of Bulgaria. Over 58 % of them reside in Group II; one quarter—located in Group III; and only one sixth of them (16.7 %)—in Group I (the most developed) cantons. By contrast, the share of respondents born in Bulgaria and residing in Group I cantons reaches 44 %—and the share of those living in the less developed (Group III) cantons is two times lower (12.5 %).

When the region of origin in Bulgaria is considered in detail, some discrepancies can be outlined regarding the Bulgarian-Swiss regional links. The majority of migrants (54 %) originating from Sofia city (Group I) are located in the most developed Swiss cantons and only about one tenth (9.6 %) report settlement in Group III cantons. A somewhat similar pattern is observed for those originating from a Group

Table 4.8 Distribution of Bulgarians by groups of Swiss cantons residence and groups of BG districts origin (%)

| District of origin in Bulgaria | Canton of current residence in Switzerland | | | |
	Group I	Group II	Group III	Total
Group I (Sofia city)	*54.0*	*36.4*	*9.6*	*100.0*
	39.0	25.8	23.0	31.1
Group II	*36.0*	*49.8*	*14.2*	*100.0*
	35.2	47.7	46.0	42.1
Group III	*45.5*	*41.1*	*13.4*	*100.0*
	24.4	21.6	23.8	23.1
Non-BG origin	*16.7*	*58.3*	*25.0*	*100.0*
	1.4	4.9	7.1	3.7
Total	*43.1*	*43.9*	*13.0*	*100.0*
	100.0	100.0	100.0	100.0

II Bulgarian district—about half of them reside in a Group II Swiss canton as well, and only 36 % are located in Group I cantons. The distribution of migrants coming from the less-developed Bulgarian regions does not follow any specific pattern regarding the Swiss allocation; moreover, its shares are estimated amid those observed for the other two groups (e.g. 45.5 % and 41 % of them report locations in cantons of Groups I and II).

These discrepancies are reflected in the structure of migrants in each Swiss cantons group obtained by groups of Bulgarian district of origin. In this respect, 39 % of the Bulgarian residents in Group I cantons come from Sofia city. This share decreases to 35 % and 24 % for Groups II and III districts of origin. At the same time, the share of Group II canton residents reporting origin in Sofia is only 25.8 %; however, those indicating a birthplace in a Group II Bulgarian district have a much larger share (47.7 %). It should be noted that the distribution of Group III canton respondents does not deviate substantially from the one estimated for the Bulgarians residing in a settlement from Group II cantons.

Even though some slight patterns are observed in the origin-residence links, there is not enough ground to suggest any distinctive relation in this aspect. As a general conclusion, the Swiss location of Bulgarians is just partially related to a correspondence between the degrees of regional development of the places of origin and current location of Bulgarian migrants.

4.9 Conclusions

This chapter presents a variety of detailed results obtained from a multi-aspect study of the "regional disparities—migration" nexus concerning two contrasting countries: Switzerland and Bulgaria. Applying a taxonomy method, the level of socio-economic development of the territorial units in both countries has been assessed and three groups of units in each country have been identified. The ranking of these units (26 cantons in Switzerland and 28 districts in Bulgaria) by groups provides different options for analyzing the regional disparities and their interactions with migration attitudes and practices of Bulgarians in both countries. The study utilizes unique datasets provided by two large sample surveys—one in Bulgaria (treating the issues of potential and return migration) and one in Switzerland (exploring the status and perspectives of Bulgarian residents). Thereafter, a summary of findings is presented along with the main conclusions.

The overall degree of regional disproportions in Bulgaria appears to be slightly lower than in Switzerland—the coefficient of variation of the integral scores is 10.5 % for Bulgarian districts as compared to 13.6 % for Swiss cantons. Nevertheless, there are various specifics in the territorial disparities in both countries that affect some of the results. For instance, Sofia city has an outlier position in the multidimensional space—its score is 40 % beyond the second ranked district which leads to its separation as a one-unit group of best-performing districts in Bulgaria. Thus, the comparative analysis frequently contrasts all other districts (partitioned in more homogeneous Groups II and III) to the capital city. This is not the case in Switzerland where Group I consists of four top-developed cantons excluding the capital city canton (Bern).

Migration variables of interest have been derived for analytical purposes, e.g. potential and return migrants per 100 district population in Bulgaria (from the sample survey) and Bulgarian residents per 10,000 canton population in Switzerland (from the official Swiss register data). For each migration variable, the correlation coefficient has been calculated with the integral score of regions' development as well as the socio-economic and demographic indicators that constitute this score in both countries. The coefficients of migration variables for Bulgarian districts with their integral scores did not show even weak correlations (values below 0.1) due to the amalgamation of various dimensions of the districts' socio-economic status. However, a moderate positive correlation for the Swiss cantons is observed (0.31), which provides particular confirmation for our initial expectation, namely, that Bulgarians in Switzerland tend to allocate regionally in search of migrant niches in relatively less developed cantons. Additionally, a negative correlation value (−0.25) is found between the concentration of Bulgarians and of total foreign residents in Swiss cantons (per 10,000 of canton population), which suggests some evidence that Bulgarians tend to avoid cantons with relatively higher concentration of migrant population.

The correlation coefficients of migration variables with the indicators of the integral score indicate several main findings regarding the postulated "regional disparity—migration" nexus in both countries. The share of people who intend to migrate is slightly higher in Bulgarian districts with higher rates of natural growth and higher risks of poverty; however, it is somehow lower in regions that enjoy better economic conditions (e.g. higher GDP per capita and better infrastructure). Also, the return migrants concentration does not substantially correlate with the districts' indicators, apart from the natural growth rate (+0.35). In consequence, we have to conclude that the regional location of mobile individuals is not clearly associated with the evaluated regional disparities in Bulgaria for the year 2012. Focussing on the Bulgarians in Switzerland, we observe that their cantonal placement is relatively proportional to the total canton population. However, contrary to our expectation, the correlations of concentration variable for Bulgarian migrants with the development indicators show that, generally, Bulgarians tend to reside in cantons with: (1) relatively higher age dependency ratio, and higher unemployment rates; (2) relatively lower income level as well as lower density of highly educated population. The negative correlation with the natural growth rate indicator provides some support for the proposition that, albeit slightly, Bulgarians avoid regions with higher-than-average natural growth rates—along with the fact that Bulgarians are dispersed more towards cantons with a relatively higher share of older population.

The sample data from the Bulgarian survey allows the identification of two main types of potential migrants—long and short term ones. The socio-economic and demographic profiles of each migrant type are explored in respect of the location of migrants by regions of different developmental levels. Similarities are observed for the long-term potential migrants in any group of districts regarding most of the demographic indicators except marital status—the prevailing share in Group I (Sofia city) is held by singles, whereas in Group II and III by married individuals. Regarding the educational structure of this type of migrant, the largest share of tertiary educated respondents is found in the mid-developed districts. As expected (see De Haas 2010), the share of individuals with basic or lower educational level is largest for Group III, which includes the most depressed Bulgarian regions. Similar shift in the "weight" of the unemployed among the long-term potential migrants is observed across the groups of Bulgarian districts—from 23 % in Group I to 37 % in Group III.

The demographic structure of potential short-term migrants is found to be more diverse across the three groups of Bulgarian districts. As a general rule, the main contrast is between Group I (capital city) and the other districts. For example, Sofia contains relatively more young male migrants, whereas Group II and III districts have a much more balanced structure by age and gender. Considering the educational structures, it can be noted that higher, plus secondary vocational categories within this type of potential migrants reach over 82 % in Sofia (Group I) as compared to 60 % in the mid-developed districts (Group III). The unemployment level also diverges substantially in the regional dimension—the share of unemployed, potential short-term migrants in Groups I and II districts is estimated at about 23 %; this share in Group III is almost twice as big (40 %). So, the depressed regions potentially recruit, more or less, relatively well-educated but unemployed, predominantly married individuals.

No substantial disparities have been found in respect of the regional profiles of Bulgarian residents in Switzerland evaluated by gender, age, and marital status. Regional differences by the administrative status of respondents (e.g. types of permit holding) are also not observed except for short-term (L) permit holders. However, the majority of those who reside in the less-developed (Group III) cantons have arrived after the year 2009, which is in conjuncture with the fact that the share of L-permit holders is largest here. Regional divergence is found regarding the distribution of Bulgarians by education and occupation in Switzerland where the contrast between the top- and low-developed cantons is most evident. For example, Bulgarians with higher education constitute about three quarters in Group I cantons, whereas the largest fraction of Group III canton residents have secondary education (47 %).

Educational differences are naturally related to the professional profile of the employed in the different canton groups, although professionals and other qualified personnel are found in all three groups. However, occupational category "Professionals" has the first place among the Bulgarian residents of Group I cantons (over one third) followed by "Service and sales workers" occupations (almost one fifth). By contrast, the leading position is observed for "Service and sales workers" (especially in Group III cantons) followed by "Elementary occupations". As expected, a substantial share (60 %) of Bulgarians with income level at or above the mean for Switzerland is located in the top-developed cantons.

Ultimately, the data did not provide substantial evidence regarding the links between the Bulgarians' districts of origin and Swiss cantons of residence. In general, Bulgarians from all three district groups are similarly dispersed in the respective Swiss cantons, although some concentration of Sofia city individuals (54 %) in the corresponding Group I cantons is found. Overall, the analysis of the "regional disparities—migration" nexus requires exploration of numerous dimensions for providing evidences in its support. This study reveals various aspects of the investigated topic in light of the available unique information about one typical European sending and one receiving country—Bulgaria and Switzerland—however, there is still work to be done for further, more in-depth elaboration of this complex social and economic phenomenon.

References

Artelaris, P., Kallioras, D., & Petrakos, G. (2010). Regional inequalities and convergence clubs in the European Union new member-states. *Eastern Journal of European Studies, 1*(1), 113–133.

Bentivogli, C., & Pagano, P. (1999). Regional disparities and labour mobility: The Euro-11 versus the USA. *Labour, 13*(3), 737–760.

Crespo-Cuaresma, J., Dimitz, M., & Ritzberger-Gruenwald, D. (2003). The impact of European integration on growth: What can we learn for EU accession? Economic convergence and divergence in Europe. In G. Tumpel-Gugerell & G. P. Mooslechner (Eds.), *Economic convergence and divergence in Europe* (pp. 55–72). Cheltenham: Edward Elgar.

De Haas, H. (2010). *Migration transitions: A theoretical and empirical inquiry into the developmental drivers of international migration* (International Migration Institute Working Paper 24). University of Oxford. Retrieved September 25, 2015, from http://www.imi.ox.ac.uk/publications/wp.

EC. (2012). *Eurostat regional yearbook 2012.* Luxembourg: EU Publications Office.

EC. (2015). *Cohesion policy data.* European Commission, Eurostat. Retrieved September 25, 2015, from https://cohesiondata.ec.europa.eu/.

Fidrmuc, J. (2004). Migration and regional adjustment to asymmetric shocks in transition economies. *Journal of Comparative Economics, 32*, 230–247.

Fischer, M., & Stirböck, C. (2006). Pan-European regional income growth and club-convergence. *The Annals of Regional Science, 40*(4), 693–721.

Harbinson, F., Manubrick, J., & Resnick, J. R. (1970). *Quantitative analysis of modernization and development.* Princeton: Princeton University Press.

Hellwig, Z. (1968). *Procedure of evaluating high-level manpower data and typology of countries by means of the taxonomic method.* Paris: UNESCO, Methods and Analysis Unit.

Isard, W. (1975). *Introduction to regional science.* Englewood Cliffs, NJ: Prentice-Hall.

Kostadinova, S., et al. (2014). *Regional profiles: Indicators for development*. Sofia: Foundation "America for Bulgaria" and Institute for Market Economy.

Kutscherauer, A. et al. (2010). *Disparities in country regional development—Concept, theory, identification and assessment* (Research Report WD-55-07-1). Ostrava: Technical University of Ostrava. Retrieved September 25, 2015, from http://disparity.vsb.cz/edice_cd/cd11_regdis_mono_angl/.

Morris, M. (1979). *Measuring the condition of the world's poor: The physical quality of life index*. New York: Pergamon Press.

Mullineux, A., & Murinde, V. (2003). Financial sector convergence in Europe. In G. Tumpel-Gugerell & P. Mooslechner (Eds.), *Economic convergence and divergence in Europe* (pp. 322–344). Cheltenham: Edward Elgar.

Narain, P., Rai, S. C., Sarup, S., & Bhatia, V. K. (2009). Inter-district variation of socio-economic development in Andhra Pradesh. *Journal of Indian Society of Agricultural Statistics, 56*(1), 52–63.

Nenovski, N. & Figuet, J. M. (2006). *Convergence and Shocks in the road to EU: Empirical investigations for Bulgaria and Romania* (William Davidson Institute Working Paper, N. 810). Retrieved September 25, 2015, from http://deepblue.lib.umich.edu/handle/2027.42/40196.

OECD. (2003). *Geographic concentration and territorial disparity in OECD countries*. Paris: OECD.

Puga, D. (2002). European regional policies in light of recent location theories. *Journal of Economic Geography, 2*(4), 373–406.

Ravenstein, E. G. (1885). The laws of migration. *Journal of the Royal Statistical Society, 48*, 167–227.

Ravenstein, E. G. (1889). The laws of migration. *Journal of the Royal Statistical Society, 52*, 214–301.

Sala-i-Martin, X. (2002). *15 years of new growth economics: What have we learnt?* (Discussion Papers 0102-47). Columbia: Department of Economics, Columbia University. Retrieved September 25, 2015, from http://www.econ.upf.edu/docs/papers/downloads/620.pdf.

Solow, R. M. (1956). A contribution to the theory of economic growth. *Quarterly Journal of Economics, 70*(1), 65–94.

Vinhas De Souza, L., & Holschner, J. (2000). Exchange rate linkages and strategies of new EU entrants. *Journal of European Integration, 23*(1), 1–27.

Yankova, N., Shopov, G., Ivanov, S., Hristoskov, Y., & Kirilova, Y. (2010). *Territorial disparities in Bulgaria—Tendencies, factors, policies*. Sofia: Bulgarian Academy of Sciences.

Chapter 5
The Impact of Policies on Migration Between Switzerland and Bulgaria

Irena Zareva

5.1 Introduction

There are different causes for migration while migration policies set a framework that affects, in a specific manner, migrant flows and integration. They are one of the determinants of international migration. Besides, migration flows are affected not only by migration policies, but also by other (non-migration) policies: labour market, social welfare, taxation, education, anti-discrimination, etc. as well as by (im) migration policies of other (third) countries and interactions between states.

Migration policies could be restrictive or expansive, aimed at regulating the levels and composition of migrants' flows.

Two main immigration policy areas could be distinguished: immigration control (immigration regulation and governing the admission of foreigners) and immigrant integration. Integration is related to the participation of foreigners in economic, social, political and cultural life.

The effects and effectiveness of migration policies could be various. In order to assess them, socio-economic and political conditions in a country and their relative importance in determining migration, policy gaps, imperfections of implementation, etc. must be taken into account.

The attitudes and responses to international migration at national level depend on the specific socio-economic, political, cultural, etc. circumstances. The international relations, the co-operation and interactions among states, as well as the regional integration processes such as the case of the EU are also important in this respect.

Wealthy and predominantly immigration countries, such as Switzerland, try to limit immigration flows to a certain extent and to regulate their composition. Countries

I. Zareva (✉)
Economic Research Institute at the Bulgarian Academy of Sciences, Sofia, Bulgaria
e-mail: i.zareva@iki.bas.bg

© Springer International Publishing Switzerland 2017
M. Richter et al. (eds.), *Migration and Transnationalism Between Switzerland and Bulgaria*, DOI 10.1007/978-3-319-31946-9_5

typical of which are intensive migration outflows of predominantly young and well-educated people, such as Bulgaria, are willing to elaborate and implement policies aimed at facilitating return migration, to attract migrants back, especially if they are characterized also by accelerated ageing of population, slower socio-economic development and lower competitiveness.

This chapter deals with the Swiss and Bulgarian migration policies and their alterations under the influence of the changing international relations and processes of European integration, and more precisely the accession of Bulgaria to the EU. It outlines specificities and the purposefulness of these policies in the two countries.

After a review of literature, addressing the issues of the nature and effects of migration policies, and of the Bulgarian-Swiss relations and migration policies, empirical findings provided by the analysis of the results of the quantitative and qualitative surveys in Bulgaria and in Switzerland are presented. They demonstrate the influence of migration policies upon migration flows between the two countries, despite their low intensity, and especially upon migration flow from Bulgaria to Switzerland.

5.2   Literature Overview

There are different theories trying to determine and explain the causes of migration as briefly outlined in Chap. 2. National and international legislations, agreements, and policies, however, set a framework which affects, in a specific manner, international migration, migration flows and migrants' integration. Migration policies, in other words states' laws, regulations, activities, etc., by which national states select and (do not) admit foreign citizens, and integrate them into their public life, are another considerable determinant of migration.

Standing on the thesis of Money (1999) that there are two separate policy types — immigration control and immigrant integration, Givens and Luedtke (2005) distinguish two policy areas and their related fields: on one side, immigration control — including illegal immigration, political asylum, family reunification, and legal labour immigration; and on the other side, immigrant integration — including citizenship and anti-discrimination. Immigration control policies deal with the problem of who could have access to a state, while immigrant integration policies are aimed at persons who have crossed national borders and do currently live in a host country.

Migration policies could be restrictive or expansive by means of: increase or decrease in quotas, requirements, fees, etc. for entry; waiting time and requirements to obtain work permit or residence; access to labour market and public services, and so on. Their aim is to regulate (control) the levels and composition (skills, for example) of migration flows. Normally, wealthy countries treat immigration (especially of low-skilled persons of poorer countries) as a problem and try to increase border control and to implement restrictive immigration policies (De Haas 2011).

Different opinions and assessments of the abilities of states to control migration and of the effectiveness of migration policies can be found in the literature. De Haas

(2011) presents two opposite stands. Some researchers argue that borders are "beyond control" and migration outflows cannot be curtailed. Therefore, national governments should reorient their policies to exploit the benefits of migration (Bhagwati 2003). Others claim that, on the whole, immigration policies have been largely effective (for example, Brochmann and Hammar 1999).

There are evidences in the literature, showing that the effects of targeted migration policies could be relatively smaller compared to other determinants of migration such as economic, social or political (non-migration policies). The arguments of those authors according to which immigration policies are often ineffective are related to the idea that international migration is driven mainly by other factors like: labour market demand, social inequalities, migration networks, etc. All these factors seem to lead to limited effects of the immigration policies.

Stephen Castles (2004), for example, claims that the most important factors that shape migration could be generalized as: (1) factors arising from the social dynamics of the migratory process, such as chain migration and migrant networks, position within the life cycle, the migration industry, migrant agency, structural dependence on emigration and on immigrant labour; (2) factors linked to globalization, transnationalism and North–South relationships; (3) factors within political systems, such as political conflicts in emigration countries, conflicts of interest in immigration countries, conflicts of interest and hidden agendas in migration policies, the political ability to control migration and the importance of rights and civil society. His conclusion is that the driving forces of international migration are very complex and are grounded on the general social transformation processes. They, however, interact with another set of forces in the processes of elaboration and implementation of policy. So, the results could be poorly conceived, narrow and contradictory policies, the consequences of which may be unintended. A conclusion of Thielemann (2004) is that some of the well-known public policy measures which aim to regulate the unwanted migration are not as effective as it has been assumed.

Yet, the effects of migration policies should not be underestimated. According to Czaika and De Haas (2013), there is empirical evidence that policies significantly affect migration and the fact that there are other factors which exert influence upon migration does not mean that policy fails. Policy should be qualified as a failure as such if it does not produce effect. Some researchers state that the effectiveness of state policies has actually increased. Broeders and Engbersen (2007), for example, contend that the effectiveness of state policies has increased, especially as far as it concerns capacity building.

The number of empirical studies in this field is growing, and some of them indicate that legislative immigration restrictions significantly reduce immigration flows. The results of the investigation of Ortega and Peri (2012) show that as countries tighten their entry conditions, immigration flows fall within the same and in the following years. These authors, as an example, give Europe and the Maastricht treaty which has significantly increased internal migration, while the Schengen treaty has decreased immigration from outside the EU. According to them, the common currency also has a significant and positive effect on the size of migration flows. They claim that regional European economic integration has had a large effect on the size and pattern of migration flows for European destinations (see also Chap. 2).

Determinants of migration are a complex system, the parts of which, including migration policies, should not be treated and studied separately, one from the others. A very important issue when trying to appraise the effectiveness of migration policies is to assess the relative significance of the effects of policies compared to the complexity of macro circumstances which determine migration. In this context, the fact should also be taken into account that the capability of the states which try to regulate migration is limited by legal, political and economic constraints (De Haas 2011).

There is a debate in the literature about the nature and evolution over the last decades of migration policies: if it has become more/less restrictive. More popular is the assumption that migration policies have become more restrictive, especially those which concern border control. De Haas et al. (2014) state that migration policies should be treated as a tool for selection of migrants rather than for affecting numbers. The results of their investigation demonstrate that migration policies have been continuously becoming more restrictive only as far as it concerns illegal migration. At present, the nationality criterion is used not as a policy tool to deny entry, but as an exemption mechanism to grant privileged access. Such are the cases of regional free mobility among EU countries, of bilateral labour migration agreements on seasonal workers, trainees or specific professional occupations. At the same time, access to regular migration options may instead be limited for those originating from countries which are not selected for these preferential policies.

Notwithstanding the existing debates in the literature and the still insufficient empirical evidence of the effectiveness and impacts of migration policies on international migration, the importance of this issue stimulates researchers of different countries to continue their investigations. A number of projects have been implemented trying to determine the effects of migration policies and to assess their influence upon migration flows and migrants' integration.

Further in this chapter, we present the EU, Swiss and Bulgarian migration policies, their specific character and purpose, as well as empirical evidence about the influence of the migration policies and their alterations on the migration flows from Bulgaria to Switzerland.

5.3   EU Migration Policy

At present, migration relations between Bulgaria and Switzerland are tied with the EU migration policy since Bulgaria is a member state and its national policy is harmonized with that of the EU, and Switzerland and the EU are bound by a number of bilateral agreements, including the one on free movement of persons.

A fundamental right within the EU is the free movement of persons. Its importance is underlined in Article 45 of the Charter of fundamental rights of the EU: "(1) Every citizen has the right to move and reside freely within the territory of the Member States. (2) Freedom of movement and residence may be granted, in accordance with the Treaty establishing the European Community, to nationals of third countries legally resident in the territory of a member State" (EP 2000). The acquisition of such a right is an example of the alterations of migration policies under the influence of changes in international relations and European integration.

The concept of free movement of persons was put into practice through the Schengen Agreement (1985) and the Schengen Convention (1990) by the abolition of border control between participating countries and was established by the Maastricht Treaty (1992) by the introduction of the notion of EU citizenship. In April 2004, the EU adopted the Directive 2004/38/EC "on the right of citizens of the Union and their family members to move and reside freely within the territory of the Member States" (EU 2004), which encourages Union citizens to exercise their right to move and reside freely within member states. According to the Directive, no visa is required to enter another member state. The right of residence for more than 3 months however is subject to certain conditions—to be engaged in economic activity, or have sufficient resources in order not to become a burden on the social services of the host member state during the stay, or be a student or be a family member of a Union citizen. Residence permits are abolished for EU citizens and after a 5-year period of uninterrupted legal residence in the host member state they acquire the right of permanent residence.

The Stockholm Programme (An open and secure Europe serving and protecting citizens) adopted by the European Council in December 2009 sets out the EU priorities for the area of justice, freedom and security for the period 2010–2014. It recalls the importance of individual rights as enshrined in the EU treaties by emphasizing that Europe must be an area in which citizens and their family members may exercise in full the right to free movement. In this context, the transformations of the EU policy on migration control are carried out together with changes in migrants' integration policies.

The right of free movement of *workers* within the EU indicates that every EU national has the right to work in another EU country without a work permit, reside there and be equally treated as nationals in access to employment, working conditions and other social and tax benefits—may have certain types of health and social security coverage and recognized professional qualifications, etc.

One of the main Regulations giving effect to that right is the Regulation (EU) 492/2011 on freedom of movement for workers within the Union (EU 2011). According to the Regulation "freedom of movement constitutes a fundamental right of workers and their families". The attainment of the objective of free movement for workers entails the abolition of any discrimination based on nationality between workers of the member states as regards employment, remuneration and other work and employment conditions. There are, however, transitional arrangements which hamper these rights by setting specific restrictions on the free movement of workers from the new EU member states for a period of up to 7 years after they join the EU. At the moment, they concern workers from Croatia which joined the EU in 2013.

Finally, as deemed relevant for this discussion, in 2011 the Commission presented a new set of measures aimed at establishing a comprehensive European migration policy (CEC 2011). One of the aspects of migration, addressed in this

Communication, concerns the integration of migrants. According to that document, the successful integration is essential for maximizing the economic, social and cultural advantages of migration, for individuals and for societies.

5.4 Swiss Immigration Policy

Having been predominantly a country of emigration, at the end of nineteenth century Switzerland became one of immigration. The number of legally resident foreigners has been growing almost permanently and in 1994 it exceeded 20 % of the total resident population for the first time.

According to data of Switzerland's Federal Office of Migration (FOM 2013/2014),[1] since World War II, over two million people have immigrated to Switzerland or live there as the descendants of immigrants; at over 23 %, Switzerland has one of the highest foreigner-to-total population ratios in Europe; one in every four employed persons in Switzerland has a foreign passport. The hardships of the naturalization process need, however, to be mentioned here to explain this data which often include first and second generation migrants who have not acquired or yet applied for the Swiss citizenship.

Switzerland is known by its decentralized government and most laws are made at canton level. The migration and integration policies are also a matter of cantonal sovereignty to a certain extent. Communes and cantons are responsible for naturalization matters and the Federal Government lays down the relevant criteria. Residence permits are issued by the Cantonal Migration Offices.

The integration actions, measures and programmes are elaborated and implemented by cantons and communes and are co-funded by the FOM (SEM). Cantonal integration programmes (CIP) are devised by cantons. Uniform performance agreements are signed with the FOM (SEM). From 2014, integration measures have been taken all over Switzerland in several areas of action (FOM 2013/2014): information and counselling (orientation and needs assessment, counselling, protection against discrimination), education and employment (language and learning, preschool support, employability), mutual understanding and social integration (intercultural interpreting, social integration).

The prevailing part of nationals immigrated to Switzerland came from EU-28 countries. In 2014 out of over 1.9 million persons, 1,328,318 came from the EU-28 (of which 5644 from Bulgaria)[2] (FOM 2014). A distinction is made in Switzerland between foreign workers when granting residence and work permits: EU/EFTA nationals and third-state nationals. Those coming from EU countries benefit from the Swiss-EU bilateral agreement on the free movement of persons, and those from

---

[1] As of 01.01.2015 State Secretariat for Migration (SEM).

[2] We refer in this chapter to the data of the SEM because they provide more detailed data for our purposes.

other states are subjected to quotas and their admission is possible mostly for persons with high professional qualifications.

Two significant policy changes took place in recent years regarding regular immigration in Switzerland. Firstly, the Federal Act on Foreign Nationals[3] (migraweb 2015) that came into force in 2008 constitutes a higher barrier for nationals of non-EU/EFTA states to enter Switzerland. Two important factors determine the quotas of persons admitted: the current economic situation and the need for labour in certain segments of the market. In order to find work in Switzerland, non-EU nationals need to be highly qualified and able to perform a job that no Swiss person can do. Without a job arranged in advance, as confirmed by the empirical work presented in Chap. 6, they cannot take up residence. As mentioned earlier, wealthy countries as Switzerland try to implement restrictive immigration policies, especially with respect to low-skilled migrants from poorer countries and in spite of the still unsatisfied needs of the lower segments of their labour markets.

Secondly, relations between Switzerland and the EU have recently also gone through significant changes. Switzerland is a large economic partner of the EU: "… over a million EU citizens live in Switzerland and another 230,000 cross the border daily for work. About 430,000 Swiss live in the EU" (EC 2014). The free trade agreement of 1972 lays the foundation of the Swiss-EU relations. In 1999, seven sectoral bilateral agreements were signed ("Bilaterals I") which include: free movement of persons, technical trade barriers, public procurement, agriculture and air and land transport (road and rail). In 2004, another set of sectoral agreements was approved ("Bilaterals II"). An agreement on Swiss participation in EU education, professional training and youth programmes was later signed in 2010. At present, the EU and Switzerland are bound by more than a hundred bilateral agreements.

In 2002, the Bilateral Agreement on the Free Movement of Persons between Switzerland and the EU member states came into force. The right of free movement is supplemented by the mutual recognition of professional qualifications and the coordination of social security systems. The Agreement was extended in 2006 to the new member states which joined the EU in 2004 (the Protocol I was signed in 2004) and to Bulgaria and Romania in 2009 (the Protocol II was approved by the Parliament in 2008). The transition period which includes the already mentioned transitional measures, as well as specific regulations for Bulgaria and Romania, however, should end in 2016. Citizens from the two countries are facing restricted access to the Swiss labour market, which means that the native labour force is given precedence and salary and working conditions may be checked by the authorities and are subject to special quotas.

The popular vote in Switzerland of 9 February 2014 in favour of the introduction of annual quotas to limit immigration, poses a question for the EU-Swiss agreement

---

[3] The Federal Act on Foreign Nationals was approved by the Swiss voters on the 24th of September 2006 and has been in force since the 1st of January 2008. The law deals primarily with the entry and residence of persons who are not EU or EFTA citizens and are not asylum seekers. The law restricts access to the Swiss employment market to those who are particularly well qualified for jobs in Switzerland but are not EU or EFTA citizens.

Table 5.1 Number of permanent foreign resident population by nationality and duration of residence (end of December 2014) (FOM 2014)

Nationality	Total	Born abroad Duration up to 10 years	Born abroad Duration 10 and more years
Total	1,947,023	995,742	951,281
EU-28 countries	1,328,318	713,392	614,926
Bulgaria	5644	4839	805

on the free movement of persons. As a result of this referendum, the extension of the agreement to Croatia was suspended and separate quotas were later introduced for the access of Croatian citizens to the Swiss labour market (see Federal Department of Foreign Affairs FDFA 2015). In July 2014, Switzerland presented a request to the EU to revise the Agreement on free movement of persons. If or until that happens, all current agreements remain[4] (see SEM 2015).

The admission of foreign workers in Switzerland is organized as a dual system. Nationals from the EU and EFTA states can benefit (gainful employment) from agreements on the free movement of persons. A limited number of qualified employees are admitted from all other countries. In 2013, 84 % of all third-state nationals who received a permit were holders of higher education qualification (FOM 2013/2014).

Anyone who works during a stay in Switzerland or who remains in Switzerland longer than 3 months requires a permit. Residence permits could be short-term (less than 1 year), annual (limited) and permanent (unlimited). At the end of December 2014, out of the total foreign population permanently resident in Switzerland (1,947,023 persons), the number of short-term residents (up to 12 months) is 28,628 (or 1.5 %), of residents 651,623 (33.5 %), and of settled residents 1,266,772 (65 %) (FOM 2014).

Most of the permanent foreign residents in Switzerland arrived from the EU-28 countries. As mentioned earlier, the number of Bulgarians is not big and the prevailing part of them has come during the last 10 years and especially after the accession of Bulgaria to the EU (Table 5.1).

Bulgarian immigrants in Switzerland have increased, mainly after the extension of the Agreement of Free Movement of Persons to Bulgaria (2009); therefore, confirming the hypothesis that changes in the migration policy have exerted influence on the size of migrants' flows. However, access to the Swiss labour market, which is still restricted, has hampered a faster growth of the number of migrants. The share of Bulgarian immigrants in the total number of the permanent foreign resident population in Switzerland is still not sizable (below 0.3 %).

---

[4] On 11.02.2015 the Federal Council approved the draft of the new legislation on foreign nationals and additional measures to make better use of the potential workforce within Switzerland. It also made a final decision on the negotiating mandate with the EU on the Agreement on the Free Movement of Persons. The new article 121a of the Federal Constitution contains two assignments for completion by February 2017, which are aimed at introducing a new immigration system and negotiating with the EU on an amendment to the Agreement on Free Movement of Persons (AFMP).

Notwithstanding the comparatively fast growing number of foreign population, Swiss immigration policy can be defined in general as restrictive, especially as far as it concerns non-EU/EFTA nationals, but not only. Despite the fact that Bulgaria is an EU member state, the specific regulations which restrict the access to the Swiss labour market and limit the free movement of persons for Bulgarian nationals are still in force. Switzerland, like some EU member states, did in fact apply the full 7-year transitional regime from the time of the extension of the Swiss-EU bilateral agreements to Bulgaria and Romania. Under the conditions of the last economic crisis, an inclination towards more restrictions is observed in the country, and it concerns also the EU member states.

As pointed out before, there are two main areas of immigration policy—immigration control and immigrant integration. In order to assess policies which promote integration (in both social and civic terms) in European societies a special index MIPEX is developed and applied[5] (MIPEX 2015). MIPEX includes policy indicators on migrant integration in several policy areas. Despite its imperfections, it is an example of the attempts to define the effects and the extent of the impact of immigrant integration policies. The strengths and weaknesses of the policies of Switzerland specify the ranks of the country by policy areas.

According to MIPEX 2015, Switzerland ranks 21st (out of 38 countries) with 49 points. Not so favourable is the assessment in the following policy areas: access to nationality and anti-discrimination—slightly unfavourable—as earlier explained by the difficulty in accessing Swiss citizenship and by the lack of an anti-discrimination framework. The areas of education, family reunion, permanent residence, political participation, and labour market mobility are assessed as halfway favourable. The only area which is considered as slightly favourable is health, probably as an outcome of the policy improvements recently introduced at national level, as well as the longstanding NGOs' practices targeting ageing migrants and more recent mixed migrant flows. No policy area is, however, scored 80 or more points which according to the MIPEX methodology means favourable.

5.5 Bulgarian Migration Policy

Bulgaria is a so-called net emigration country with permanent negative migration increase for the period 2007–2014 (Fig. 5.1). The most unfavourable period in this respect was 2009–2010, after the beginning of the economic crisis in the country. Since 2012, the "refugee wave" to the country[6] (State Agency for Refugees with the

---

[5] The research is undertaken by Barcelona Centre for International Affairs (CIDOB) and the Migration Policy Group (MPG) in cooperation with the research partners (37 national-level organizations are integrated with the MIPEX project).

[6] According to data of the State Agency for Refugees, the main refugee flow to Bulgaria comes predominantly from Syria, Iraq and Afghanistan. Since 2012, and especially in 2013 and 2014, the

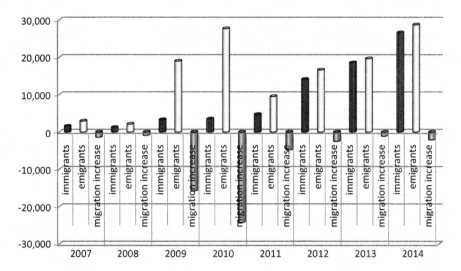

Fig. 5.1 External migration (number). Data on external migration include only persons who have declared to the administrative authorities a change of their present address in the country to a new one outside; and a change of an address outside the country to a new one in the country. Source: Bulgarian National Statistical Institute (NSI Accessed 14 Sept 2015)

Council of Ministers 2015) and emigration from Bulgaria which is again growing have led to a relative balance and small negative migration increase.

Because of the fact that the country is a predominantly sending one, it is trying to elaborate adequate policy towards its citizens living abroad. New national strategies in this area are developed and implemented. Notwithstanding these efforts, the migrant outflow from Bulgaria is not diminishing.

The state policy towards the Bulgarians living abroad is aimed at: assistance to the Bulgarian citizens and communities outside the country, inclusion of Bulgarian migrants in the country's public life, and attraction of persons of Bulgarian origin back to Bulgaria. It is regulated by the Law on Bulgarians Living outside the Republic of Bulgaria, adopted in 2000.[7] According to the Law, the Bulgarian state assists the creation of favourable conditions for free development of the Bulgarians living outside the country with the purpose of assistance and protection of migrants' rights and legal interests, and also the preservation and development of the Bulgarian linguistic, cultural and religious traditions.

For the purpose of preservation of the national, cultural and spiritual identity of Bulgarians abroad, a National Programme "Native language and culture beyond border" has been implemented since the 2009/2010 school year. The aim of the Programme is to assist the study of Bulgarian language and literature, history and geography by the children of Bulgarian migrants. Furthermore, the Employment Promotion Law (2002) regulates social relations in promotion and support of

---

number of asylum seekers sharply increased; having been 890 persons in 2011, it reached 1387 in 2012, 7144 in 2013 and 11,081 in 2014.

[7] Because of the change in conditions since 2000 and the accession of Bulgaria to the EU, a new up-to-date law is expected to be devised.

employment, including intermediation for furnishing information and placement of Bulgarian citizens abroad.

After the accession of Bulgaria to the EU, the country has been striving to be in line with the new international conditions, relations and arrangements, and with the new developments in migration and protection issues. Several national strategies in the field of migration have been adopted since then.

The National Strategy on Migration and Integration (2008–2015) sets two main objectives: (1) attracting Bulgarian nationals and foreigners of Bulgarian origin to permanently settle in Bulgaria; (2) pursuing a modern policy for receiving third-country nationals with a view to contributing to the development of the Bulgarian economy and effectively regulating and controlling migration. Some of the envisaged activities are: maintaining stable connections with the Bulgarian communities and their organizational structures abroad; consistent activities for the defence of the rights of Bulgarian citizens staying and working in other countries; analysis of the attitudes of the young highly qualified Bulgarian emigrants for repatriation and professional realization in the homeland; permanent and steady activities for the opening of schools for learning Bulgarian language, history and culture, etc. (pp. 20, 21).

The Strategy was revised and remains in effect in the form of a Migration and Integration Programme (2008–2015) after the adoption of the new National Strategy on Migration, Asylum and Integration (2011–2020). The latter is one of the strategic Bulgarian documents the purpose of which is to develop a policy framework providing a comprehensive and sustainable regulatory and institutional basis for ensuring successful management of legal migration and integration while preventing and counteracting illegal migration. Its main feature is the strong accent on security issues. Notwithstanding this peculiarity, the Strategy again sets the aim of attracting back Bulgarian citizens who have left the country in the last two decades, to prevent their emigration becoming permanent, so that it is followed instead by a return (p 3).

In mid 2014, Bulgaria's Council of Ministers adopted a National Strategy for Bulgarian citizens and Bulgarian communities worldwide. The aim of the Strategy is to establish a political framework for the creation of a complex, long-term and integrated state policy for the Bulgarian citizens and historical Bulgarian communities outside the country. According to the Strategy, the state policy should be orientated towards the achievement of the four following strategic goals: (1) attraction and inclusion of Bulgarian citizens—temporary or permanently living abroad—in the public and political life in Bulgaria; (2) preservation of the Bulgarian ethno-cultural area outside the country; (3) improvement of the migration balance in the country; (4) establishment and maintenance of a Bulgarian lobby abroad.

A year later (in June 2015) the Bulgarian government approved another strategic document—the National Strategy in the Field of Migration, Asylum and Integration (2015–2020) which unites the previous analogical strategies and updates them according to the changes in the country and in the EU that have occurred after the refugee crisis in 2013. Some of the main priorities of the national policy in the field of migration, embedded in the Strategy, include once more return and permanent resettlement options in Bulgaria for highly qualified Bulgarian emigrants and foreigners of Bulgarian origin, as well as assistance to Bulgarian citizens in terms of their EU citizens' free movement rights in the EU and EEA.

Being a country characterized by constant negative migration increase during the past years (see Fig. 5.1), Bulgaria is also the country with the highest negative natural increase of the population in the EU (−5.7‰ in 2014, while the indicator for the EU-28 is 0.2‰ in 2013). These negative trends have necessitated the elaboration of a National Strategy for Demographic Development in the Republic of Bulgaria (2012–2030).[8] The Strategy formulates guidelines and priority tasks in the area of the demographic policy, as well as in ensuring high quality human capital, while some of them are aimed at formulation of adequate migration policy (including attraction of Bulgarians living abroad) and significant decrease in the emigration of young people of reproductive age.

The institutional framework for the implementation of the state policy towards Bulgarian living abroad, which has been established since the accession of Bulgaria to the EU, is broad. A number of governmental institutions are involved in this issue which include, among others, the Council of Ministers, Ministry of Foreign Affairs and Agency for Bulgarians Abroad, Ministry of Labour and Social Policy, Ministry of Education and Science, Ministry of Culture, Ministry of Justice, Ministry of Internal Affairs, etc. Each of these institutions is, however, connected with different aspects of the activities and some of them have certain specific competences.

The State Agency for Bulgarians Abroad has the main task of implementing the state policy for Bulgarians abroad. It coordinates the work of the state institutions in this field. The Ministry of Labour and Social Policy is responsible for the signing of bilateral employment agreements and social security agreements with third countries, for assisting Bulgarian nationals in exercising their employment and social security rights. The Employment Agency (an executive agency under the Minister of Labour and Social Policy) assists Bulgarian nationals for their employment abroad in line with the international treaties and employment agreements, as well as within the EURES (European Employment Services) information and mediation network. A network of Labour and Social Affairs' Offices has been established in the Bulgarian embassies in other EU member states to contribute to the practical implementation of the free movement of Bulgarian nationals and to help them exercise their rights as EU citizens.

In 2011, a National Council on Migration Policy was first established as a linking unit between the respective ministries, local authorities, NGOs, and international organizations on the territory of the country engaged in the management of migration processes, with a view to improving the co-operation and coordination between the different actors in the field of migration policy.

The efforts of the Bulgarian state to attract Bulgarian nationals and foreigners of Bulgarian origin back to the country, however, seem to be without sizable effect. Policy gaps and imperfections, ways of implementation, etc. are important in this respect. Yet attracting emigrants back, especially young and well-educated persons, is not only an issue of migration policy, but also of creating favourable living and working conditions in the country, adequate to their needs and aspirations.

---

[8] The strategy builds upon the National Strategy for Demographic Development 2006–2020.

5.6 Bilateral Bulgarian-Swiss Relations

This section aims at linking the Swiss and Bulgarian migration policy framework by briefly exploring the evolution of the bilateral relations between the Republic of Bulgaria and the Swiss Confederation across time and in light of the changing political and socio-economic realities.

The diplomatic relations between the two countries were established in 1915 when consulates were opened, which about 20 years later were given the status of legations. In 1963, the legations were transformed into embassies. To promote and support bilateral economic relations an Agreement on economic relation was signed in 1972.

At present, the contractual and legal basis of the bilateral relations in different areas has been set up and the agreements between the two countries are mainly in the spheres of trade, economic and financial relations.

From the beginning of the transition process to a market economy, more specifically from 1992, till the admission of Bulgaria to the EU (2007), the collaboration between the two countries had been focused on Swiss assistance to the transition in Bulgaria. With the accession of Bulgaria to the EU, the contractual and legal basis has been gradually adapted to the bilateral agreements, signed between Switzerland and the EU, which are applied in the relations with the newly accessed countries. The character and the forms of the Swiss assistance have changed as a result. From 2009 the support of the Swiss Confederation to Bulgaria has been directed towards the decrease of economic and social disparities inside the enlarged EU. That support is performed within the framework of the Memorandum of Understanding between the Council of the EU and the Swiss Federal Council, which envisaged a Swiss financial contribution for the benefit of the member states (2006), and the Addendum to the Memorandum, stating the additional financial contribution to Bulgaria and Romania (2008).

A bilateral Framework Agreement between the government of the Republic of Bulgaria and the Swiss Federal Council concerning the implementation of the Swiss-Bulgarian Cooperation Programme to reduce economic and social disparities within the enlarged EU was approved in 2010. The Swiss-Bulgarian Cooperation Programme, among the several areas to foster further cooperation between the two countries, focuses on the reduction of economic and social disparities between dynamic urban centres and structurally weak peripheral regions in Bulgaria in order to achieve sustainable economic and social balanced development.

In the economic sphere, the Bulgarian-Swiss Chamber of Commerce was established at the end of 2004 with the purpose of assisting and promoting bilateral economic and trade relations. The Chamber submits information, contacts and services to its partners from both countries. The development of bilateral economic relations and their institutionalization through the Chamber of Commerce favour the movement of persons.

While supporting the economic and social development of Bulgaria, which is also related to migration (social inequalities, as mentioned above, are one of the most important determinants of migration), Switzerland has not yet removed some restrictions regarding the free movement of persons and especially labour mobility and migration.

In order to facilitate the movement of citizens of the two countries at the end of 2003 (applied from the beginning of 2004), an Agreement between the Bulgarian government and the Swiss Federal Council for mutual removal of visa requirements was signed. According to the stipulations of this agreement, citizens of each of the two countries, with valid passports, could enter without a visa into the other country and stay there up to 90 days within a 6-month period with no right to gainful employment. This was the first most important step to facilitate the free movement of persons between the two countries.

The next steps were made after the accession of Bulgaria to the EU. A "Transitory Agreement" between the EU and Switzerland on the free movement of persons was signed in 1999 in Luxembourg and applied with effect from 2002. In 2008, a Protocol to the Agreement was approved to recognize Bulgaria and Romania as negotiating countries. However, according to its Protocol II, Bulgarian citizens need a permit in order to have access to the Swiss labour market. To obtain a work permit, a request from a Swiss employer is necessary, who has to prove that there are no other suitable local workers or specialists from the EU, living in the country, for that job.

The Swiss labour market is not open for free access for Bulgarians and the limitations will probably stay in place until 2016. There are, however, possibilities for further restrictions that could result from the Swiss popular vote "against mass immigration" (2014). Besides, the number of work permits is also limited by quota.

There is an Agreement signed in 1995 and amended in 2003 between the governments of the Republic of Bulgaria and the Swiss Confederation on the exchange of a limited number of young professionals (trainees) in the age group 18–35 years with completed vocational education (secondary or tertiary). Directly related to labour mobility, the Agreement gives the opportunity to exchange Bulgarian and Swiss citizens, with acquired professions, to work for a limited period of time in the other country in order to improve their professional (occupational) and linguistic skills. The work permits are for the period of 12 months with a possibility of a maximum prolongation of 6 more months and the job must be in the profession studied by the applicant. Despite the opportunities the Agreement affords, its practical effects are minimal. According to data of the Bulgarian Employment Agency (at the Ministry of Labour and Social Policy), only three persons in 2011 and seven persons in 2012 received permission to work in Switzerland under this Agreement.

Another aspect of the changes of migration policies, which facilitates the movement of persons between the two countries, is related to Annex II to the Agreement between the EU and the Swiss Confederation on free movement of persons which foresees coordination between the social insurance schemes. A bilateral Insurance Agreement was first signed in 2006. The agreement concerns the equal rights and obligations of the citizens of the two countries, their families and inheritors, ensuing from the respective national legal regulations of social insurance. It ensures equal access to social insurance systems and foresees mutual recognition and recapitulation of insurance periods. After the admission of Bulgaria to the EU, the above-mentioned agreement was replaced by an EU-Swiss Agreement on coordination of social security schemes, which provides common rules for protection of social security rights. From 2009, the Regulation (EC) 1408/71 has replaced the Bulgarian-Swiss Insurance Agreement.

The bilateral Bulgarian-Swiss relations are regulated by a number of agreements which are shortly described in this section. Two important actions to facilitate the free movement of persons which took place in the last few years need to be emphasized: the visa removal in 2003 and the extension of the Agreement between the EU and Switzerland on the free movement of persons to Bulgaria in 2008. Notwithstanding these policy changes, the access of Bulgarians to the Swiss labour market is still limited, which poses some barriers for migrant flows.

5.7 Impact of Migration Policies: Empirical Evidences

Following the description of the migration legislative and policy frameworks linking Switzerland and Bulgaria in the context of wider European integration processes, in this section the collected empirical data from the Bulgarian and Swiss quantitative surveys is presented. These data highlight the behaviour of Bulgarian potential and actual (currently living abroad) migrants, which allows us, firstly, to outline the influence of migration policy upon the decision whether and where to migrate. Secondly, this information helps in elucidating the extent of migrant integration, according to the opinion of the respondents, in the societies abroad, and especially in Switzerland. Finally, reference to selected qualitative analysis will enrich these data.

5.7.1 Bulgarian Potential Migrants

The results provided by the Bulgarian quantitative survey demonstrate that migration policies have sizable impact upon the decision of the Bulgarian migrants where to migrate. A substantial part of the potential migrants do not want to choose Switzerland as a destination country (nearly 96% of the respondents) and some of the main reasons for more than 31% of them are: Switzerland is not an EU member state, and it is difficult to find a job there (official or unofficial). Other important barriers are the lack of an ethnic network and the high cost of living in the country (Fig. 5.2).

The groups of potential migrants for which the fact that Switzerland is not an EU member state is important when deciding where to migrate are women and persons of the age groups above 45 years. The Swiss restrictive work regime is of significance for persons of the most active age groups 30–44 and 45–59, and for those with higher levels of education and income. The difficulty in finding unofficial work, however, is a problem for women, persons of the age groups 30–44 and 60–65 years, as well as for those with lower incomes.

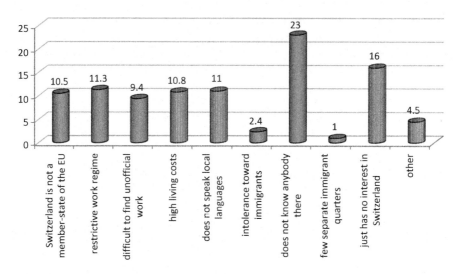

Fig. 5.2 What are the main reasons for NOT choosing Switzerland? (%)

Another potential barrier for migration to Switzerland where there are specific regulations, and the access to the labour market is still restricted for Bulgarians is the fact that Bulgarian migrants rely mainly on their relatives or friends abroad to find a job and to a lesser extent on labour offices or other employment institutions (see Chap. 6). Answering the question "How do you plan to find a job abroad?", 17.1 % of the potential migrants say that they count on the Bulgarian employment agency or labour office (those are predominantly persons of higher age groups— above 45 years, as well as young people below 29 years, and with higher education), 5.3 % on a local labour office or other institution (elderly people above 60 years of age and with higher education), and 3.7 % on Bulgarian employers who are there (mainly men, of higher age groups, with a high level of education and income).

Notwithstanding that the number of Bulgarian potential migrants who prefer Switzerland as a destination country is not very big compared to the total number of that group of respondents (39 and 971, respectively), their views could illustrate the influence of the Swiss immigration policy.

These persons are mainly women 53.8 % (the average percentage of women within the group of Bulgarian potential migrants is 45.4 %); people of the age group 31–40 years (32.5 %), but also 21–30 (27.5 %) and 41–50 years (25 %); with secondary vocational (40 %) and higher education (30 %); employed in private or public companies (46.2 %); students (10.3 %); but also unemployed (33.3 %).

Most of them intend to work in Switzerland (82.1 % compared to 78.6 % of the whole group of potential migrants), 10.3 % intend to study (compared to 8.8 % of all potential migrants) and 7.7 % claim that they do not know what to do and will decide once there (a smaller percentage compared to 10.3 % for the total group). The strict Swiss legislation limits the number of persons who want to migrate but do not know what to do abroad.

Bulgarian potential migrants who prefer Switzerland as a destination country would rely to a greater extent, compared to the others, on Bulgarian employers in

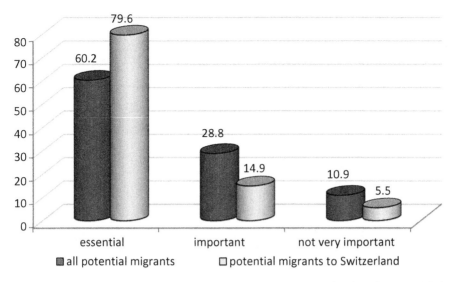

Fig. 5.3   To what extend is it important to you for your job abroad to be legal (under contract)? %

Switzerland (respectively 12.5 and 3.8 %), Bulgarian recruiting companies (21.3 and 12.4 %), local labour institutions (8.5 and 5 %) and to a lesser extent on Bulgarian colleagues and acquaintances working there (17 and 30.2 %), and relatives and family (8.2 and 13.4 %) to find work in the destination country.

It is important for the Bulgarian migrants to find a legal job (under a contract with an employer), (Fig. 5.3). Such an attitude is even stronger for those who prefer Switzerland as a destination country. Almost 95 % of them claim that for them it is very important, and even essential, to find legal work. Legal work is equally important for men and for women, but for men it is predominantly essential (53.8 %) while for women it is very important (75 %). It is not so important for elderly people above 50 years of age and for persons with lower levels of education (primary or lower and secondary general).

The possibilities for and the differences in the ways and extent of integration of the migrants in the destination countries illustrate the influence and the effects of migration policies concerning the scale, intensity and directions of migration flows. The legal barriers that Switzerland's migration policy poses before the access of the Bulgarians to the Swiss labour market obviously impact upon their decision to move to Switzerland.

5.7.2   Bulgarian Migrants in Switzerland

The views of the Bulgarian migrants in Switzerland, provided by the Swiss quantitative survey, confirm the influence of the Swiss migration policy on the possibilities to move there and the position and the extent of their integration.

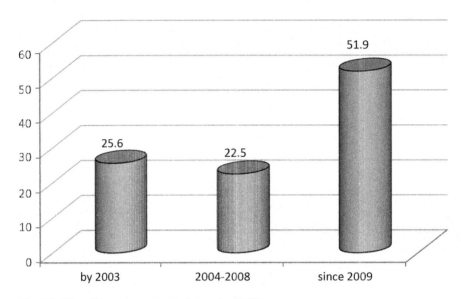

Fig. 5.4 When did you first arrive in Switzerland? (%)

The admission of Bulgaria to the EU and the Agreement on the free movement of persons extended to the country exerted influence on the Bulgarian migration flows to Switzerland. Most of the Bulgarians arrived in Switzerland after 2009. The visa removal in 2003 is also important, but did not play such a big role[9] (Fig. 5.4).

The results from the analysis of the Swiss qualitative survey give another touch to this picture. They support those from the quantitative survey that one big part of the Bulgarian migrants arrived in the country after the visa removal and the other, after the accession of Bulgaria to the EU. Earlier migrants are rare and they came by very individual ways, such as a diplomat working for the UN who is now managing a small international organization, or with some help from Swiss friends.

With the changes in the migration flows, alterations in the profiles of the Bulgarian migrants occur. Among those who arrived before 2003, women, persons from higher age groups, level of education and income prevail. After 2009, more young persons and students have come and thus the structure of the migrants by age, level of education, income and current activity changes (Table 5.2).

The residence permit of almost two-thirds of the Bulgarians in Switzerland is mid-term[10] (FOM 2014). The prevailing part of the Bulgarians who settled in Switzerland before 2003 are residents, while those who arrived after 2003 (after the mutual removal of visas requirement) and 2009 (the extension of the Agreement on free movement of persons to Bulgaria) have mainly mid-term permits (Fig. 5.5).

---

[9] The data correspond to the official statistics. According to FOM (SEM) data, the duration of stay of 3796 persons out of 5644 Bulgarian immigrants is between 0 and 4 years, 1043 persons between 5 and 9 years, 492 persons between 10 and 14 years, 185 persons between 15 and 19 years and 128 persons more than 20 years (FOM 2014).

[10] The official statistical data of the Swiss State Secretariat for Migration show that at the end of 2014 the share of the short-term residents (L) of Bulgarian origin is 7.7%, of the residents (B) 73.5% and of the settled residents (C) 18.8%.

Table 5.2   Profiles of Bulgarian immigrants in Switzerland (%)

		Up to 2003	2004–2008	Since 2009	Total
Gender	Male	32.2	23.6	42.8	35.7
	Female	67.8	76.4	57.2	64.3
Age groups	Up to 30	7.7	21.6	36.8	25.9
	31–40	34.3	52.7	37.5	40.1
	41–50	36.9	19.1	19.1	23.6
	Above 50	21.2	6.6	6.7	10.4
Education	Primary or lower	2.2	2.5	5.9	4.2
	Secondary general	9.1	8.3	15.9	12.5
	Secondary vocational	27.2	20.3	21.8	22.9
	Higher	61.6	68.9	56.4	60.5
Current activity in Switzerland	Work	78.7	71.3	70.6	72.9
	Education	3.7	9.3	14.7	10.7
	Taking care of family members	9.7	15.6	10.6	11.5
	Other	7.8	3.8	4.0	5.0
Groups by income per capita (CHF)	Up to CHF 2100	42.0	38.3	50.6	45.7
	CHF 2100–4200	34.0	39.3	31.6	33.9
	CHF 4200–6300	13.0	11.9	10.8	11.6
	Above CHF 6300	10.9	10.4	7.0	8.8

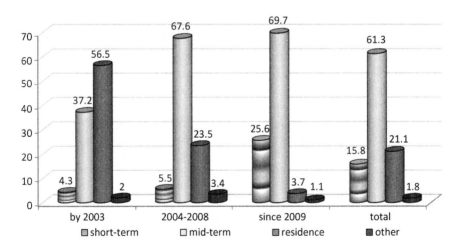

Fig. 5.5   If you are not a Swiss citizen, what type of permit do you have? (%)

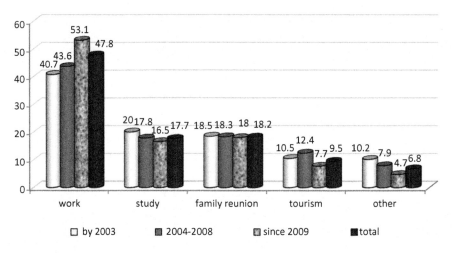

Fig. 5.6 What was the initial purpose of your first visit to Switzerland? (%)

The group of the Bulgarian settlers in Switzerland consists mainly of persons of the age above 40 years, with higher education, and with a slightly prevailing share of women. Those who hold short-term permits are mostly younger men with secondary or higher education.

The predominant part of the Bulgarian migrants—89.5 %—possesses Bulgarian citizenship, 4 % have dual citizenship (Swiss and Bulgarian) permitted by the Bulgarian law,[11] 0.4 % Swiss, and 6 % other. As mentioned already, the difficult access to Swiss nationality (in conformity with the Swiss migration policy) is an essential premise for that.

With the unfavourable Swiss migration policy and the restricted access to the labour market, almost half of the Bulgarian migrants arrived for the first time in Switzerland with the purpose of getting a job; they are mainly men of the age groups above 30 years with higher education. That phenomenon is more obvious after 2008 with the facilitation of free movement of persons between the two countries (Fig. 5.6).

The data from the qualitative survey in Switzerland also show that Bulgarian migrants enter the country as students and as skilled workers, who apply for a job directly from Bulgaria and often find the job through their company. There is also the possibility of entering Switzerland without a regular permit or with temporary arrangements. The distinction is not always clear, and the migrants often try later to regularize their status either through marriage or through a longer lasting work contract, which entitles them first to a permit and later to a permanent permit. Other ways for access to the country are through marriage and family reunion, the same as among other nationalities.

The latter entry's ambition and the Swiss legal requirements, especially those concerning the labour market, determine the way of moving and settling in Switzerland. Swiss employers, together with friends and relatives in Switzerland

---

[11] The Law on Bulgarian Citizenship (1999) allows dual nationality in specific cases.

(see also Chap. 6), are the main supporters of those Bulgarians who actually moved to Switzerland: 35.7 % of the respondents declare that they were supported by an employer in Switzerland (21.7 % by friends in Switzerland, 19.2 % by relatives in Switzerland).

The situation is the same concerning support for settling in Switzerland. Most of the Bulgarian migrants (37.8 %) confirm that they have received assistance by Swiss employers to settle in the country (32.4 % by friends in Switzerland and 25.6 % by family).

The share of the Bulgarian migrants whose purpose for arriving in Switzerland is family reunion is about 18 % (see Fig. 5.6). It does not change significantly in the different periods although these persons have increased as an absolute number since 2009, together with the increase in the total number of Bulgarian migrants. The absence of more obvious changes suggests that no positive developments in this respect have occurred in the Swiss migration legislation.

After 2009, the number of those who have arrived in Switzerland to study increases considerably. Almost half of the respondents of this group have arrived since 2009 (92 persons) while up to 2003 the number was 55 persons and 43 in the period 2004–2008. The policy changes after 2008 have wielded influence in this direction too. The share of these persons, however, slightly decreases due to the higher increase in the number (296, 112 and 105 persons for the respective periods) and, respectively, in the share of those who arrived with the purpose of getting a job (see Fig. 5.6).

Another area of immigrant integration policy is the anti-discrimination actions whose relevance and lack thereof has been introduced earlier by the MIPEX findings. Parts of the Bulgarians in Switzerland think that they have no equal rights in the Swiss labour market because they are foreigners—they had a lower chance to get a job compared to the local people, got a lower payment for the same job, got a job and a position lower than their qualifications and skills, the attitudes of the employers/superiors at work were bad/rude. These are mainly women, persons with secondary or lower education, from lower income groups, migrants who had arrived before 2003, but not only (see Table 5.3 and also Chap. 3 for cross findings).

The still restricted access of Bulgarians to the Swiss labour market and the existing strict regulations and requirements for employment of foreign citizens are a possible explanation of the higher percentage of Bulgarian migrants who reported smaller chances of getting a job compared to local people and of the lower percentage of those who claim that the attitude of employers is bad.

A certain proportion of Bulgarians claim that they are discriminated against in the Swiss labour market. These are persons mainly of the following groups: women, lower educated, from lower income groups and to a comparatively higher extent those who have arrived before 2009 which suggests that the changes in migration policies after the accession of Bulgaria to the EU have led to a decrease in discrimination acts (Table 5.4).

The restrictive immigration policy of Switzerland presupposes a relatively good knowledge of its requirements on the part of the migrants before their departure for the country. About two-thirds of the Bulgarians who had arrived in Switzerland

Table 5.3 Did you face any of the following obstacles at work in Switzerland because you are a foreigner? (Answer YES—%)

	Gender		Income per capita groups (CHF)				Education				Years in Switzerland			Total
	Male	Female	Up to 2100	2100–4200	4200–6300	Above 6300	Primary or lower	Secondary general	Secondary vocational	Higher	Until 2003	2004–2008	Since 2009	
Had a lower chance to get a job compared to the local people	34.1	42.5	42.1	40.5	46.3	34.6	38.3	42.9	44.6	37.2	44.7	42	36.6	39.5
Got a lower payment for the same job compared to local people	19.9	17.4	21.3	20.6	17.6	9.9	22.4	15.8	24.5	16.3	16.5	19.7	19	18.3
Got a job and a position lower than my qualifications and skills	12.1	18.0	17.9	17.4	10.2	8.6	4.1	10.5	15.3	18.1	16.5	18.1	15.1	15.9
The attitudes of the employers/superiors at work were bad/rude	5.8	8.0	8.2	7	5.6	8.6	4.1	6.8	7.6	7.4	8.4	8	6.5	7.2

Table 5.4 Have you experienced any of the following practices while working in Switzerland? (Answer YES — %)

	Gender		Income per capita groups (CHF)				Education				Years in Switzerland			
	Male	Female	Up to 2100	2100–4200	4200–6300	Above 6300	Primary or lower	Secondary general	Secondary vocational	Higher	Until 2003	2004–2008	Since 2009	Total
Working without a contract	5.6	11.0	12.1	9.2	8.3	2.5	16.3	13.5	11.2	6.8	9.9	13.4	7.2	9.0
Fully or partially not paid insurance contributions from employers	4.5	7.6	10.4	4.1	5.6	2.5	10.2	9.8	10.8	3.9	7.3	4.6	7.2	6.5
Increased working time/overtime/shift work/night work without compensation	16.2	16.1	19.9	17.1	15.7	8.6	22.4	23.3	18.5	13.4	14.7	16	17.6	16.1
Insults, physical/psychological abuse	4.8	8.1	8.7	8.2	0.9	4.9	2	8.3	8	6.6	9.9	6.3	5.9	6.9

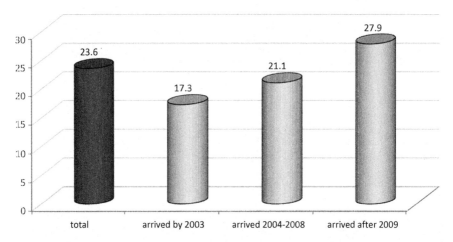

Fig. 5.7 How do you keep track of changes in migration legislation in Switzerland and Bulgaria? Answer "I don't" (%)—total and according to the time of the arrival

before the visa removal and the accession of Bulgaria to the EU claim that they keep track of changes in the Swiss migration legislation. These are mainly persons holding a residence permit and of higher age groups (above 40 years). However, a significant number of migrants do not keep track of changes in migration legislation, especially those who have arrived in the country after 2009 (after the admission of Bulgaria to the EU and the changes in the agreements between the countries), who hold short-term permits and are of lower age groups, especially under 30 years (Fig. 5.7).

It has to be mentioned that persons with higher education levels less frequently follow the changes in the legislation (25–26 % of those with university or higher education do not keep track of changes compared to 22–21 % of the migrants with secondary education or primary or lower education, respectively).

A possible explanation of the above-mentioned phenomena is that these groups of migrants feel more secure because they belong to settled groups or because they have arrived after 2009, which supports the assertion that migration policies and their alterations exert not a small influence upon migrants.

The most frequently used sources of information about the changes in legislation are the Internet (61.3 %), TV (40.1 %) and newspapers (30.7 %). Elderly people use more frequently TV and newspapers, but still the Internet is a quite commonly used channel of information among all groups of migrants.

Relatively high is the percentage of the Bulgarian migrants who claim that they have not experienced any changes in migration policies since living in Switzerland. Those persons are mainly short-term migrants and persons who have arrived in the country after 2009, i.e. after the extension of the Agreement on the Free Movement of Persons to Bulgaria (Fig. 5.8), as well as people of lower age groups (under 30 years). The share of the settled migrants who have experienced changes in migration policy is higher. This observation adds support to the statement that migration policies exert influence upon migration flows and migrants' life.

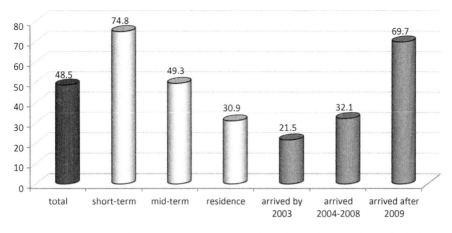

Fig. 5.8 Have you experienced any changes in migration policies since you have been living in Switzerland? Answer "NO" (%)

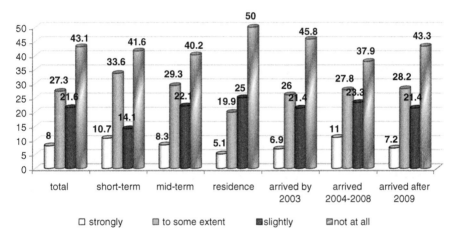

Fig. 5.9 Do the migration policies impact on your daily life? (%)

In accordance with the previous observation, about 43 % of the respondents state that the migration policies do not impact on their daily life. Those are predominantly resident persons, who arrived before 2003, and to a lesser extent—immigrants after 2009 (Fig. 5.9). Not surprisingly, migrants with short-term permits report a stronger impact of legislation on their lives.

According to the results from the quantitative survey, a considerable part of the Bulgarian migrants in Switzerland claim that they are not aware of the changes in migration policy and do not follow them. This part consists predominantly of settled residents, who to a great extent do not depend on migration policies any longer, and persons who have arrived after the accession of Bulgaria to the EU, who probably rely on the agreements between Switzerland and the EU, but who at the same time were directly affected by the changes in the migration policies which made their access to Switzerland easier.

The results from the analysis of the qualitative survey draw a similar picture: changes in policies are not of great interest for Bulgarian migrants. The persons interviewed state that they have encountered difficulties when applying for a permit but are not always fully aware of the policies' consequences. They acknowledge the bureaucratic obstacles but less the general political framework. There is, however, an understanding of broader political changes, such as the accession of Bulgaria to the EU and its effects on the Bulgarians in Switzerland, as well as the limitations on the access to the labour market and the lack of many privileges related to labour mobility. Concerning the most recent movement towards policy change, the popular vote of February 2014 against "mass immigration", there is no unanimity among Bulgarians because of different personal motives—some of them express understanding, feeling their position in the labour market threatened by the arrival of more migrants, while others are unsettled by similar developments thinking that their position is not very secure as they await prolongation of their permits.

5.8 Conclusions

The chapter treats the issues of migration policies as one of the important determinants of migration, of choice of destination and immigrant integration, as a framework which affects migrants in different ways.

There is a debate in the literature about the nature and evolution, the effects and effectiveness of migration policies. Still, a number of empirical studies indicate that migration policies have significant influence on the direction and intensity of migration flows, as well as on the extent of immigrant integration.

The changes in international relations, state interactions and regional integration together with those in socio-economic and political conditions lead to alterations of migration policies. An example is the EU. During the last decades, the concept of free movement of persons has gained more adherents and at present this right is fundamental within the EU.

Switzerland and the EU are tied by more than a hundred bilateral agreements, including that on the free movement of persons. However, Switzerland being a country of immigration, its policy has some specific characteristics. Swiss immigration policy can be classified as restrictive, especially as far as non-EU/EFTA nationals are concerned. Despite the fact that Bulgaria is an EU member state and the Agreement between the EU and Switzerland on the free movement of persons was extended to the country, there are some temporary regulations which reflect those formerly applied by the EU-15 to the new member states from Central and Eastern Europe and more recently to Croatia. They restrict access to the Swiss labour market and limit the free movement of persons for Bulgarian nationals.

Bulgaria could be classified as a net emigration country and is also characterized by the highest negative natural increase of the population in the EU and by accelerated ageing of its population. Despite its efforts to develop an adequate policy towards its citizens living abroad to facilitate return migration and to attract back migrants with Bulgarian origin, especially young and well-educated persons, the country still remains a sending one. However, the general socio-economic conditions in the country and their relative magnitude in determining migration, policy gaps, existing imperfections, ways of policy implementation, etc. are important when considering the policy effectiveness.

The empirical data from the Bulgarian and Swiss quantitative and qualitative surveys, as well as the official statistics on the number and profiles of the Bulgarian migrants in Switzerland give examples of the effects of migration policies and their influence on migrants' decision whether and where to migrate, on the size of migrant flows from Bulgaria to Switzerland and their integration into the Swiss society.

Bulgarians in Switzerland are small in number though increasing after the visa removal and especially after the extension of the Agreement on the free movement of persons to the country—the two important political actions aimed at facilitating the free movement of persons.

The surveys' results indicate that migration policies have a sizable impact upon the decision of the Bulgarian migrants where to migrate. They show that among the main reasons for both real and potential migrants not to choose Switzerland as a destination country is the fact that it is not an EU member state and implements restrictive migration policies, especially concerning access to the labour market and the difficulties in finding a job (including an unofficial one).

Those Bulgarians who have migrated to Switzerland are also subjected to the influence of migration policies. More than half of the respondents have arrived in Switzerland since 2009. The prevailing part of those who settled in Switzerland before 2003 are residents while those who arrived after 2003 (the mutual visa removal) and 2008 (the extension of the Agreement on free movement of persons to Bulgaria) have mainly mid-term permits (almost two-thirds of all migrants). Only 0.4 % possess Swiss citizenship, a reason for which is the difficult access to Swiss nationality.

About half of the Bulgarian migrants arrived for the first time in Switzerland with the purpose of getting a job and, in accordance with the Swiss regulations, most of them were supported by Swiss employers.

A proportion of the migrants find that they have no equal rights in the Swiss labour market because they are foreigners and some of them claim that they are discriminated against. The access of Bulgarians to the Swiss labour market, which is still restricted, and the existing strict regulations and requirements for employment of foreign citizens are a possible explanation of that phenomenon.

Notwithstanding that migrants are directly affected by the changes in migration policies, as the data show, a considerable number of them claim that they are not aware of these changes and do not follow them. This part, though, consists mainly of already settled residents, as well as of persons who have arrived during the last few years and who probably rely on the agreements between Switzerland and the EU. That situation, however, in its essence leads again to consequences from the regulations and migration policies and could be changed as a result of their possible alterations.

References

Bhagwati, J. (2003). Borders beyond control. *Foreign affairs*. January/February 2003. Retrieved January 20, 2015, from http://www.foreignaffairs.com/articles/58622/jagdish-n-bhagwati/borders-beyond-control.

Brochmann, G., & Hammar, T. (Eds.) (1999). *Mechanisms of immigration control: A comparative analysis of European regulation policies*. Oxford: Berg.

Broeders, D., & Engbersen, G. (2007). The fight against illegal migration: Identification policies and immigrants' counterstrategies. *American Behavioral Scientist*, August 2007. 50(12).1592–609. Retrieved January 16, 2015, from http://www.godfriedengbersen.com/wp-content/uploads/The-Fight-Against-Illegal-Migration.pdf.

Castles, S. (2004). Why migration policies fail? *Ethnic and Racial Studies, 27*(2), 205–227.

CEC (2011). *Communication from the Commission to the European Parliament*. The Council, the Economic and Social Committee and the Committee of the Regions. Communication on migration, COM (2011)248, Brussels, 4 May 2011.

Czaika, M., & De Haas, H. (2013). The effectiveness of immigration policies. *Population and Development Review, 39*(3), 487–508.

De Haas, H. (2011). *The determinants of international migration: Conceptualising policy, origin and destination effects* (IMI/DEMIG Working Paper No. 32). Oxford: University of Oxford, International Migration Institute.

De Haas, H., Natter, K., & Vezzoli, S. (2014). *Growing restrictiveness or changing selection? The nature and evolution of migration policies* (IMI/DEMIG Working Paper No. 96.) Oxford: University of Oxford, International Migration Institute.

EC (2014). *Press release database*. MEMO, EU-Swiss relations, Brussels, 10 February 2014. Retrieved November 27, 2015, from http://europa.eu/rapid/press-release_MEMO-14-100_en.htm.

EP (2000). *Charter of fundamental rights of the European Union*. Official Journal of the European Communities, 18.12.2000. C 364/20. Retrieved November 27, 2015, from http://www.europarl.europa.eu/charter/pdf/text_en.pdf.

EU (2004). *Directive 2004/38/EC of the European Parliament and of the Council of 29 April 2004 on the right of citizens of the Union and their family members to move and reside freely within the territory of the Member States*. Official Journal of the European Union. 30 April 2004.

EU (2011). *Regulation (EU) 492/2011 of the European Parliament and of the Council of 5 April 2011 on freedom of movement for workers within the Union*. Official Journal of the European Union, 27 May 2011.

Federal Department of Foreign Affairs, FDFA (2015). *Directorate for European Affairs DEA. Swiss policy on the European Union*. Retrieved September 04, 2015, from https://www.eda.admin.ch/dea/en/home/bilaterale-abkommen/ueberblick/personenfreizuegigkeit.html.

FOM (2013/2014). *Migration report 2013, July 2014*. Retrieved November 27, 2015, from https://www.sem.admin.ch/dam/data/sem/publiservice/berichte/migration/migrationsbericht-2013-e.pdf.

FOM (2014). *Online statistical data*. Retrieved June 10, 2015, from https://www.bfm.admin.ch/bfm/fr/home/publiservice/statistik/auslaenderstatistik/archiv/2014/12.html.

Givens, T., & Luedtke, A. (2005). European immigration policies in comparative perspective: Issue salience, partisanship and immigrant rights. *Comparative European Politics, 3*, 1–22.

National Strategy on Migration and Integration/Migration and Integration Programme (2008–2015). Retrieved from http://www.strategy.bg.

National Strategy on Migration, Asylum and Integration (2011–2020). Retrieved from http://www.mvr.bg.

migraweb (2015). *Living in Switzerland—Information and counselling online*. Retrieved November 27, 2015, from http://www.migraweb.ch/en/themen/auslaenderrecht/auslaendergesetz/.

MIPEX (2015). *Migrant integration policy index 2015*. Retrieved November 27, 2015, from www.mipex.eu.

Money, J. (1999). *Defining immigration policy: Inventory, quantitative referents, and empirical regularities*. Annual Meetings of the American Political Science Association, Atlanta, GA, September 2–5.

National Strategy in the Field of Migration, Asylum and Integration (2015–2020). Retrieved from http://www.strategy.bg.

Ortega, F., & Peri, G. (2012). *The effect of income and immigration policies on international migration* (NBER Working Paper No. 18322, August 2012.).

SEM (2015). *Controlling immigration: Federal Council approves draft legislation and negotiating mandate*. Press Release, The Federal Council, 11.02.2015. Retrieved June 02, 2015, from https://www.bfm.admin.ch/bfm/en/home/aktuell/news/2015/ref_2015-02-110.html.

State Agency for Refugees with the Council of Ministers (2015). Retrieved June 01, 2015, from http://www.aref.government.bg/?cat=8.

Thielemann, E. (2004). *Does policy matter? On governments' attempts to control unwanted migration* (Working paper 112 (December 2004)). San Diego: Center for Comparative Immigration Studies, University of California. Retrieved June 16, 2015, from http://personal.lse.ac.uk/thielema/Papers-PDF/CCIS-WP-112-2004.pdf.

Chapter 6
Social Networks and Transnational Migration Practices

Dotcho Mihailov, Marina Richter, and Paolo Ruspini

6.1 Introduction

One of the important changes migration induces in the social tissue concerns the relationships between people—migrants as well as non-migrants. The construction of new networks and the maintenance and eventually loss of old ones result in specific practices in the actual country of residence as well as in transnational patterns including those towards Bulgaria. We will therefore discuss interactions between the Bulgarian migrants and the local communities, but also interactions inside the migrants' community itself. The leading question is how networking models develop during the process of migration—starting from organizing the travel, going through the challenges of finding a job and ending up with shifts in transnational practices, resulting from the migration experience. Therefore, we will also look at the way these interactions, with their national as well as transnational scope, change across time and space. That means time spent in Switzerland and space in geographical terms according to newborn connections with Bulgarian friends and relatives in other countries or old and new friends from different nationalities in several locations across the globe.

Networks have been recognized long ago as an important resource for migrants as they provide channels to enter a desired country and to help to find their way in a new society. Several studies have therefore adopted a network approach to understand

D. Mihailov (✉)
Agency for Socioeconomic Analyses, Sofia, Bulgaria
e-mail: dmihailov@asa.bg

M. Richter
Social Policies and Social Work, University of Fribourg, Fribourg, Switzerland
e-mail: marina.richter@unifr.ch

P. Ruspini
Faculty of Communication Sciences, University of Lugano (USI), Lugano, Switzerland
e-mail: paolo.ruspini@usi.ch

© Springer International Publishing Switzerland 2017
M. Richter et al. (eds.), *Migration and Transnationalism Between Switzerland and Bulgaria*, DOI 10.1007/978-3-319-31946-9_6

how people migrate and how they can mobilize resources to live and work in the society they arrive (see, for instance, Brettell 2000; Kearney 1986 or Grasmuck and Pessar 1991). Networks provide information about the migration process and about possible destination countries. They help to guide migrants to areas where they can expect other migrants from their own origin (ethnical, religious or national) to reside, which then helps them in having access to support from people with previous migration experience.

According to the pertinent literature, there are three types of social networks which usually shape the migration processes and consist of labour, personal (family) and the so-called illegal migrant networks. All three types provide benefits and costs for migrants which are quite well explored by scholars (Boyd and Nowak 2012). For the purpose of our discussion, we will mainly focus on the labour and personal types of migrant networks. In this context, it is important to remember that, although networks are relevant vectors for employment and social opportunities particularly for the most vulnerable individuals, not all migrants depend on labour networks to find employment, nor do all of them rely on personal networks during the settlement process.

The concepts developed in social network, social capital and social identity theories help to analyse migrant networks in a more nuanced way. Social networks as a form of social capital always constitute potential resources that need to be activated. Belonging to a group gives access to a network, but the access to the resources (such as help in finding a job, financial or moral help) needs to become active and depends therefore on the individual and his or her position in the network (Bourdieu 1986). At the same time, not all ties are equally powerful. What Granovetter (1973) coined as weak and strong ties refers to the notion, that ties to relatives and close friends (Granovetter 1983) are strong in the sense that they are unquestionable but often they don't provide access to substantially new resources for the individual. Weak ties include ties to more distant persons like acquaintances, where the relationship requires more "work" to become activated, but may provide access to substantially different resources. In this sense, the weak ties could be more valuable than the strong ones for gaining access to socially important resources.

A prime discussion about migrant networks has also dealt with the issue of remittances. Mainly, remittances are understood as financial resources or goods that are transferred from migrants back to people in their country of origin. Since remittances convey exchange of money across borders, they are also well described as financial networks where the flow of money and earnings relies on the networks developed by labour migrants with their families and communities (Boyd 1989; Boyd and Nowak 2012). An important change in perspective stresses the need to understand remittances as financial help that can also flow reversely to the migrants (Mazzucato 2011). In this sense, remittances represent also a long-standing recognized form of migrant transnational practice (Vertovec 2004).

Transnational practices have been explored not only in terms of remittances but in several habits which extend beyond household and family networks to include organizations that link the home country with one or more societies in which its migrant population has moved and settled (Glick Schiller et al. 1995). The notion of transnational social spaces as developed by Thomas Faist (1998) is quite relevant for the purpose of our analysis. Faist (2000) later introduced the idea of "community without propinquity" by linking migrant social and symbolic ties to positions in networks and organizations in different geographical locations covering two or more nation-states. Time-space compression is what makes similar social configurations possible.

As networks are strongly linked to questions of belonging to groups, migrant networks and in particular transnational practices and transnational networks are also discussed in relation to questions of citizenship, identity and belonging (Ehrkamp and Leitner 2006; Richter and Nollert 2014; Smith 2007). The debate whether transnationalism just provides another disputable category in the discussion around integration, assimilation and multiculturalism can only be mentioned here. Available data suggests that transnationalism does not inevitably hinder social integration or imply a negative correlation between feelings of belonging and engagement in transnational activities (Vermeulen 2006; Snel et al. 2006). As research on transnationalism has focused strongly on the notion of simultaneity of contacts, exchanges and networks (Levitt and Jaworsky 2007), changes over time, concerning the networks but also forms of belonging, have received less attention (Waters 2011). Schans (2009) has however described a negative effect concerning the duration of stay on frequency of contact with relatives in the country of origin. Other researchers have instead focused on the notion of belonging among migrants and how they can become double (as in dual nationality), multiple (Wodak and Krzyzanowski 2007) and hybrid (Bhabha 1994) to name just a few of the concepts introduced into this debate. Whereas early assimilation studies described a path of inclusion in society that also led towards a change in the feelings of belonging towards an identification with the host society (for instance, Gordon 1964), present research acknowledges a variety of forms of belonging and simultaneous embeddedness in multiple societies (Bilgili 2014).

Further empirical research is needed, however, concerning the durability of transnational ties linked with the length of migrant stay and its impact on the feeling of belonging, particularly as far as the newer migrant generations are concerned. This research need is also due to a predominant qualitative methodology because the transnational framework poses important logistic problems in assessing a mobile population.

The chapter is structured by the networking practices along a migration path, outlining the specific phases in the networking process while settling down abroad. The particular practices addressed are such as related to preparing the travel, looking for a job, keeping contacts with the home country, interacting with the national community, networking with the Bulgarians abroad, interacting with the local people, as well as to selected transnational practices, such as the exchange of goods and remittances. Another angle for looking at networking is the "reverse" perspective of the people who are left behind. Finally, a particular section deals with the shifts in social identity and sense of belonging driven by the migrants' experience. The analyses are based on the findings from all four data sets that were collected in the course of the project: the Bulgarian and Swiss quantitative surveys as well as the interviews conducted in Switzerland and in Bulgaria.

6.2   Networking Before Migrating

Migrants make use of networks long before arriving in their country of choice. This section shows different networking patterns related, in particular, to the social strata of migrants. The first section discusses the networking patterns of Bulgarian migrants including returnees (based on the Bulgarian quantitative survey and on the interviews conducted in Bulgaria with return migrants), while the second section concentrates on the specific case of migration to Switzerland (based on the Swiss quantitative survey and the interviews conducted in Switzerland).

6.2.1   Overview of Bulgarian Migrants' Networks

How migrants travel to the receiving country, whether they travel alone, with a family or in a group is considered as deeply related to the social networks available afterwards in the host country, and therefore it constitutes a factor that may later influence networking and adaptation patterns to the host society. When asked about how migrants arrived in the receiving country, about half of the migrants[1] (47.2 %) respond that they travelled with *someone*. Most of the co-travellers are acquaintances (12.5 %), colleagues (8 %), fellow citizens (3.2 %) and others (0.6 %). This data outlines a non-family pattern of co-travelling, comprising a broader circle of colleagues and acquaintances, and accounting for altogether 24.3 % of the responses. Alternatively, there is a family pattern of arriving abroad, involving the spouse (10.8 %), children (5.2 %), the whole family (1.3 %) and other relatives (5.5 %). This pattern altogether makes up in total a similar though slightly lower share—22.8 %. The third way of travelling is of course, departing *alone* (52.8 %), which certainly does not exclude previous or future networking interactions with relatives, friends and colleagues from home.

However, the available survey data on the initial travel discloses two distinct patterns of networking that serve travellers for their migration project: a non-family pattern and a family pattern. The first one, which is slightly prevailing, sets up opportunities for a wider networking as it involves a wider variety of participants, presuming a collective or a group pattern of networking and subsequent adaptation in the host country. The alternative pattern is to migrate with the family or the spouse, limiting the scope of networking to a more individualistic or family-centred type of ties. This results in differences in the social resources these networks constitute and has an impact on work opportunities in the host country (see also Chap. 3).

Are there any specific socio-demographic profiles of those two patterns and what are the adaptation consequences following one or the other way of getting abroad? The wider, or group pattern of networking is typical for people coming from smaller communities—villages (20.9 %, travelling with friends) compared to Sofia (11.6 %,

---

[1] Base: number of responses in a multiple question.

travelling with friends). The group pattern we observed in smaller communities was either through informal networks of friends/acquaintances and neighbours or through migration agents. These migrant workers formed networks to provide each other with information and also lived together in the country where they worked. In some cases, they were very efficient in pooling information about how the social security system works in the country where they work and how they can secure their rights. The agents also collected workers mainly from villages and took advantage of their limited job opportunities on the local labour market in order to attract them to work in a foreign country.

Further, this type of networking is particularly important for men (17 % vs. 8.6 % for women) and for younger people (18.2 % of those 15–29 % vs. 1.7 % for those 60–65). The level of education (people of lower and secondary education) as well as the low level of income matches the picture of migrants coming from smaller communities and—in particular when attracted by agents—with few opportunities on the local labour market. A good example is a Roma community we visited and where we interviewed several return migrants. They described how they were excluded from the Bulgarian job market because of their ethnicity and how it was therefore difficult for them to make a living with the little money they could earn in Bulgaria. The ethnic discrimination in the Bulgarian labour market makes these people particularly vulnerable to exploitative contracts of agents.

Alternatively, the family networking pattern (travelling with a spouse) is typical for women (16.7 % women, 8.9 % men) and middle age migrants (16.2 %, age group 30–44). Understandably, this family model comprises a bigger part of migrants who have children (17.7 %). As far the other socio-demographic determinants are concerned, there are, however, no significant differences with the group networking model. Both patterns comprise migrants of comparatively lower education, and of predominantly Roma and Turkish ethnic identity. The family networking migrants are, however, of significantly higher financial status. Because of their higher age or better professional realization, the financial status of the family networking migrants is much better. So, 27 % of the migrants travelling with a spouse consider their financial situation as "better than other people in Bulgaria", compared to only 3 % of the networking migrants group travelling with friends/acquaintances. On the other hand, only 11.3 % of migrants travelling with a spouse consider themselves poorer than the majority, compared to 29.6 % of the migrants travelling with acquaintances/friends. The better financial status provides migrants greater self-sufficiency, explaining why they can afford to look for a job more independently, and why they can afford to take their spouses abroad even without a secured occupation.

Being more self-sufficient, the family networking pattern constitutes a resource for migrants from different socio-economic and regional contexts during the migration process. We found Roma families who had built a family network they used for migrating. Similarly, we found people, scattered across the interviews conducted in Bulgaria, who had taken advantage of having family members abroad in order to facilitate their migration. The choice of a country of destination very often was determined by the fact that a member of the family had already migrated there.

Table 6.1 Networking patterns

		Responses		Percent of cases (%)
		N	Percent (%)	
Multiple(a)	How did you find work abroad the last time?	12	2.2	2.6
	My relatives/family were there	106	18.7	22.2
	People from my home town/region were there	76	13.3	15.8
	Bulgarian colleagues/acquaintances, working there	197	34.7	41.3
	Bulgarian employer there	25	4.5	5.3
	Recruiting company in Bulgaria	59	10.4	12.4
	Labour office in Bulgaria	10	1.7	2.1
	Local labour office/institution there	21	3.6	4.3
	Internet job search engine	12	2.2	2.6
	In another way	50	8.8	10.5
Total		569	100.0	119.2

There is one type of migration that is often coupled with the family networking pattern; women working as care givers abroad, often organize their stay by sharing a job with a relative (for instance, mother and daughter) to be able to return to Bulgaria for some months while the other person would migrate as caregiver for the same elderly person.

These different networking patterns are also visible in the means migrants use to find a job when abroad. The group networking pattern of planning the migration in general turns out to be more effective in terms of finding a job. Table 6.1 shows the means that were used for job search. Almost half of the migrants relied on non-family networks (48 %) for finding a job, whereas only 20.9 % relied on their family and relatives, which points to the non-family pattern as weak ties. Other means such as recruiting companies based in Bulgaria (10.4 %) or Internet engines (2.2 %) were of less importance.

While the non-family networking type leads faster to a job than travelling alone or in a family pattern, the identified jobs are usually lower-paid and require lower qualifications. This is understandable taking into account that migrants' groups are normally organized on the demand of construction or agricultural companies abroad. Therefore, Bulgarian migrants interact among each other, forming groups and travelling collectively from their home places directly to the hosting construction company, for example, in Germany or to the agricultural fields in Spain, Italy or Greece. This means, that these networks are based on weak ties, but ties that nevertheless do not bridge the ethnic group to the hosting community. Talking to return migrants in Bulgaria revealed, that getting to know people outside their ethnic group usually meant a step towards better and more stable employment.

These assumptions are confirmed by the data on return migrants. The low socio-demographic profile of the group pattern of travel suggests that such migrants tend to engage in low-qualified jobs. Cross-tabulations show that travelling with acquaintances significantly determines (Chi Square Sign ≤0.00) higher frequency of involvement in elementary occupations requiring no qualification once the migrant starts working—41.1% of the migrants who have arrived in a group with acquaintances are later occupied in elementary jobs compared with 24.1% of those who have not arrived that way. There are, instead, no significant correlations for this low profile migrant pattern that arriving with a spouse or with the family predicts higher occupational status.

Alternatively, the individual model of settling down abroad is typical for higher positions. This is understandable taking into account the better financial status of the family migrants described, assuming higher professional skills and a better start up once arriving abroad. Moreover, companies, not surprisingly, do not invite managers, specialists or applicants for highly paid positions in groups. That is why only 1.6% of those who have arrived abroad in group networks are later occupied as managers, compared to 5.1% of those travelling with their spouses.

The return-migrants data on job search confirms that group networking is typical for jobs requiring middle and lower qualifications. For example, 72% of the machine operators and assemblers have found their job via Bulgarian colleagues (working there) compared to only 17.3% of the managers. Similarly, relatives are more effective in finding work for middle-level qualification jobs like "Employees in services for the population, trade and security" (29.7% of them found jobs via relatives) and "Qualified workers on rural, forestry, fishery and hunting" (22.7%). Alternatively, recruiting companies are more effective for professions of occupational groups with higher competence such as assistants and administrative personnel (50.2%), or technicians and applied specialists (34.5%), requiring formal qualifications or references, but not so much for managers (17.1%) and specialists (15.5%).

Though some of the job-searching goes through recruiting companies, there is no general formalization or institutionalization in the networking process. These findings seem to reinforce those of similar empirical research on the informal and selective role of agents and intermediaries in assisting post-accession migration from CEE countries to the United Kingdom (Jones 2014). The collected data speaks about a generally informal process of finding a job and settling down abroad, it being based on a group or individual pattern of networking.

The qualitative data stories collected in Bulgaria among return migrants show how networks are important in selecting the country. In particular, it seems important to go to places where they already know somebody and that knowing somebody and in particular knowing different people is a reason to choose a destination. For instance, one of the migrants described how his uncle had already been working in Greece for some years when he got there. He then helped him with housing, money and work. When he was searching for a better paid work, he received help from a relative. Another migrant described how her sister-in-law had already been in Italy for long and that there was also a Bulgarian family from a village near her own village. They helped her when she went the first day to find housing, to get food, to obtain some money to start and also to find work. She even stresses how everyone was keen to help her and that she only had to ask.

What is also clear from the data collected in Bulgaria is that networks are often specific to the ethnic groups. Roma rely on Roma networks (as well as Roma agents), whereas the Bulgarian-Turkish population relies on networks that often encompass Turkish people. This can lead to a first migration to Turkey as another migrant narrates. She had been to Turkey because she had a contact there. As she speaks the language (Bulgarian-Turks also speak Turkish apart from Bulgarian), she had no problems in communicating and even thought of staying there for good. These contacts can also result in transnational networks as the same migrant explained. Through her contacts in Turkey she went twice to Switzerland to work there for a limited time.

6.2.2 Networks of Current Migrants in Switzerland

The Swiss quantitative survey provides a sample of comparatively higher status migrants both in terms of employment and education. The difference in the social strata also translates into other networking patterns. While the return-migrants data showed a group or individual/family pattern of settling abroad, the dominating support here comes from the employers. Bulgarian migrants have received support for moving to Switzerland mainly from Swiss employers (35.7 %), only then followed by friends (21.7 %) and relatives (19.2 %) who are already located there. The higher support given by the employers is quite specific for the data from the Swiss quantitative survey since other data, based on return (mostly circular) migrants show that initial migration is supported basically by local friends, relatives and workers from the same regions, who are already established there. The higher level of employers' support here means that migration has been arranged or negotiated in advance by the employer and the potential migrant. This indicates a specific demand and prominent interest of the employers, which must be related to high or specific qualifications and skills. In fact, this is to some extent confirmed by the data showing that employers' support rises to 43.8 % for university graduates and even to 55.1 % for Ph.D.s, compared to only 17.0 % of people with basic education. As shown in Chap. 5, this is strongly related to Swiss legislation and policy towards regulating the entry of new migrants and the selective process of admission into the Swiss labour market further discussed later.

That employers' support increases with the skills and qualifications of the migrants is also mirrored in tabulations along the type of occupation. So, employers' support is given for the initial migration to 60 % of the current managers and 56.3 % of the current professionals compared to only 35.7 % of the machine operators and 9.4 % of migrants (consequently) occupied in elementary jobs. In total, the employers' support is given for 43.7 % of the workers, compared to 11.1 % of the students.

When looking at the different social strata, we identify the same patterns discussed for Bulgarian migration in general. Support given by friends is the highest among migrants with basic education (12.8 %) and nearly missing for the Ph.D.s (0.9 %). Another significant factor of the employer's support is age, which is the highest for the middle or rather the active older young (45 % aged 31–40 years, compared to 35.2 % above 40). Networks and support structures originating in

Bulgaria are rather unimportant for the migrants. The data by occupation verifies the hypothesis that while employers' support is distinctive for the higher profile of migrants (managers and professionals), the networking process, facilitated by previously settled friends, relatives and colleagues is typical for lower strata of migrants. Such a support from established friends, for example, is received by 32.1 % of the migrants, occupied in elementary professions and 35.7 % of the machine operators, compared to only 18.0 % of the managers and just 15.8 % of the professionals. Even more salient is the data on the support provided by established relatives—it goes up to 42.9 % of the machine operators compared to only 6.3 % of the professionals and 4 % of the managers. Therefore the informal, networking support that snowballs migration via established relatives and friends is a migration route only for the low- and medium-skilled workforce.

The support received for settling down in terms of finding work, finding a place to live, dealing with the administration, follows a similar pattern as the support for the initial move to Switzerland. It is mainly provided by the employers (37.8 %), followed by friends who are already based there (32.4 %) and the family (25.6 %). Data shows similar determinants as for the initial move, indicating, for example, that support from employers distinguishes migrants of higher education, while the ones of lower education are supported mainly by local friends already established in Switzerland. Similarly, low-skilled workers such as those engaged in elementary occupations (57.1 % vs. 20.0 % of managers) or mid-level machine operators (45.0 % vs. 22.4 % of technicians) are more commonly supported by friends who have settled down. Managers predominantly find a job, instead, with the support of employers (54.0 %), compared to 18.9 % of migrants consequently employed in elementary jobs. In general, the processes of initial move and settling down include either migrants of identical profiles or simply the respondents do not perceive them as different episodes.

A more nuanced picture concerning the role of networks in facilitating migration comes from the persons we interviewed in Switzerland. The research findings show that these Bulgarians did not make extensive use of networks for assistance in their migration decision contrary to the return migrants interviewed in Bulgaria. Of course, Bulgarian migrants used their contacts for information about the country, the educational possibilities or to learn about how "things" work in Switzerland. But as many—at least in the German and French speaking part of the country— arrived as skilled workers or for educational reasons, they relied less on networks than what is known from less skilled workers. Those Bulgarians interviewed in Southern Switzerland have provided instead a more complex picture where support of friends often comes into play together with help from relatives as far as some family migration patterns are concerned. Students and those who are working at the level of their skills are, however, less prone to networking for migration.

Social networks are instead important for finding jobs and information about how to deal with administrative issues such as health insurance and the Swiss authorities. The networks comprise mainly Bulgarians. Interestingly, the middle class Bulgarians relate more to other Bulgarians (exceptions exist, such as students in an international environment), whereas the few Bulgarians from lower social strata, even with an irregular situation, rely on people from different nationalities. It is not clear from the interviews, whether these migrants just rely on who they find and cannot choose their networks, or whether it is a strategy to diversify their networks and have access to a wider array of resources.

6.3   Networking with Bulgaria

While the previous section described the type of networks during the initial phase of migration, the particular modes of keeping ties with Bulgaria once migrants arrive in the host country is the basis on which networks are maintained and is therefore explored in this section.

6.3.1   Migrants' Ties with Bulgaria

Practically, all return migrants keep close ties with Bulgaria while abroad. Just 3.6% of the return migrants respond that they have not kept any contacts with Bulgaria at all. In general, there are two ways to keep in touch with the people left behind: on the one hand, there is the possibility of travelling and being geographically close; on the other hand, it is possible to bridge the distance by communication technologies such as phone, mail or Skype.

Travelling is not the most frequent but nevertheless an important way of maintaining the networks. About half of the migrants travel back home at least once per year. Migrants travel home once a year (20.1%) or several times per year (15.9%) and even as frequently as "every month" (1.9%). Contrariwise, 48.1% of the migrants report not going back home since they had left the country. These are migrants who stay for longer periods and seem to reduce their frequency in travelling home although this correlation is not always supported by similar research on transnational practices (Snel et al. 2006; Schans 2009; Bilgili 2014).

Who are the most frequent travellers back home among the migrant community? The determinants of choosing travel instead of other communication channels are socio-economic rather than demographic or personal. No salient correlations are identified with normally strong demographic determinants such as gender, age and ethnicity. Alternatively, a higher level of financial status (in terms of self-perception) correlates to more frequent travel home. There are however contradictory indications that very rare travelling (less than once per year) may increase with income and welfare perception, indicating that travel could be related to the type and level of the specific occupational position.

Migrants use a combination of various communication channels. The most typical communication channel is Phone or VoIP (71.0%) and Skype or other computer programmes (66.1%), followed by Facebook and other social media. In fact, calculated as a multiple response item,[2] the number of responses related to computer use is bigger than all others—55.4 % comprising a share of 35.4 % for Skype, 12.1 % for Facebook and other social media and 6.5 % for e-mails. Migrants are relying on computer or smartphone-driven communication, whereas only 3.1 % still make use of postal letters. These findings are also reflected in some of the goods given by migrants to family members who stayed in Bulgaria. Several times we were told during the qualitative interviews that they had bought smartphones for their parents back home in order to have access to cheap communication.

The duration of stay abroad does not affect the communication via telephone or Skype but matters for using ordinary post or e-mails—these more formal channels of communication increase with the duration of stay abroad. So, only 9 % of the migrants who stay up to 1 month abroad use e-mails for interacting with Bulgaria, while this channel surges up to 18.4 % for those who stay above 12 months. For written communication, the data points to a development towards faster and less wordy means of communication, such as social networks or short messages. For verbal communication, the shift is towards cheaper solutions than standard phone, such as VoIP or Skype. Bulgarian migrants' communication therefore mirrors current, modern communication practices. These findings thus represent further evidences of the way the ICT revolution has dramatically accelerated migrants' means of interacting in comparison to long-standing but less frequent transnational migrant practices of past migrations (Cerase 1974).

Modern communication tools such as Skype are more frequent among younger and more educated migrants coming from more developed communities though they are well spread among all demographic and socio-economic groups. However 74 % of the young return migrants (15–29) and 70 % of the Sofia citizens use Skype compared to 45.2 % of the older ones (60–65 years) and 54.6 % of those coming from villages. Alternatively, there are indications that (though more expensive) telephone communication is used more frequently by more disadvantaged persons coming from less developed communities (74.6 % for the richer group, compared to 79.2 % for poorer group). Similarly, 38.5 % of Sofia return migrants use the telephone for communicating with Bulgaria from abroad, compared to 80.6 % coming from villages.

6.3.2 The Case of Bulgarian Migrants in Switzerland

For the Swiss case, where we encountered more settled migrants from higher social strata, migrants also maintain their networks with Bulgaria on a regular basis—only 2.0 % report not keeping any ties with Bulgaria. The data verifies the return-migrants data, showing that modern Internet communication is already dominating the communication channels of migrants with Bulgaria—82.8 % use Internet-based video

---

[2] In a multiple response calculation, if the base is the number of responses, the sum of the various options results in 100 %.

communication tools such as Skype. Alternatively, 72.1 % are using VoIP or Phone communication and only 7.3 % write conventional letters when interacting with Bulgaria. As expected, the Internet communication is most typical for younger people, reaching 73.9 % for Facebook among the youngest age group up to 30 years old, and particularly for the young women. Contrariwise, the use of phone is typical for the older people, rising up to 78.7 % for the oldest group of above 40 years old. In comparison to the Bulgarian returnees investigated above where socio-economic disparities and regional differences more played a role, a demographic divide seems instead at play in Switzerland in access to communication technology between the older—still dependent on phone—and the younger generations of Bulgarian migrants—used to the newest ICT. From the in-depth interviews we additionally understand that Bulgarian migrants in Switzerland do not only stay regularly in contact with relatives and friends in Bulgaria but also with those all over the world thanks to the easy availability of new communication technologies. These patterns recall similar well-researched practices of other communities of CEE migrants in Europe (Sandu 2005; Eade et al. 2006; Anghel 2008).

While the ICT revolution shows the same positive impact on Bulgarian migrants in Switzerland as for other communities of Eastern European migrants all over Europe (Kropiwiec and King-O'Riain 2006), travelling back to Bulgaria remains a frequent way of communication applied by 96.8 % of the sample. Most of the Bulgarian migrants travel several times per year (42.6 %) or once per year (36.9 %). There are 16.5 % who travel less than once per year while only 0.8 % travel every month. Frequent travel is typical for the younger migrants, particularly students. More than half of the younger people (50.7 %) and students (50.4 %) travel several times per year to Bulgaria, compared to 38.4 % of the older people above 40 and 47.2 % of the workers.

Although the return-migrants survey provided support but also some contradictory evidences concerning the travel habits of the highly skilled, it is however clear from both the Swiss and Bulgarian quantitative surveys that travels to Bulgaria of those migrants occupied in low-qualification positions are less frequent—21.1 % of the workers engaged in elementary occupations travel "several times per year" to Bulgaria, compared to 60.0 % of the managers, 56.7 % of the professionals and 35.7 % of the plant and machine operators and assemblers. In this way, the Swiss survey confirms that travelling is a form of networking segmented by the availability of time and above all financial means. This is illustrated by the fact that 34.3 % of the migrants with a middle income travel several times per year to Bulgaria, compared to 49.7 % of the migrants of the highest income group. In general, the number of visits to Bulgaria is comparatively low and is generally similar to the number of returns indicated by the Bulgarian survey data—a median frequency of once per year for both samples.

The duration of visits to Bulgaria also depends on whether migrants are settled in Switzerland or rather are of the circular type. Research on transnational practices of Eastern European migrants in Europe shows evidences that the lack of secure legal status due to short permits of stay and restricted labour migration regimes might instil circular migration (Ruspini 2011). Bulgarian short-term (circular migrants) stay up to 3 months in Bulgaria, while migrants with a residence type of permit stay 1.2 months. The latter also corresponds with the usual holidays one receives with a regular working contract. Again, recent migrants (that have come to Switzerland after 2007) are keeping tighter bonds with Bulgaria, spending 2.1 months compared to 1.5 months of earlier arrivals.

Generally speaking, the standard form of transnational visits we know, spending more or less every holiday and every day of vacations in Bulgaria in order to visit friends and family seems however overcome by new forms of mobility. In particular, families with young children but also people who have established their lives in Switzerland start to have other wishes and practices about their vacations. They reduce their visits to maybe once or twice a year (in general Easter and Christmas, or also during summer time) and prefer to spend the rest of their vacations in other countries by visiting other parts of Europe and the world. At the same time, parents are also visiting their children in Switzerland, in particular, those who have small children: for example, during the summer break, when day care closes, the grandmother can be of great help taking care of the children.

6.4 Networking with Bulgarians and the Local Community in the Host Country

As we just have described for the networking with people in Bulgaria, networks change over time and according to the way social interactions are lived and used. We therefore concentrate in this section on the networking that happens in the host country with Bulgarians as well as with the local community. The focus lies thereby on the development after an initial phase of finding a place to live, a job, etc. These steps pertain to changes in ties and interactions because of the duration of stay abroad as well as socio-economic and other factors (like age, education, etc.) migrants are encountering when they are away or when they return home.

6.4.1 Experiences of Bulgarian Migrants

Interacting with the Bulgarian Community. The majority of migrants regularly (at least once a week) interact with representatives of the Bulgarian community. There are only 10.2 % who do not keep any contacts with other Bulgarians. It is interesting that the number of interactions (Table 6.2) increases with the duration of stay abroad, starting from about 6 and ending up at more than 12 meetings per month. The duration of stay therefore leads to a more intense networking among Bulgarians. There is however no significant correlation with the type of migrants, e.g. whether they are circular, not-circular or of another type.

Table 6.2 Approximately, with how many Bulgarians living there did you keep regular contact (at least once per month) outside work while you were abroad?—Number

Duration of stay abroad	Mean
Up to 1 month	5.9
1–3 months	6.7
4–12 months	11.7
Over 12 months	12.6
Total	10.2

Data from the qualitative fieldwork in Bulgaria prove that return migrants keep contact not only with people back home when they are abroad, but they also stay in touch with people they met abroad once they return. Most stated that they kept contact with Bulgarians but also with citizens of the country where they had worked, in particular colleagues from work, sometimes also their supervisor. They maintain these contacts in order to have a network to rely on when they need to migrate again.

In terms of demographic determinants, stronger interactions with the Bulgarian community are typical for lower social strata, described by variables such as lower education (10 interactions per month for up to secondary education vs. 5 for university graduates), worse financial self-estimation (6 vs. 3.68 for the better off), ethnic minorities (10 for Roma vs. 5 for Bulgarians) and smaller settlements (7 for villages vs. 3.9 for Sofia).

The social status of people, with which migrants interact while abroad, calls for some attention. Is it higher or lower—in other words, is the communication socially stratified, enclosed in separate status circles or is it socially diluted? The data speaks about a "stratified communication"—the big majority of migrants (80.8 %) interact with people who have the same social status—15.0 % communicate with people of lower status and only 4.2 % with people of higher status. The correlation indicates that the "poorer" you think you are, the more frequently you consider other people (from the local Bulgarian community) to be of higher social status (your status is lower than theirs). This recalls previous findings about the group networking type, which because of its weak ties leads more quickly to employment but rarely to skilled and well-paid types of employment.

An additional, more general, indicator of the networking pattern is derived by a question about whom migrants approach in a problematic situation. Table 6.3 verifies the hypothesis that, for settling down, migrants rely predominantly on interacting closely within the Bulgarian community. The data also validates previous findings that networking is based almost entirely on personal, not institutional counterparts and interactions.

Interacting with the Local Community. While abroad the frequency of interacting with the local community is much lower than with the Bulgarians. The number of migrants who do not interact with any people from the local community is 33.1 %, compared to 10.2 % not communicating with Bulgarians. The average number of contacts is, however, identical—once per week.

Table 6.3 Networking patterns in problematic situations

Multiple response	%
Friends—Bulgarians	45.9
Friends—foreigners	15.5
Bulgarian clubs/associations	1.4
Churches of my conviction	0.4
Official Bulgarian representations	0.5
Civil/Non-government/ organizations in the country	0.2
The authorities in the country	2.9
I had no difficulties (I managed on my own)	49.1

Base: return migrants

The variety of socio-demographic determinants, influencing the interactions with the local community is smaller, compared to the interactions with the Bulgarian community. While interactions with Bulgarians were found typical for the lower social strata, there is a significant correlation of interactions with locals with the income indicator: migrants of higher monthly income per capita (81.4%) tend to interact more frequently with locals than the ones of lower incomes (BGN up to 200, 53.2%). The duration of stay is also an important factor for the interaction with locals. Following well-known models of migration studies, the longer the stay, the more frequent is the interaction with the local community (Castles and Miller 2009). Alternatively, the length of stay in Bulgaria (when return migrants are back) has a negative impact on the interactions with the locals of the country of migration— (80% up to 1 month vs. 65% after 12 months staying back home in Bulgaria).

Regarding the perceived social status in terms of communication with the local community, migrants tend to evaluate their own status as lower than the local people they communicate with (49.7%). Alternatively, there are 47.2% who think that their social status is equal to the locals and, respectively, only 3.1% consider themselves as of higher social status than the locals. This "inferiority" self-perception is particularly typical for the people of lower social strata such as those holding lowest education degrees.

6.4.2   The Case of Bulgarian Migrants in Switzerland

The Swiss survey reveals a higher level of interaction with the host social networks. While migrants communicate mostly with the family (63%), most also spend their free time with Swiss friends (42.8%) and less with Bulgarians in Switzerland (26.9%). Students, in particular, spend time much more often with Swiss friends (60.7%) than with migrant workers (43.3%).

Networking with locals depends very much on the type of stay. Therefore, resident migrants are better integrated in the host social network compared to short-term migrants. On the whole, the most significant factor of interaction with the local community seems to be education. In combination with young age and studying activities, university graduates (32.3 %) communicate more frequently with local people in comparison with migrants with secondary (22.7 %) or even basic education (14.9 %). By verifying that communicating with the Swiss community is about qualification and not just a side-effect of being in a university, data shows that 52.0 % of the managers and 41.1 % of the professionals spend free time with Swiss friends, compared to only 24.5 % of the migrants occupied in elementary occupations. This correlation however is not so linear, indicating that the highest frequency of communication with Swiss locals is among mid-level workers such as clerical support workers (56.7 %).

The local language is spoken fluently by 59.6 % of the Bulgarian migrants, partially by 32.3 % of them, whereas only 8.0 % respond that they are not fluent in a local language at all. As expected, fluency in the local language varies significantly on nearly all socio-demographic variables, including education, gender (higher among women), age (higher among younger groups), but surprisingly excluding incomes. There are indications that fluency in the local language is the highest among middle income groups (65.3 %), while people of lower and higher incomes report comparatively similar frequency in language fluency. People working in higher income employments are able to communicate in English in their working environment and therefore do not need to speak a local language for work. Similarly, students are found often in courses where English is the teaching language and have therefore a relatively low fluency in the local language (59.5 %).

The fieldwork with qualitative instruments in Southern Switzerland proves to result in contrasting findings concerning the interactions between Bulgarians and the others in relation to their level of education. As time goes by, Bulgarians mainly rely on, and spend their time with their Bulgarian friends, some Russians or other foreigners. The latter is particularly true for those who work in highly skilled positions. There are, of course, exceptions which are related to the level of integration originating also from marriages with Swiss people and the resulting acquisition of Swiss citizenship. In general, the Bulgarians in Southern Switzerland being also a very small community, their level of association is marginal, and they mainly get along by small groups across a sort of cultural divide between the successful migrants and the less fortunate who sometimes are not working at the level of their original skills.

6.5   The Perspective of the People Left Behind in Bulgaria

This section gives an opportunity for a "reverse" angle on transnationalism since it deals with networking and intercultural practices tackled via the perspective of people close to the migrants based in Bulgaria. As such, it aims at revealing the impacts of intercultural behaviour and networking on the social capital in the sending community. There are mainly two patterns of relationships to people abroad which also relate to specific social characteristics. The first is having family members abroad; the second is migration of friends.

In general, 82.5% of the non-mobile population in Bulgaria respond that they have at least one acquaintance of Bulgarian origin who lives abroad. The average number of such persons is 8 (median value), rising to 16 persons in terms of arithmetic average. The number of known persons living abroad is particularly high among the ethnic Turks (10 people, median), which is understandable taking into account the large number of ethnic Turks that emigrated from Bulgaria to Turkey during the last three decades, including during the socialist regime and the transition period. This data reveals that the pattern of transnational networking in Bulgaria is definitely oriented towards people living abroad.

Therefore, first of all, the scope of migration intensity in Bulgaria can be estimated. Almost every second person (46.6%), left behind in Bulgaria, has a close friend or a relative that is currently abroad. Is there a specific socio-demographic profile of the people that are left behind by migrants? The migrants' survey does not elicit significant evidences for particular socio-economic strata though there are some demographic specifics: the people left behind are both from Sofia (45.1%) and the villages (45.6%), having medium incomes and holding various education degrees. Having someone close abroad is, however, more typical for younger people (52.1% among 15–29 years old compared to 33.6% for the oldest age group of 60–65 years), but also for people who have children under 18 (52.6%) and women (48.9% vs. 44.2% for men). In general, the data suggests that younger people in Bulgaria have a bigger number of people living abroad who are close. Most probably, this is due to education factors (friends studying abroad) rather than a specific socio-economic status. The young people may also represent potential migrants and in turn know many other young people who have left the country.

Therefore, in our case, migration dismantles family relationships most often, depriving family members of older sons/daughters and household members. By differentiating along the type of relationship with the migrants abroad, we can first discern those people who have family members abroad. According to the data, 17.9% of Bulgarians have a family/household member abroad such as a spouse or a son/daughter. Additionally, another 13.6% have another close family member abroad such as an adult son/daughter and mother/father (Table 6.4).

Together these two responses account for 31.5% or almost one-third of the sampled population. It is particularly important that this third is actually among the most vulnerable social strata. People who have household members abroad are predominantly from the poorest regions (North-west, 20.1%, South-east, 22.8%); coming from villages (23.1%) and district towns (21.6%), compared to 8.4% in Sofia; older people (34.8%, 60–65) compared to 13.5% (15–29 age group); without education degree (25.7% compared to 12.6% university graduates), mainly Bulgarian Turks (26.3%) and Roma (23.3%) rather than Bulgarians (16.6%); people of lower incomes (20.1% up to BGN 200 per capita compared to 13.0% for the highest income group) and with a self-perception of lower social status. This data confirms therefore that the most vulnerable and lowest social strata are those who

Table 6.4 Close person abroad

The close person is:		Education groups			
		Without education or up to secondary	Secondary	University	Total
He or she is	Household member	25.7%	18.2%	12.6%	17.9%
	Other close family member (adult son/daughter; mother/father)	18.6%	11.9%	14.8%	13.6%
	Other close relative (sister/brother)	17.4%	19.7%	23.2%	20.2%
	Friend	19.6%	29.2%	30.1%	28.0%
	Another close person	18.7%	21.1%	19.3%	20.2%
Total		100.0%	100.0%	100.0%	100.0%

because of migration mainly suffer both the rupture of intimate networks and the loss of valuable social capital.

Then, the second most frequent relationship which is dismantled by migration regards friends (28%). Having a friend abroad is particularly frequent among the active and comparatively better-off social strata, comprising university graduates (30.1%), younger people (38.4%), but also among people of higher incomes (32% for the above BGN 300 per capita group compared to 25.5% of the poorest), people that can afford to pay a 1-week holiday (30.6%) and men (33.7%). Therefore, the active and better-off people tend to lose friends because of migration rather than family members in their social networks.

6.6 Exchanging Goods and Remittances

Exchanging goods and financial resources falls into those forms of transnational practices which link migrants and the people of their networks across national boundaries. Similar practices do therefore delineate cultural and transnational impacts in both directions—from and to the migrant—which are explored in our Bulgarian-Swiss research endeavour. Returnees and people left behind in Bulgaria plus current migrants in Switzerland are investigated for this purpose.

6.6.1 Receiving and Sending Goods

About one-third (32%) of the people left behind in Bulgaria have received some consumer goods (food, drinks, clothes, detergents) from migrants. However, only 3.7% receive such goods "regularly". The frequency of receiving goods is understandably higher among respondents from less developed regions, as well as people living in district towns, women, younger and older people (versus middle age people), and finally people of lower education. The contrasts among ethnic groups are particularly striking: 12.0 % of the Roma families receive goods from those abroad who are close to them in comparison with only 3.5 % among the Bulgarians and the Turks. Understandably, the receiving of goods depends on the income levels though the differences were expected to be bigger—4.2 % of the people of up to BGN 200 per capita receive goods compared to 3.9 % of all the others.

In short, the profile of the beneficiaries of goods sent by Bulgarian migrants delineates the most vulnerable social groups, comprising people living in underdeveloped areas, very young and very old people, women, ethnic minorities and people of lower incomes. Therefore, the transfer of goods serves as a tool for direct social support. It is hard to estimate its national impact on the reduction of social contrasts and inequality. The data however indicates that if 46.6 % of the population have a person abroad who is close and 32.0 % of them receive goods, then the beneficiaries are about 15 % of the entire population.

Contrariwise, 14.5 % send some goods abroad to the migrant. This is about half of the number of local people receiving goods (32 %). The sending of goods is also with much lower frequency. Less than 1 % (0.9 %) regularly send goods abroad, while the majority of people close to the Bulgarian migrants do this irregularly. The sending profile is different from the receiving although the socio-demographic characteristics are of lower significance here. These are people mainly of middle and higher age (18 %, yes, highest age group 60–65 years old), of higher education (16.6 %, yes, University education) and people of higher income (15.7 %, yes).

6.6.2 Receiving and Sending Money: Remittances and Return Migrants

Most of the money is sent as remittances from abroad to Bulgaria. Only 1.8 % of the people based in Bulgaria send money to those close to them abroad. By contrast 19.8 % respond that they receive remittances. On the sending side, 47.8 % of the returnees had transferred money to Bulgaria, and respectively 5.3 % of them respond that they had received financial support from home.

As with the profile of receiving goods, the beneficiaries of the financial support in Bulgaria are categorized by the lowest social strata: people living in villages (24.6 % vs. 9.9 % in Sofia), women (22.8 % compared to 16.3 % men), very young (22.0 %, 15–29 years) and, particularly, very old people (25.8 %, 60–65 years) compared to middle age (17.3 %, 45–59 years), people without education or up to secondary degree (26 % vs. 14.7 % with university degree), understandably people of lower incomes (22.7 %, up to BGN 200 compared to 18.8 % of above BGN 300) and particularly Roma (30.6 %) in comparison with Bulgarians (19.0 %).

The overall importance of this support for the households is, however, comparatively low although for the poorest households it is quite significant. In general, most of the people respond that the remittances comprise a "very small part" of their household budget (44.0 %) or "less than half of it" (20.6 %). There are however 9.2 % for whom remittances comprise "almost all" of the financial income. This type of family rises to 15.7 % of the very young people, obviously the migrants' children left behind in Bulgaria. Similarly, the complete dependence on remittances rises to 15.4 % of the Turkish households and 11.2 % of the Roma households, compared to 8.2 % of the Bulgarian families. Understandably, the impact is the highest for the poorer households reaching 19.4 % of the households with up to BGN 200 per capita. Therefore, the data proves similar research by confirming that the higher intensity of the social support is again typical for the most vulnerable social strata and contributes to the reduction of social inequality (see, for instance, De Haas 2007). Anecdotal evidence of the importance of remittances for lower social strata was given in a Roma community. The migrant interviewed told how when abroad he sometimes used to answer the phone by saying, "I have no money" instead of a greeting because he already knew why his family was calling him.

On the other hand, the profile of the people sending money abroad is less definite. It is characterized by higher social strata, but it is also related to sending money to students studying abroad, which is also typical for the better-off parents. Therefore, the profile here is opposite to the beneficiaries of the remittances, comprising middle-age people (instead of younger and older), Bulgarians (1.9 % instead of 0 % Roma) and people reporting higher incomes per capita (1.7 %, above BGN 300).

6.6.3 Receiving and Sending Money: Remittances and Migrants in Switzerland

According to the Swiss survey, 44.4 % of the sampled migrants in Switzerland send money to Bulgaria. This percentage, although a bit lower, is generally consistent with the information derived from the return-migrants survey (47.8 %). The migrants who send money from Switzerland are predominantly working there, but there are also 18.9 % students, who also send money to Bulgaria. Data from Switzerland verifies previous observations based on return migrants that the frequency of sending money does not vary significantly by the level of income or the qualifications of migrants.

This confirms that remittances are a matter of the needs on the receiving side rather than of the opportunities at the sending side. Remittances, however, increase among the older migrants reaching 58.5 % among the groups of above 40 years in comparison with 25.5 % of the youngest group up to 30 years. Bearing in mind that there are no significant differences in income, this could be demographically explained by the advanced age of parents of the older migrants, who normally need higher support. The hypothesis that sending is determined by the "receiving demand" rather by the "sending supply" is also confirmed by the higher frequencies of sending money to Bulgaria among the (marginalized) ethnic minorities — 58.6 % among Bulgarian Turks, reaching 100 % sending money among the Roma, compared to only 45.2 % of the ethnic Bulgarians.

A significant determinant of sending remittances is the duration of stay in Switzerland. Remittances increase among the migrants who had arrived in Switzerland by 2007 (52.9 %), compared to the ones that have arrived there after the accession of Bulgaria to the EU (38.7 %). The duration of stay goes together with the type of permit, which speaks about a more secure economic and legal status of some migrants in Switzerland. In fact, migrants holding residence permits (51.6 %) more frequently send money to Bulgaria in comparison with the ones who have short-term permits (47.8 %). This could be explained by the higher incomes among the resident migrants, as well as by their higher age. As this seems to contradict earlier findings that remittances are driven more by the needs of the receivers and less by the opportunity of the senders, a possible explanation can be that established migrants travel less frequently to Bulgaria than circular migrants. The latter may not need to send money if they can bring cash when returning to Bulgaria.

Finally, only 7.4 % of migrants in Switzerland receive money from Bulgaria. Understandably, these are mainly students and young people since 29.5 % of the students receive money from home compared to only 4.6 % of labour migrants.

6.7   Identity and Belonging Among Return and Potential Migrants

As discussed in the introduction to this chapter, in the current migration literature there are few empirical evidences concerning the durability of transnational ties linked with the length of migrant stay and its impact on the sense of belonging. Feeling Bulgarian, Swiss or both may be eventually related to the time and quality of migration experience, migrants' age and social status, inclusion in the destination country and ties or lack thereof with the home country, as well as the availability of political rights through naturalization as a consequence of long-term residence in Switzerland or life events like mixed marriages.

An important aspect that is linked to questions of belonging, cultural and ethnic identity is the factor of whether a foreign person possesses political rights. Citizenship in both countries may bring about a dual sense of belonging, as supported by the statement of a migrant in Southern Switzerland who feels both Bulgarian and Swiss:

(…) *since I can now vote either here or in Bulgaria, although to cast a ballot for Bulgaria is more difficult since one must go to Zurich, Geneva or Bern* (female, 59, unemployed in Switzerland).

The lack of official papers is, understandably, a serious obstacle for developing a sense of belonging or a new cultural identity. Another younger interviewee stresses that political rights have something to do with a sense of belonging.

(At last) I do feel more Bulgarian because I still don't have my Swiss papers. Although it is a formality, they make someone feel more [at home], (female, 23, student in Switzerland).

At the same time, it is not only political rights that induce a sense of belonging but also social networks, as we have discussed in the previous sections of this chapter. An absence of family and roots in Switzerland can make people feel that they belong more to Bulgaria.

At the other end of the spectrum, there are positions that instead report alienation from Bulgaria. These are people who have established a new life in Switzerland and feel that their life has moved them away from how things are done and experienced in Bulgaria.

No. Bulgaria personally does not miss me, when I get there and stay a week then I say "I have to go home", (male, 30, construction worker in Switzerland).

The question of belonging also becomes important for people returning to Bulgaria. Their experience of having lived abroad changes the way they look at their home town or city and can make them feel alienated. Return migrants described their place of origin in contrast to the place they had lived abroad pointing out the out-dated and decaying infrastructure or the grey and depressing buildings in Bulgaria.

Belonging is also about perception and stereotypes with which return migrants are faced once they go back home. Interviewees describe how they perceive being regarded as different from other people in the village or town and how people look at them, as if they were haughty. Re-establishing relationships with neighbours and former acquaintances requires time and effort, which is not expected when returning "home".

The above observations describe various possible outcomes of how belonging and identity is shaped by the experience of migration. We find a variety of other shifts in belonging and cultural identity also in the quantitative data. The issues of social and cultural identity and belonging are addressed by comparing self-definition in terms of regional, ethnic and national categories along various migration types (Table 6.5). The data shows that a significant part of the Bulgarians in the survey state that they feel something other than Bulgarian—19% describe themselves either as European (11.7%) or World (7.3%) citizens.

Table 6.5 points to a very strong correlation between migration status and the type of cultural identity. The general trend is that migration practices and the very intention of migration correlate to non-national modes of identity, such as European and Cosmopolitan (World) identity. The highest number of respondents who identify themselves as World citizens is found among the most decided potential migrants, e.g. the ones who would like to settle down abroad (24.7%). On the other hand, the lowest frequency of *world* identity is among the people who do not foresee migrating in the near future (4.7%). Similarly, the non-mobile population scores lowest for the EU identity mode, while the highest number of EU citizens is found among the current circular migrants (33.2%) and the return migrants (23.3%). Therefore, European identity seems to result from actual migration experience. It is typical for the mobile groups who have particular migration practices, while *world*

Table 6.5 Which one of the following identities best describes the way you feel about yourself?

	Return migrant	Circular migrant	Not potential migrants	Potential migrants			Total
				Short-term labour migrant	Long-term labour migrant	Potential settlers	
I am a citizen of the World	15.9%	12.2%	4.7%	13.2%	11.1%	24.7%	7.3%
I am European	23.3%	33.2%	9.2%	20.5%	20.0%	22.0%	11.7%
I am a citizen of the host country	6.2%	5.3%					
I am Bulgarian	48.1%	41.9%	74.6%	56.6%	58.3%	42.1%	69.6%
I am from (my) region in Bulgaria	3.8%	3.2%	8.5%	4.2%	6.5%	6.8%	8.0%
I am from (my) ethnic group	2.2%	4.2%	2.1%	4.1%	3.0%	3.7%	2.4%
I am … my profession	0.5%		1.0%	1.4%	1.0%	0.7%	1.0%

identity can be aligned with the vague and unspecified wish of the potential migrants to migrate *somewhere in the world*. The data suggests that migration practices correlate with the wish to be different from Bulgarians, rather than with a feeling of a new belonging. That is why only 6.2 % of the return migrants and 5.3 % of the circular migrants identify themselves as citizens of the host country. Alternatively, the non-mobile respondents, who do not wish to migrate anywhere, rank the highest as Bulgarians (74.6 %).

The self-categorization into a European or World identity frame among potential migrants suggests that the motivation for migration goes together with an open-mindedness towards other parts of the world and in particular towards the countries where people would like to migrate to, which lay mainly in Europe. Value transformations such as identifying with a World or European identity serve as a mental tool for supporting the decision to migrate. On the other hand, people who strongly identify with the region they come from and answer that they are not planning to migrate, match their frame of action with their frame of belonging.

What are the socio-demographic determinants of selecting a supranational or national pattern of identity? The socio-demographic profile of return migrants indicating a supranational pattern is characterized, first of all, by the group of young people (European identity, 25.5 % for the age of 15–29 vs. 9.6 % for the oldest age group), but also by the size of the settlement (European identity, 46.9 % bigger cities vs. 14.8 % small towns) and by higher education (European identity, 26.7 % university graduates vs. 18.2 % of up to secondary education). There are no significant correlations with gender and demographic variables such as number of children.

Men, for example, tend to identify more frequently with the European category but less frequently with the World citizen category in comparison with women.

There are also ambivalent correlations by financial self-perception, which is a significant determinant and income per capita, which is not a statistically significant factor for the World identity. While there is a strong correlation between income per capita and World identity, the links of the incomes with a European identity are not so evident. For example, World identity surges from 5.6 % among the lowest income group (≤200 BGN) up to 16.6 % for the highest income group (≥BG300). The dynamics for EU identity are similar but it increases in a more slanting manner, from 19.8 % to 25.8 %, respectively. The alternative Bulgarian national identity, however, strongly declines with income and financial self-evaluation.

The distribution of cultural identity by ethnic groups is then particularly intriguing. Interestingly, the return migrants of Turkish ethnic identity appear as the strongest "Europeans" (25.5 % European identity), followed closely by Bulgarians (23.7 %). Contrariwise, the Bulgarians emerge as the most distinctive citizens of the World (17.8 %) among the three main ethnic groups. In turn, the Roma come out as more decidedly "Bulgarians" (59.1 %) than the ethnic Bulgarian themselves (49.4 %).

6.8   Conclusions

This chapter has described specific patterns of networking, defined by three different circles of interactions such as the family circle, the circle of home friends in the host country and the host community circle comprising networking with the locals. In terms of time, the process of networking of Bulgarian migrants has been discussed in three different circumstances: before leaving, during the process of arrival and then during the period of settlement in the destination country. The ensuing discussion includes such transnational practices as communication and ties with the people left behind as well as the exchange of goods and remittances. The description of these different transnational patterns of Bulgarian migration is then linked to the shifts in identity and sense of belonging induced by the migration experience.

Networking facilitates the migration process even before it starts — already at the moment when potential migrants are planning migration, organizing the travel and arranging future employment and accommodation. For the Bulgarian migrants in general, we found two main types of networking regarding the initial travelling and the preliminary search for a job: an individual networking pattern via family and relatives, and a group networking pattern of colleagues, fellow citizens or acquaintances already based in the receiving country. The latter seems more effective for finding a job, but is typical for lower social strata and generally results in finding low-qualification occupations. Looking individually for a job through agencies and the Internet is typical instead for the better-off socio-demographic groups. This, however, has to do very much with the type of job sought, since occupations requiring comparatively low qualifications and skills are more often found via the group-networking channels, while better jobs are identified through other channels.

In the Swiss case, there is a third pattern of networking, based on support coming from the employers. This support is, however, typical for the higher strata of migrants, comprising qualified and highly educated migrants. The group- and informal networking support for settling down via relatives and friends is instead typical for the low- and medium-skilled workforce. The "managerial" and "professional" profile migrants are however facilitated by (and therefore in demand among) the employers. These research findings prove also the segmentation of the Swiss labour market for different cohorts of Bulgarian migrants along social and ethnic lines as well as the asymmetrical character of the Swiss admission policy. In this way, our surveys seem to confirm the observations made by previous research (Boyd and Nowak 2012) about the diversity of the social relationships that facilitate the migration process from its very initial phases, comprising labour and personal networks.

Networking with Bulgaria starts instead as soon as migrants arrive in the destination country. Both surveys prove that interacting with the home country is intensively sustained by migrants. The increasing share of non-travel communication proves to be among the dominating modes of interactions with home although both surveys reveal that migrants return back to Bulgarian about once per year on average. Travelling is also connected to the type of migration, the residence type of permit and most importantly to the distance in terms of time that separates the migrant from home both in terms of arrival date and age. An important factor is welfare indicators, showing more frequent returns among better-off people.

There are instead no clear indications that a longer time spent abroad and a more settled pattern of living in a foreign country would downgrade the frequency of communications with Bulgaria. Interactions based on the Internet are, however, dominating the interactions of all types of migrants, disregarding their types of permits, welfare or income status. This observation confirms other research according to which the Internet has also opened a completely new era of communication for the migrants, in which spatial distance can be bridged by cheap and simple means of remote communication (see, for instance, Nedelcu 2009).

As time in the destination country goes by, social interactions evolve both with local Bulgarians and the local community. As proven by the return-migrants survey, interactions with Bulgarian circles increase with the duration of the stay. This communication pattern with the local Bulgarian community is typical for the lower social strata and is socially closed, based on people from one and the same social segment. It is even stronger in situations of difficulty where a wide social network would increase the potential resources of the migrants. Bulgarian migrants tend also to evaluate their own status as lower than the local people they communicate with. In terms of the social identity theory (Tajfel and Turner 1979), the self-categorization in a lower social stratum, combined with a group networking pattern, oriented towards Bulgarian circles (or to the group of an identical nationality such as Roma or Turks) speaks about a drive for a positive distinctiveness via isolation from the "local superior", as the host environment is perceived by migrants. These social identity factors are aggravated by the shortness of the return stay and particularly for circular migrants—the shorter migrants stay abroad, and the longer they stay in the home country, the weaker are their interactions with the local communities and the stronger is the propensity to withdraw within the networking circles of the Bulgarian community abroad.

In practice, the lack of interaction with the local community is particularly pronounced for groups of circular migrants, occupied in seasonal activities such as construction, agriculture and other low-skilled occupations. Such a working environment combined with inferiority perceptions, lack of language proficiency and social communication skills restricts the networking process within the native boundaries of the Bulgarian community. This is a finding that matches the relevant literature on labour networks, their benefits in terms of finding employment but also costs like, for instance, deskilling, "herd behaviour" and sometimes exploitation in recruitment or recruiting for exploitative purposes (Boyd and Nowak 2012; Epstein et al. 2002; Anderson and Calzavara 1986).

The reverse angle, explored by researching the people left behind, shows that every second person in Bulgaria has a close friend or a relative that is currently abroad. As a consequence, migration causes the dismantlement of intimate networks and breaks valuable social capital in terms of separating families and relatives. This is particularly valid for the most vulnerable and lowest social strata, while younger and better-off social layers most often lose only friends from migration.

Mobility apart, the research in Switzerland has documented a number of transnational practices including remittances to Bulgaria particularly for migrants of the lower strata, gifts to/from relatives in Bulgaria and frequent contacts via different communications means like Skype with families back home or with friends all over the world (since in several cases friendship ties have vanished as time in Switzerland has passed by).

Finally, our research has highlighted a number of interesting findings, revealing migration as a driver of shifts in national and ethnic identity and the related sense of belonging. The qualitative findings revealed that identifying with notions of being Bulgarian, Swiss or international very much depends on different situational components such as the time and place and social context. The quantitative surveys have in addition identified interesting shifts in the different dimensions of identity and sense of belonging, showing that migration experience is often coupled with shifts in the articulation of identity. Firstly, the number of people who state that they have a World or European identity is much bigger among the mobile population and the potential migrants. Either: in terms of social identity theory, migration practices and attitudes bring a positive self-identification with a broader and economically better-off socio-economic status—or: people who also are more open to a wider frame than their ethnic and national boundaries are also more inclined to migrate. Secondly, having a World identity is based on an active socio-demographic profile, comprising higher education, lower age, living in bigger settlements and having a positive self-evaluation of the financial status. This shows that the young and the economically active social strata are particularly active in employing migrant status as a psychological tool for gaining a positive self-perception. Thirdly, the data speaks about ethnic identity shifts, coupled with migration experience and leading to a self-identification into other more positively perceived ethnic groups. The migrant groups of ethnic Roma and Bulgarian Turks tend to identify themselves less frequently as ethnic groups, compared to these groups in the non-mobile sample. Therefore, migrant Roma tend to self-identify more often as Bulgarians than Roma; Bulgarian Turks more often as EU citizens than Turks; and Bulgarians are the strongest adherent of a World identity. This indicates that the migration experience does not only broaden the frame of reference for social identity, but it can also provoke transformations in national identity and ethnic identities, proving that identity can be situational and based on stereotypes (Shih et al. 1999; Ajrouch and Kusow 2007).

References

Ajrouch, K., & Kusow, A. M. (2007). Racial and religious contexts: Situational identities among Lebanese, and Somali Muslim immigrants. *Ethnic and Racial Studies, 30*(1), 72–94.

Anderson, G., & Calzavara, L. (1986). Networks, education and occupational success. In K. Lundy & B. Warme (Eds.), *Work in the Canadian context: Continuity despite change* (2nd ed., pp. 314–327). Toronto: Butterworths.

Anghel, R. G. (2008). Changing statutes: Freedom of movement, locality and transnationality of irregular Romanian migrants in Italy. *Journal of Ethnic and Migration Studies, 34*(5), 787–802.

Bhabha, H. K. (1994). *The location of culture*. London: Routledge.

Bilgili, Ö. (2014). Migrants' multi-sited social lives. Interactions between sociocultural integration and homeland engagement. *Comparative Migration Studies, 2*(3), 283–304.

Bourdieu, P. (1986). The forms of capital. In J. Richardson (Ed.), *Handbook of theory and research in the sociology of education* (pp. 241–258). Westport: Greenwood Press.

Boyd, M. (1989). Family and personal networks in international migration: Recent development and new agenda. *International Migration Review, 23*(3), 638–670.

Boyd, M., & Nowak, J. (2012). Social networks and international migration. In M. Martiniello & J. Rath (Eds.), *An introduction to international migration studies: European perspectives* (pp. 79–105). Amsterdam: Amsterdam University Press. IMISCOE Textbooks.

Brettell, C. B. (2000). Theorizing migration in anthropology. The social construction of networks, identities, communities, and globalspaces. In C. B. Brettell & J. F. Hollifield (Eds.), *Migration theory. Talking across disciplines* (pp. 97–135). London: Routledge.

Castles, S., & Miller, M. (2009). *The age of migration. International population movements in the modern world* (4th ed.). Basingstoke: Palgrave-Macmillan.

Cerase, F. P. (1974). Expectations and reality: A case study of return migration from the United States to Southern Italy. *International Migration Review, 8*(2), 245–262.

De Haas, H. (2007, October). *Remittances, migration and social development. A conceptual review of the literature*. United Nations Research Institute for Social Development. Social Policy and Development Programme Paper Number 34.

Eade, J., Drinkwater, S., & Garapich, M. P. (2006). *Class and ethnicity. Polish migrants in London* (Research Report for the RES-000-22-1294 ESRC project). Guildford: Centre for Research on Nationalism, Ethnicity and Multiculturalism (CRONEM), University of Surrey.

Ehrkamp, P., & Leitner, H. (2006). Rethinking immigration and citizenship: New spaces of migrant transnationalism and belonging. *Environment and Planning A, 38*, 1591–1597.

Epstein, G. S., Bauer T., & Gang I. N. (2002). *Herd effects or migration networks? The location choice of Mexican immigrants in the United States*. Bonn: Institute for the Study of Labor. Retrieved August 25, 2015, from https://www.iza.org/iza/en/papers/transatlantic/1_gang.pdf.

Faist, T. (1998). Transnational social spaces out of international migration: Evolution, significance, and future prospects. *Archives of European Sociology, 39*(2), 213–247.

Faist, T. (2000). *The volume and dynamics of international migration and transnational social spaces*. Oxford: Oxford University Press.

Glick Schiller, N., Basch, L., & Szanton Blanc, C. (1995). From immigrant to transmigrant: Theorizing transnational migration. *Anthropological Quarterly, 58*(1), 48–63.

Gordon, M. (1964). *Assimilation in American life. The role of race, religion, and national origin.* New York: Oxford University Press.

Granovetter, M. (1973). The strength of weak ties. *American Journal of Sociology, 78*(6), 1360–1380.

Granovetter, M. (1983). The strength of weak ties: A network theory revisited. *Sociol Theory, 1,* 201–233.

Grasmuck, S., & Pessar, P. R. (1991). *Two islands. Dominican international migration.* Berkeley: University of California Press.

Jones, K. (2014). It was a whirlwind. A lot of people made a lot of money: The role of agencies in facilitating migration from Poland into the UK between 2004 and 2008. *Central and Eastern European Migration Review, 3*(2), 105–125.

Kearney, M. (1986). From the invisible hand to visible feet. Anthropological studies of migration and development. *Annual Review of Anthropology, 15,* 331–361.

Kropiwiec, K., & King-O'Riain, R. C. (2006). *Polish migrant workers in Ireland.* Community Profiles Series. Dublin: National Consultative Committee on Racism and Interculturalism (NCCRI).

Levitt, P., & Jaworsky, N. (2007). Transnational migration studies. Past development and future trends. *Annual Review of Sociology, 33,* 129–156.

Mazzucato, V. (2011). Reverse remittances in the migration-development nexus: Two-way flows between Ghana and the Netherlands. *Population, Space and Place, 17,* 454–468.

Nedelcu, M. (2009). *Le migrant online. Nouveaux modèles migratoires à l'ère du numérique.* Paris: Ed. L'Harmattan. Collection Questions sociologiques.

Richter, M., & Nollert, M. (2014). Transnational networks and transcultural belonging: A study of the Spanish second generation in Switzerland. *Global Networks, 14*(4), 458–476.

Ruspini, P. (2011). Conceptualising transnationalism: East-West migration patterns in Europe. In C. Allemann Ghionda & W. D. Bukow (Eds.), *Orte der Diversität: Formate, Arrangements und Inszenierungen* (pp. 115–127). Wiesbaden: VS Verlag.

Sandu, D. (2005). Emerging transnational migration from Romanian villages. *Current Sociology, 53*(4), 555–582.

Schans, D. (2009). Transnational family ties of immigrants in the Netherlands. *Ethnic and Racial Studies, 32*(7), 1164–1182.

Shih, M., Pittinsky, T. L., & Ambady, N. (1999). Stereotype susceptibility: Identity salience and shifts in quantitative performance. *Psychol Sci, 10*(1), 80–83.

Smith, M. P. (2007). The two faces of transnational citizenship. *Ethnic and Racial Studies, 30*(6), 1096–1116.

Snel, E., Engbersen, G., & Leekers, A. (2006). Transnational involvement and social integration. *Global Networks, 6*(3), 285–308.

Tajfel, H., & Turner, J. C. (1979). An integrative theory of intergroup conflict. In W. G. Austin & S. Worchel (Eds.), *The social psychology of intergroup relations* (pp. 33–47). Monterey, CA: Brooks/Cole.

Vermeulen, F. (2006). *The immigrant organising process: The emergence and persistence of Turkish immigrant organisations in Amsterdam and Berlin and Surinamese organisations in Amsterdam, 1996–2000.* Amsterdam: Amsterdam University Press.

Vertovec, S. (2004). Migrant transnationalism and modes of transformation. *International Migration Review, 38*(3), 970–1001.

Waters, J. (2011). Time and transnationalism: A longitudinal study of immigration, endurance and settlement in Canada. *Ethnic and Migration Studies, 37*(7), 1119–1135.

Wodak, R., & Krzyzanowski, M. (2007). Multiple identities, migration, and belonging: Voices of migrants. In C. R. Caldas-Coulthard & R. Iedema (Eds.), *Identity trouble* (pp. 95–119). Basingstoke: Palgrave MacMillan.

Chapter 7
Analysis and Conclusions: Research and Policy Challenges Ahead

Paolo Ruspini, Dotcho Mihailov, and Marina Richter

Bulgaria and Switzerland are connected by a rather weak migration pattern. Nevertheless, we have taken the case of these two countries situated in the broader context of migration from Central Eastern Europe towards Western Europe to further our understanding of factors and issues that are linked to these processes. The case, being small in numbers, allows the acquisition of a deep understanding of what is happening. And, in addition, it also provides a very particular case, as the migrants arriving in Switzerland represent a selection of the general population leaving Bulgaria. We have used the various data (quantitative and qualitative) obtained during the course of our research project to explore the interlinkages of migration, social inequalities, regional disparities and their contextual contingency in the field of national and European migration policies.

Potential and current migration, including circular and return flows between Switzerland and Bulgaria, are the result of a combination of economic, social and political factors at micro, meso and macro levels that the research instruments have combined to capture. Similar factors concern Bulgarian migrants as individual agents, their social networks and structural elements such as migration policies either in Switzerland or Bulgaria. The latter policies are then embedded in broader supranational processes of globalization and European integration which affect both countries differently. Bulgaria joined the EU in 2007 and Switzerland has remained

P. Ruspini (✉)
Faculty of Communication Sciences, University of Lugano (USI), Lugano, Switzerland
e-mail: paolo.ruspini@usi.ch

D. Mihailov
Agency for Socioeconomic Analyses, Sofia, Bulgaria
e-mail: dmihailov@asa.bg

M. Richter
Social Policies and Social Work, University of Fribourg, Fribourg, Switzerland
e-mail: marina.richter@unifr.ch

© Springer International Publishing Switzerland 2017   181
M. Richter et al. (eds.), *Migration and Transnationalism Between Switzerland and Bulgaria*, DOI 10.1007/978-3-319-31946-9_7

outside the European polity although has historically negotiated its place in the European context through bilateral agreements with the EU since 2002.

Contextualizing Bulgarian-Swiss migration within the European political and historical framework reminds us that there is a necessity to discuss the findings outlined in the previous chapters with reference to knowledge about East–West migration within Europe. At the same time, these concluding remarks also aim to contribute to interlinkages we have studied empirically and conceptualize them further to, finally, highlight the theoretical and empirical challenges which lie ahead.

Pertaining topics for comparative analysis include, firstly, the differences and specificities of the Bulgarian-Swiss case in the context of pre- and post-EU enlargement processes of Bulgarian migration in Europe. Elements of convergence and divergence between similar cases of Bulgarian and East–West migration in Europe are briefly introduced along with the presented findings of our research. Bulgarians are, in fact, evenly scattered in traditional European countries of immigration like Germany and Austria. Since the EU accession they are also present in large communities in Southern European countries like Spain or Italy. Reference to recent and older Bulgarian migration flows and transnational configurations in these countries helps in contrasting and understanding the peculiarities of the Swiss-Bulgarian case studied.

Secondly, the level of theoretical knowledge concerning the interrelation of migration processes with social inequalities, regional disparities and migration policies remains an open field for further investigation. In this sense, our work has provided a contribution in considering these theoretical concepts in a comprehensive way by relying on the transnational approach. The latter approach aims at capturing the impact of these concepts on the ongoing mobility processes, both virtual and real, by virtue of an array of communication, networking practices and economic transfers including the flow of goods and remittances between Switzerland and Bulgaria. All these transnational practices help also with investigating the link between migration and those demographic and economic factors which facilitate or delay the regional development in the country of origin. Additionally, circular and other patterns of Bulgarian migration are also the result of the type of admission (liberal or conservative), labour and citizenship policies aimed at present and prospective migrants in both the sending and receiving country as well as at longstanding communities of Bulgarians abroad.

Thirdly, we have thoroughly researched the extent of potential and current migration between Bulgaria and Switzerland and the determinants of migration, moving from the relevant theory which distinguishes between aspirations, capabilities and opportunities for mobility (De Haas 2011). In this context, potential migration remains a controversial issue, but correct estimations can actually assist in preparing adequate demographic and development policies for the sending country and balanced integration strategies for the receiving country. Findings from the different chapters are combined in a discussion of the various drivers of migration, in particular demographic factors of inequality as well as regional factors of disparity. In this sense, this work aims at building upon that tradition of regional migration research that the EU expansion processes have actually reinvigorated. Lastly, by differentiating the researched categories of Bulgarian migrants in terms of ethnicity, nationality and time of migration, we have attempted to overcome from within the risks of methodological nationalism which a single case-study can actually incur.

The following sections will briefly assess the above comparative, theoretical and empirical perspectives inherent in our Bulgarian-Swiss case-study by looking, firstly, at the timing of migration and distinguishing between long-term and short-term migration. Stratified patterns of migration are, secondly, explained by showing the role of inequality in permeating similar social processes and further enlarging the real and self-perceived divide between more and less successful Bulgarian migrants. The latter point leads, thirdly, to processes of reproduction of inequality and downward mobility that Bulgarian migrants have experienced in Switzerland. Deskilling and downward social capital are therefore compared to similar processes that CEE migrants have reported in recent East–West migration. Voluntary deskilling is contrasted with accidental factors of inequality and social exclusion as per the Bulgarian case. In what follows, the networking and transnational dimensions in connection with inequalities, regional disparities and, fourthly, migration policy are addressed. Bonding or bridging social capital in networks of Bulgarian migrants as well as individual vs. institutional migrant configurations in Bulgaria or Switzerland are among the elements considered. They explain, to a great extent, the degree of inclusion or exclusion as well as the perceived sense of identity and belonging of different categories of Bulgarian migrants currently in Switzerland and circular/repeat migrants or returnees back in Bulgaria.

7.1 Timing in Migration: Or Long-Term Versus Short-Term Migration

Different time patterns of migration have been explored in this book, which result in different modes of networking and socio-economic personal approaches for adaptation in the host society. The recent East–West post-accession migration experience indicates a complexity and diversity of underlying causes which make any potential and actual migration forecast difficult, as well as the reduction of these recent intra-European mobility patterns under any single explanatory framework (Okólski and Salt 2014). East–West temporary and circular migration seems historically to prevail where the borders are open and the local labour markets provide attractive conditions for migrant workers. Bulgaria could be classified as a net emigration country and is also characterized by the highest negative natural increase of the population in the EU and by accelerated ageing of its population. The country's negative demographic outlook coupled with the selective admission policy of the non-EU member state Switzerland are among the concurring factors in establishing a special case in this intra-European mobility framework.

Potential migrants included in our sample, either long or short term, share a common demographic profile: they are mostly men, younger individuals and persons without family commitments. They tend to express a higher aspiration to migrate, which is also confirmed by the regression analysis. The outmigration aspirations of the youngest Bulgarians are widely spread, but since their share in the total population is quite low, it is probable that actual migration will gradually decrease in the near future. The latter expectation is largely coherent with the CEE post-accession migration experience although there are clearly differences from country to country in view of the respective demographic, economic and social features.

The comparison of capability characteristics of the two temporal types of potential Bulgarian migrants reveals that migration aspiration is driven to a great extent by education, it being the higher educated people who aspire more for long- as well as for short-term migration. Migration in the Bulgarian context does not represent a phenomenon that is linked to certain social strata since individuals from all income ranges aspire towards migrating. The differentiation lies rather in the type of occupation, because students and unemployed people aspire, to a high degree, to migrate, either long or short term. The same applies to those persons who are occupied in agriculture and who probably dispose of low earnings and little security in these positions. Other occupational sectors like the public sector seems to hold people back home, as these jobs represent fairly stable and secure positions. It is therefore rather job insecurity that acts as a driver for migration and less the level of income.

As supported by former migration research, another strong determinant of migration aspiration includes the availability of networks between countries. In general, the fact of having once migrated may be a strong determinant of having further aspirations to migrate for good or engage in circular migration. It is, however, hard to say whether the aspiration to migrate again results in circular migration or in a migration for long term or even for good since the data recorded people's aspirations and former experiences regarding migration but could not provide any information about the fulfilment of these aspirations. Such research would require a longitudinal approach.

When we switch from the aspirations of potential to those of actual return migrants, the labour market context in Bulgaria emerges as an important element for consideration. Younger respondents, unemployed people and those working as freelance usually express an aspiration to migrate anew in comparison to people who have obtained a more stable position after their return. This clearly indicates that, having experienced migration, the young and better qualified individuals feel the gap between their return expectations and the unsatisfactory absorption by the Bulgarian labour market which drives people again to search for better job opportunities elsewhere. Therefore, the prior experience of migration acts in this case as a driver for repeated migration in combination with the insecurity of jobs on the Bulgarian labour market as discussed before.

Networks together with geographic proximity (and in the case of Romanian migrants, linguistic proximity to Italy and Spain) have proved very important pull-factors in the EU-2 countries' post-accession migration (Kahanec et al. 2010). Similar proximity networks based on a shared language can be found for the Bulgarian Turks in Turkey. When it comes to networking in terms of time, our Bulgarian-Swiss research findings point to three different circumstances: before leaving, during the process of arrival and then settlement in the destination country.

Networking already facilitates the migration process at the moment when potential migrants are planning migration, organizing the travel and arranging future employment and accommodation.

Networking with Bulgaria starts as soon as migrants arrive in the destination country as proved by all the survey tools. Transnational practices include remittances to Bulgaria from Switzerland particularly for lower strata migrants, gifts to/from relatives in Bulgaria and frequent contacts via different communications means like Skype with families back home or with friends all over the world but also those travelling to Bulgaria. Although migrants return back to Bulgaria about once per year on average, the increasing share of non-physical contact is among the dominating modes of interaction with home. The Internet is already a prevailing channel of communication for all types of migrants, regardless of their types of permits, welfare or income status. This kind of interaction will probably increase its share in connecting with home, taking into account the 'active' socio-economic profile of its users.

Travelling back to Bulgaria is instead not only a matter of income, though this is statistically the most salient factor since the data sets reveal significant correlations with welfare indicators, showing more frequent returns among better-off people. Keeping ties with Bulgaria is the outcome of a multiplicity of economical, legal and individual factors connected to the type of migration, the residence type of permit and most importantly to the distance in terms of time that separates the migrant from home. There are instead no clear indications that having spent more time abroad and living in a more settled pattern in a foreign country would downgrade the frequency of communications with Bulgaria.

Living in a foreign country for long brings also an evolution of the social interactions both with local Bulgarians and the local community. As proven by the return-migrants survey, interactions with fellow nationals increase with the duration of the stay, indicating for a pro-Diaspora pattern of adaptation in the host country. This communication pattern with the local Bulgarian community is typical for the lower social strata and is socially closed, based on people from one and the same social segment.

Finally, our research highlights different patterns of networking stemming from the patterns of stay in the host country. The data, which cover a wider sample of Bulgarian returnees from different European countries, show that the lack of interaction with the local community is particularly typical for groups of circular migrants, occupied in seasonal activities such as construction, agriculture and other low-skilled occupations. Such a working environment combined with inferiority perceptions, lack of language proficiency and social communication skills restricts the networking process to the native boundaries of the Bulgarian community. Bonding capital seems thus to prevail over bridging social capital by relegating these temporary and low-skilled migrant workers to close community relationships such as those which usually take place in ethnic networks. As already pointed out, similar closed labour network configurations, while useful for gaining employment, may eventually cause 'herd behaviour' or exploitation in recruitment and recruiting for exploitative purposes (e.g. Boyd and Nowak 2012).

Research on the people left behind shows instead that every second person in Bulgaria has a close friend or a relative that is currently abroad. As a consequence of migration, the most vulnerable and lowest social strata suffer the dismantlement of intimate networks and the loss of social capital deriving from families and relatives. At the same time, the members of their families abroad provide a stable network to build upon when migrating. Younger and better-off social layers most often lose only friends instead. This also points to the fact that with increased resources, migrants manage to acquire more stable jobs and may be able to take their family with them.

7.2 Stratified Patterns of Migration: Or About 'Losers' and 'Winners'

Production and reproduction of inequality for Bulgarian migrants have been a special concern throughout the book. The stratification of incomes stems in particular from education, gender and ethnicity. While working abroad increases the incomes of all social strata, there remain also income gaps and inequality generated by the level of qualification and occupational status. The income level abroad among low-qualified workers rises compared to Bulgaria. Contrariwise, middle and upper qualification groups tend to be penalized through processes of deskilling although they experience a smaller increase in income with respect to Bulgaria. This results in an income gap among lower and higher qualified groups which decreases abroad. Nevertheless, the middle and upper qualification groups manage to improve their situation significantly over time which increases the income gap again.

Our study shows that inequality shifts are not universal among all migrants. Changes in inequality are stratified along social strata and are particularly associated with higher occupational skills and professional positions. For example, the distribution of property and financial assets verifies the stratified pattern of inequality. While working abroad increases inequality measured by high value assets such as real estate property, welfare gaps actually decrease abroad compared to Bulgaria if measured by lower value assets such as vehicle or availability of deposits. This points towards a general rise in the level of lifestyle that includes certain lower value assets for most migrants.

The various migration patterns and socio-demographic profiles highlighted by our research correspond to particular patterns of networking. The return-migrants data extrapolated from the Bulgarian survey, based on short-term migration and carried out by comparatively less qualified migrants points to two main types of networking regarding the initial travelling and the preliminary search for a job: an individual networking pattern via family and relatives and a group networking pattern of colleagues, fellow citizens or acquaintances already based in the receiving country. Although more effective for finding a job, the latter networking pattern is typical for lower social strata and generally results in finding low-qualification occupations. Looking individually for a job through agencies and the Internet is instead typical for the better-off socio-demographic groups. In this sense, our research confirms the role of 'private subcontractors' as migration intermediaries in recent East–West migration within the whole neoliberal model (Jones 2014).

As proved by the Swiss data, support coming from the employers represents instead a third pattern of networking, typical for the higher strata of migrants, comprising qualified and higher education migrants. The Swiss research findings prove also the segmentation of the Swiss labour market for different cohorts of Bulgarian migrants across social and ethnic lines as well as the asymmetrical character of the Swiss admission policy. Though Bulgaria is an EU country and by now has access to the EU labour market, entry to Switzerland is still restricted by transitional arrangements. Factually, as regards the Swiss labour market Bulgarians are treated the same way as citizens from the so-called third countries, i.e. non-EU countries. Their entry is only allowed if they are highly skilled and if the labour market requires their contribution or if they can migrate in the context of family reunification. At the same time, there has also been an increase in short-term permits issued for low-qualified people from 'third countries', as Bulgaria is presently considered. We have detected this in our data; the analysis of the reasons and functioning behind these findings remains open to further analysis.

While potential migrants are more or less evenly distributed across the different Bulgarian regions, long- and short-term patterns of migration are associated with specific regional patterns. Among long-term migrants the differences lie mainly in the level of education: the largest share of tertiary educated respondents is found in the mid-developed districts. The share of individuals with a basic or lower educational level is largest instead for the group which includes the most depressed Bulgarian regions. Similarly, unemployment is also a stronger driver for long-term migrants in depressed regions than in economically more prosperous regions such as the capital Sofia. For short-term potential migrants, the picture is more diverse: from the capital, short-term migrants are predominantly male, whereas the gender distribution is more balanced in the other regions. At the same time, the short-term migrants from Sofia are better educated than the ones from other districts. And the share of unemployed migrants is much higher in the depressed regions than in other parts of the country. In summary, the depressed regions potentially have, more or less, relatively well educated but unemployed, predominantly married short-term migrants.

Also in Switzerland, the level of development of the region of residence is coupled with patterns of migration and levels of wealth. Educational differences are linked to the professional profile of the employed in the different Swiss canton groups. In this context, a substantial share (60 %) of Bulgarians with income level at or above the mean for Switzerland is located in the top-developed cantons. The percentage of Bulgarians with intentions to circulate between the two countries is instead highest in the less developed cantons (14.7 % compared to 8.6 % in the top developed ones). Although empirical evidence on circular migrants is scarce (Constant et al. 2012), the unsettled working and living conditions of Bulgarian migrants in selected Swiss cantons seem to be a factor for repeated movements.

7.3　Reproduced Inequalities: And/Or Downgrading Social Capital

Inequalities between migrants are generally reproduced in the host country and fostered back home. As we stated before, the inequality between low and higher skilled groups decreases when abroad in the short term. In the longer run, higher skilled groups manage to secure their positions and climb the social ladder with the result that inequality increases again. By contrast, gender and ethnic inequalities tend to decrease rather than increase in the host country. Therefore, it seems that migration may be able to mitigate deep poverty and social contrasts, in particular when abroad. As we have also observed, the less qualified workers often remain without employment when returning to Bulgaria. In fact, unemployment rises drastically among return migrants compared to the rate of unemployment before leaving. As we have stated before, migration can lead to a downgrading of the occupational level for the upper social layers while abroad. The latter deskilling process proves to be a well-known fact for the whole recent East–West migration configurations in Europe as highlighted by other empirical research (see, for instance, Parutis 2011).

Whether the cost-benefit analysis is an appropriate tool to assess advantages and disadvantages of migration in the inequality-migration framework, in terms of import of cheap high-skilled labour for the host country and export of unemployment for the home country, remains an open question. In any case, future research should be aware that migrants who fail abroad often turn back, and the absence of adequate return policies might even reinforce current social problems.

The analysis of the regional disparities–migration link confirms the Bulgarian migrants' search for a less developed socio-economic environment. The data points to a trend to settle down in less developed locations in Switzerland. Unexpectedly, Bulgarian migrants tend to reside in cantons in which the age dependency ratio and the unemployment rates are relatively higher, whereas the income level and the density of highly educated population are relatively lower. Bulgarians seem instead to avoid regions with higher-than-average natural growth rates, and they are more dispersed towards cantons with relatively higher share of elder population. This latter finding may possibly bring us to suppose a growing need for elderly caretakers in selected Swiss cantons, and this need has been actually confirmed by our qualitative interviews with Bulgarian women in Southern Switzerland. Other sources also report that agencies organizing elderly care on a live-in basis in private households also recruit Bulgarians for their services (Schwiter et al. 2015), a fact that contributes to the distribution discussed.

Data correlation for the Swiss cantons provides confirmation that Bulgarians in Switzerland tend to locate regionally in search of migrant niches in relatively less developed cantons, and additionally they tend to avoid cantons with relatively higher concentration of migrant population.

According to the survey carried out in Switzerland, the main reasons for leaving Bulgaria are the improvement of the occupational and income situation followed by a general perception of a missing development perspective in their home country. Similar motivations do not differ from those of other income-seeking CEE migrants in the post-EU accession era (e.g. Morawska 2008). In the recent East–West large-scale migration experience either to a specific country like Great Britain or within comparable contexts, it is hard to generalize on the explanatory framework because of the combination of different structural factors in the destination and sending countries (Okólski and Salt 2014). Even though the Swiss survey indicates some upward mobility, most migrants experience downward mobility to lower occupational positions and low-skilled economic sectors. Thus, in comparison to Bulgaria the shares in lower status occupations and in elementary occupations increase sharply in Switzerland. Downward mobility is, however, often not linked to an economic worsening in the transnational sense. On the one hand, compared to the Swiss population, many migrants experience downward mobility, on the other hand, compared to their previous status and in particular to their income back in Bulgaria, they experience an improvement.

The intentional or unintentional character of the downward mobility remains an issue for further discussion. There are many examples in the literature that show that an apparent low status and low income job can provide valuable resources from the migrants' perspective. For instance, in the case of Polish workers in Britain, they were ready to take low-status and low-paid jobs due to different motivations like a future return to Poland where they were keen to finally settle and start their professional life after 1 or 2 years of international experience (Waldinger and Lichter 2003; Jones 2014). Many Bulgarian migrants are, however, able to compensate for the status decline in the course of their stay in Switzerland and many migrants realize the development goals of their career at a later moment.

The data of the return migrants suggests that migration pays out for the host country as its employers win a highly skilled workforce whose education is paid for by the Bulgarian state. On the other hand, Bulgaria profits from the export of unemployment. If the migrants return home, they are often pushed into lower social positions or even unemployment, whose social costs weigh on the sending country.

Our research shows a polarization in terms of professional status: while many well-qualified Bulgarian returnees can preserve or even improve their occupational status, the low-skilled return-migrants risk the experience of downward mobility. Similar shifts in the occupational and respective social status of migrants often results in inferiority self-perceptions in regard to the local community.

However, only few Bulgarian migrants in Switzerland report an experience of discrimination. Those persons who report cases of discrimination include mainly women, lower educated, from lower income groups and those who have arrived after 2009 (after the Swiss-EU bilateral agreements were extended to Bulgaria). In the foreground is the reported lack of recognition of equal rights on the Swiss labour market because of either lacking and non-accredited certificates or unacknowledged skills. In addition, low-skilled migrants as well as Turks and Roma are particularly affected.

7.4 Migration Policies: And the Institutional vs. Personal Perspective

Migration policies have a significant influence on the direction and intensity of migration flows, as well as on the extent of immigrant integration. Changes in international relations, state interactions and regional integration processes (such as the EU) together with changes in socio-economic and political conditions have an impact and cause changes in migration policies.

Switzerland and the EU are tied by more than a hundred bilateral agreements, including that on the free movement of persons. Swiss immigration policy can be classified as restrictive, especially as far as non-EU/EFTA nationals are concerned. Despite the fact that Bulgaria is an EU member state and the agreement between the EU and Switzerland on the free movement of persons was extended to this country, aforementioned temporary regulations restrict the access to the Swiss labour market and limit the free movement of persons for Bulgarian nationals. They reflect the 7-year transitional arrangements applied by the EU member states to the CEE countries and more recently to Croatia.

Despite Bulgarian efforts to elaborate adequate policy towards its citizens living abroad to facilitate return migration and to attract back migrants of Bulgarian origin, especially young and well-educated persons, the country still remains a sending one. When considering migration policy effectiveness, the general socio-economic conditions in Bulgaria, and their relative importance in determining migration, policy gaps, existing imperfections and ways of policy implementation are important factors reported by our work which are grounded in comparative theory of migration policymaking (e.g. Zincone 2011).

The empirical data from the Bulgarian and Swiss quantitative and qualitative surveys, as well as the official statistics on the number and profiles of the Bulgarian migrants in Switzerland, give examples of the effects of migration policies and their influence on migrants' decisions whether and where to migrate, on the size of migrant flows from Bulgaria to Switzerland and their integration in the Swiss society. Bulgarians in Switzerland are small in number although they have increased after the implementation of the free movement of persons' regime: the visa removal and especially the extension of the Agreement on the free movement of persons to the country. The surveys' results confirm the sizable impact that migration policies have upon the decision of the Bulgarian migrants where to migrate. They show that among the main reasons for both real and potential migrants not to choose Switzerland as a destination country are: that it is not an EU member-state; that it implements restrictive migration policies, especially concerning access to the labour market; and the difficulties in finding a job (including an unofficial one).

Migration policies do also have an impact on the lives of those Bulgarians who have actually migrated to Switzerland. More than a half of the respondents have arrived in Switzerland post-2009. The prevailing part of those who settled in Switzerland before 2003 are residents while those who arrived after 2003 (the mutual visa removal) and 2008 (the extension of the Agreement on free movement of persons to Bulgaria) have mainly mid-term permits (almost two-thirds of all migrants). Only 0.4 % possess Swiss citizenship, a reason for which is difficult access to Swiss nationality. About half of the Bulgarian migrants arrived for the first time in Switzerland with the purpose of getting a job and, in accordance with the Swiss regulations, most of them were supported by Swiss employers. This is also linked to the fact stated before that higher skilled migrants in Switzerland are supported by employers in finding a job, more than by family and friends. The still restricted access of Bulgarians to the Swiss labour market and the existing strict regulations and requirements for employment of foreign citizens is another possible explanation to be added to the reported cases of discrimination.

Notwithstanding the importance of the policy and institutional factors, additional findings validate a networking pattern based almost entirely on personal, not institutional counterparts and interactions. These personal networks are also mostly focused on other Bulgarians. The frequency of interacting with the local community is in fact about three times lower than with Bulgarians, while abroad. Furthermore, Bulgarian migrants tend also to evaluate their own status as lower than the local people they communicate with.

These research outcomes are therefore grounded in the propositions of Tajfel's and Turner's (1979) social identity theory according to which the self-categorization in a lower social stratum, combined with a group-networking pattern, oriented towards fellow nationals, demonstrates a drive for a positive distinctiveness via isolation from the 'local superior', as the host environment is perceived by migrants. The short length of return stay and particularly with circular migrants, results in aggravating factors: the shorter migrants stay abroad, and the longer they stay in the home country, the weaker are their interactions with the local communities and the stronger is the propensity to close-in within the networking circles of the Bulgarian community abroad. Bulgarians living in Switzerland and who represent a higher social stratum, prove the above observations that less educated migrants and low-skilled workers confine themselves to within the Bulgarian social network, while more educated people tend to communicate in wider and culturally more diverse networks.

Finally, migration also implies shifts in national or ethnic identity and the related sense of belonging. In terms of social identity theory, migration practices and attitudes not only bring a positive self-identification with a broader and economically better-off socio-economic status but also cause transformations in national identity and ethnic identities, proving that identity can be situational and based on stereotypes (Shih et al. 1999; Ajrouch and Kusow 2007). While qualitative findings revealed that feeling Bulgarian, Swiss or international very much depends on different situational components such as the time and place, the quantitative data also shows identity shifts leading to a self-identification with other more positively perceived ethnic, national and supranational groups.

Interestingly, these shifts in ethnic self-identification show a pattern along the ethnic or national groupings identified in our sample. For instance, the number of people who state that they identify as being citizens of the World or as having a European identity is much bigger among the mobile population and the potential migrants: being a migrant justifies you as a citizen of the World or as a European citizen, easing the stigma of being a member of a less developed Bulgarian or ethnic community such as the Roma. At the same time, one could also argue that being interested in a broader identity frame than only the ethnic or the national also provides fertile ground for migration. Further, the World identity includes persons with higher education, lower age, living in bigger settlements and who have a positive self-evaluation of their financial status. Finally, ethnic identity shifts are reported as a consequence of migration, which leads to a self-categorization into other more positively perceived ethnic groups. Roma and Bulgarian Turks tend to identify less frequently as ethnic groups after migration, compared to these groups in the non-mobile sample. Migrant Roma tend to self-identify more often as Bulgarians than Roma, Bulgarian Turks more often as EU citizens than Turks, and Bulgarians strongly support a World identity.

The elusion from the stigmatic self-perception of being a foreign national or a national associated with perceivably inferior social strata by the local community in the foreign environment represents a justification for these statements of identity shifts. This concerns particularly the Roma who, while abroad, manage to avoid the ethnic stigma of being a Roma in Bulgaria. Furthermore, they feel the opportunity of stopping being called a gypsy as another positive incentive for leaving Bulgaria.

7.5 Final Thoughts

A number of challenges to understanding the composition and extent of migration and mobility of Bulgarians in Switzerland and more broadly East–West migration in Europe lie ahead for further research. They include, firstly, the significance of circular migration: What are migrants' motivations behind such a type of migration? What role do the Bulgarian migrant networks play? And what is the impact of changing policy frameworks in propelling these migratory flows? Secondly, as stressed earlier by our work, causes and consequences of the migration and inequality nexus are far from being fully explored: What is the impact of migration on inequality and vice versa? And in particular what is the effect as far the welfare system of the sending country is concerned? Drivers of migration at the regional level and the link between migrant sending and receiving localities are also a fertile ground for further research in this respect. Thirdly, return migration to Bulgaria has been considered in different guises and policy frameworks. Nevertheless, a comprehensive model which links the return needs of the different cohorts of Bulgarian migrants with the receiving country's current demographic and social outlook would be useful not only for the acquisition of further knowledge but also for the whole country's development.

These three specific challenges are briefly discussed herein. Since migration nowadays has to be regarded as a continuum of different forms of movement, understanding circular and transnational migration patterns is important not only for scientific reasons but also for demographic, economic and political aspects concerning both sending and receiving countries. The circulation of persons, goods and ideas has in principle the potential of being beneficial either for the Bulgarian migrants themselves, their households or persons left behind in Bulgaria. It can also be beneficial in terms of skills, knowledge or labour force transfer for a receiving country like Switzerland. There are, however, different types of circulation, which are socially stratified since they involve migrants with various skill levels. For instance, less skilled migrants often experience temporary work permits and precarious living conditions in the host country. These migrants are characterized by bonding social capital and closed ethnic networks, such as those described by our research. Although for these social strata this type of migration often provides a possible means of securing the well-being of their families, it is open to exploitative conditions of all sorts. Similar circular migrant configurations are also the result of social exclusion paths in Switzerland which need to be adequately considered. To some extent one could also argue that for the receiving countries, these circular migrants replace the former guest workers, used as a buffer in the labour market in low-skilled and labour-intensive, often seasonal jobs. For the migrants, to acquire bridging social capital with the local communities, for instance, in Switzerland and with Bulgarians abroad, provides a valuable resource to overcome the closed circles generated by ethnic support groups that structure the circular migration we analysed.

As for the inequality-migration nexus, our research has explored many interlinkages of inequality and migration. Nevertheless, the nexus needs further theoretical explanations due to the scattered character of the current empirical investigations. There is a need for further investigation to grasp the functioning of this nexus: to understand how inequality acts as a driver of migration and how it structures migration paths and patterns. And, vice-versa, we also need to understand the impact migration has on social inequality in sending and receiving countries. This makes it necessary to take a transnational approach to inequality in order to bridge the divide between the different social positions of the migrants in different countries. While avoiding any possible deterministic research attitudes in linking sending and receiving regions, the exploration of the local drivers of migration can further assist in understanding migrants' aspirations and also in preparing adequate integration paths for the receiving countries. Related more to the field of social policy, one peculiar area of attention concerns the welfare systems of both Bulgaria and Switzerland. Bulgaria should be prepared to adjust its social integration framework not only for the successful migrants returning to Bulgaria who are welcomed because of the *brain gain* and the resources they bring after migration. It is of utmost importance also that the Bulgarian social welfare is prepared to provide a fair reintegration path for those less successful migrants with different ethnic backgrounds. These migrants should be addressed not as a 'burden' for the system but as individuals who may also bring manual or technical competences much in need in selected niches of the national labour market. Self-help structures, with the use of mediators such as migrants' facilitators drawn from ethnic and social networks in Bulgaria, can be considered for drawing on similar migration experiences.

The migration-development nexus moreover points to the importance of a comprehensive investigation into the patterns of return migration. Re-migration patterns and migrants' aspirations for circular/repeat migration have been considered in our quantitative and qualitative works. Linking circular, return and transnational flows to understand their motivations and the socio-demographic profiles of the migrants involved has been accomplished to a large extent in our research. The multivariate causes of the return migration processes require, on the other hand, further attention as far as the most vulnerable individuals are concerned and along ethnic lines including migrant groups as the Roma and the Bulgarian Turks. Addressing the determinants for (re)migration aspirations and circular/transnational patterns of migration requires further qualitative research. Nevertheless, we encountered clear evidence for the difficult reintegration of low-skilled circular migrants in the Bulgarian labour market. For these migrants, often also from minority groups, the difficult labour market situation in Bulgaria acts as a driver for migration. After their return, their labour-related networks in Bulgaria have weakened, and they experience even stronger exclusion from the labour market. Demographic, development and local repatriation programmes which address the needs of these migrants at the local and community level are therefore another possible way to create synergies with current transnational practices at the individual and household level such as the transfer of money and remittances. A prerequisite for this endeavour is, first of all, the understanding of return migration as a new start, a new life. It may be thought of as the final step in migration or a new step towards circulation in between two or more countries—but with all the knowledge, skills and experiences that mobility brings about.

The EU enlargement process has been changing the migration landscape of European countries, including also non-EU countries such as Switzerland. New patterns of migration have emerged; cheap and fast modes of transport and communication are supporting these patterns together with the current EU and national migration policies. In addition, there is a financial crisis and currently a refugee crisis. These changes have opened a rich field for research. At the same time, evidence from research is also needed as a basis for policy to address the social potentials and challenges emerging.

References

Ajrouch, K., & Kusow, A. M. (2007). Racial and religious contexts: Situational identities among Lebanese, and Somali Muslim immigrants. *Ethnic and Racial Studies, 30*(1), 72–94.

Boyd, M., & Nowak, J. (2012). Social networks and international migration. In M. Martiniello & J. Rath (Eds.), *An introduction to international migration studies: European perspectives* (pp. 79–105). Amsterdam: Amsterdam University Press. IMISCOE Textbooks.

Constant, A. F., Nottmeyer, O., & Zimmerman, K. F. (2012). *The economics of circular migration* (IZA Discussion Paper No 6940).

De Haas, H. (2011). *The determinants of international migration: Conceptualising policy, origin and destination effects* (IMI/DEMIG Working Paper No. 32). Oxford: University of Oxford, International Migration Institute.

Jones, K. (2014). It was a whirlwind. A lot of people made a lot of money: The role of agencies in facilitating migration from Poland into the UK between 2004 and 2008. *Central and Eastern European Migration Review, 3*(2), 105–125.

Kahanec, M., Zaiceva, A., & Zimmermann, K. (2010). Lessons from migration after EU enlargement. In M. Kahanec & K. F. Zimmermann (Eds.), *EU Labor Markets after Post-Enlargement Migration* (pp. 3–45). Berlin: Springer.

Morawska, E. (2008). *East European westbound income-seeking migrants: Some unwelcome effects on sender- and receiver- societies* (Working Paper Series of the Research Network 1989, Working Paper 16/2008).

Okólski, M., & Salt, J. (2014). Polish emigration to the UK after 2004, why did so many come? *Central and Eastern European Migration Review, 3*(2), 11–37.

Parutis, V. (2011). 'Economic Migrants' or 'Middling Transnational'? East European migrants' experiences of work in the UK. *International Migration, 52*(1), 36–55.

Schwiter, K., Berndt, C., & Truong, J. (2015). Neoliberal austerity and the marketisation of elderly care. *Social and Cultural Geography*, 1–21.

Shih, M., Pittinsky, T. L., & Ambady, N. (1999). Stereotype susceptibility: Identity salience and shifts in quantitative performance. *Psychological Science, 10*(1), 80–83.

Tajfel, H., & Turner, J. C. (1979). An integrative theory of intergroup conflict. In W. G. Austin & S. Worchel (Eds.), *The social psychology of intergroup relations* (pp. 33–47). Monterey, CA: Brooks/Cole.

Waldinger, R. D., & Lichter, M. I. (2003). *How the other half works: Immigration and the social organisation of labour.* Berkeley: University of California Press.

Zincone, G. (2011). Conclusion. Comparing the making of migration policies. In G. Zincone, R. Penninx, & M. Borkert (Eds.), *Migration policymaking in Europe. The dynamics of actors and contexts in past and present* (pp. 377–441). Amsterdam: Amsterdam University Press. IMISCOE Research.

Index

CPSIA information can be obtained
at www.ICGtesting.com
Printed in the USA
LVOW04*0907160816

500590LV00011B/155/P